THE DRIVE ACROSS CANADA

THE DRIVE ACROSS CANADA

The Remarkable Story of the Trans-Canada Highway

Mark Richardson

DUNDURN
PRESS

Copyright © Mark Richardson, 2025

All rights reserved. No part of this publication may be reproduced, stored in a retrieval system, or transmitted in any form or by any means, electronic, mechanical, photocopying, recording, or otherwise (except for brief passages for purpose of review) without the prior permission of Dundurn Press. Permission to photocopy should be requested from Access Copyright.

Publisher: Meghan Macdonald | Acquiring editor: Kathryn Lane | Editor: Michael Carroll
Cover designer: Karen Alexiou
Cover image: Mark Richardson
Back cover images: left: Courtesy of Lorne Findlay; right: Courtesy Library and Archives Canada a029908
Interior maps: Eric Sweet

Library and Archives Canada Cataloguing in Publication

Title: The drive across Canada : the remarkable story of the Trans-Canada Highway / Mark Richardson.
Names: Richardson, Mark, 1962- author.
Description: Includes bibliographical references and index.
Identifiers: Canadiana (print) 2024051467X | Canadiana (ebook) 20240518721 | ISBN 9781459754928 (softcover) | ISBN 9781459754935 (PDF) | ISBN 9781459754942 (EPUB)
Subjects: LCSH: Trans-Canada Highway. | LCSH: Trans-Canada Highway—History. | LCSH: Automobile travel—Canada—History. | LCSH: Roads—Canada—History. | LCSH: Richardson, Mark, 1962-—Travel.
Classification: LCC HE357 .R53 2025 | DDC 388.10971—dc23

We acknowledge the support of the Canada Council for the Arts and the Ontario Arts Council for our publishing program. We also acknowledge the financial support of the Government of Ontario, through the Ontario Book Publishing Tax Credit and Ontario Creates, and the Government of Canada.

Care has been taken to trace the ownership of copyright material used in this book. The author and the publisher welcome any information enabling them to rectify any references or credits in subsequent editions.

The publisher is not responsible for websites or their content unless they are owned by the publisher.

Printed and bound in Canada.

Dundurn Press
1382 Queen Street East
Toronto, Ontario, Canada M4L 1C9
dundurn.com, @dundurnpress

*For Perry Doolittle and Bert Todd,
who dreamed of the Trans-Canada Highway*

Contents

Prologue	1
1: Newfoundland and Labrador	15
2: Nova Scotia	35
3: Prince Edward Island	55
4: New Brunswick	71
5: Quebec	91
6: Ottawa	107
7: Southern Ontario	121
8: Northern Ontario	143
9: Manitoba	163
10: Saskatchewan	179
11: Alberta	195
12: Mainland British Columbia	213
13: Vancouver Island	241
Epilogue	255
Acknowledgements	267
Appendix: Rules for the Todd Medal	271
Selected Bibliography	273
Image Credits	275
Index	277
About the Author	281

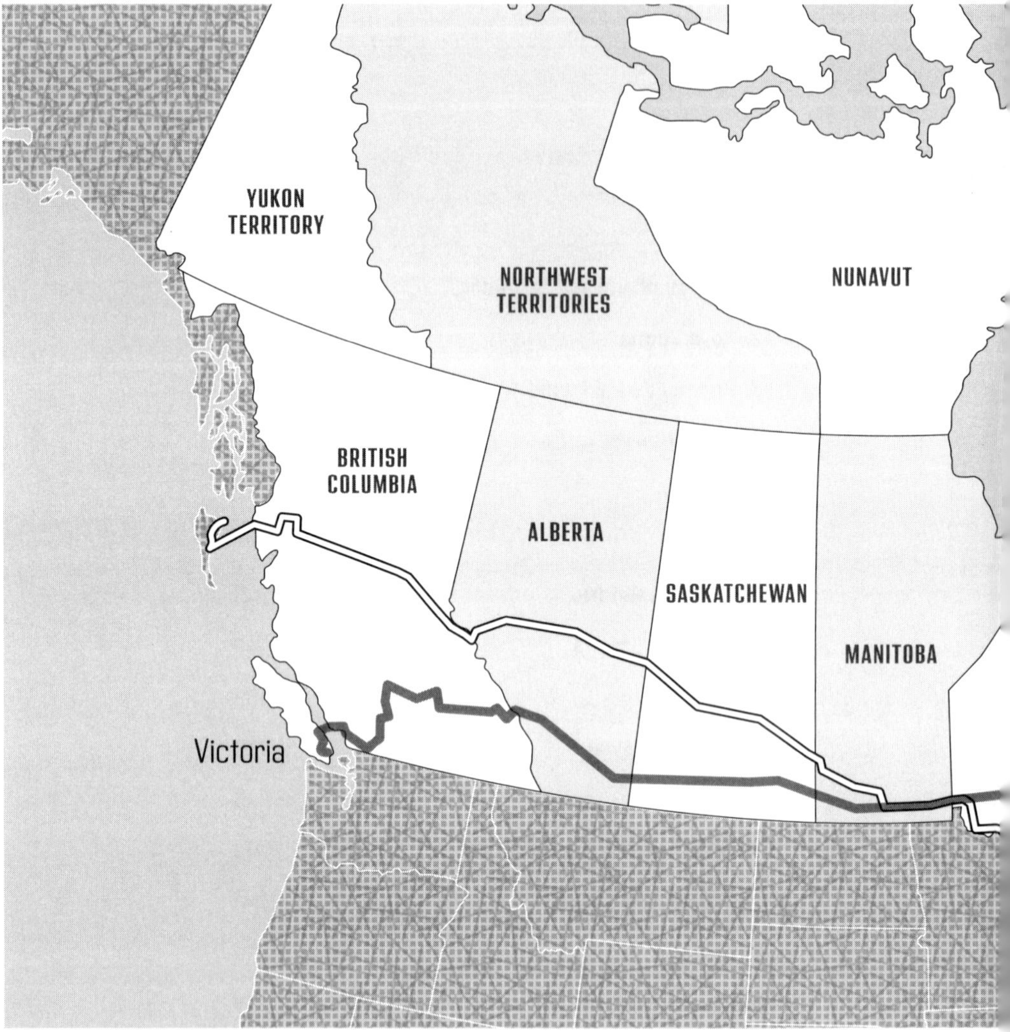
YUKON
TERRITORY
NORTHWEST
TERRITORIES
NUNAVUT
BRITISH
COLUMBIA
ALBERTA
SASKATCHEWAN
MANITOBA
Victoria

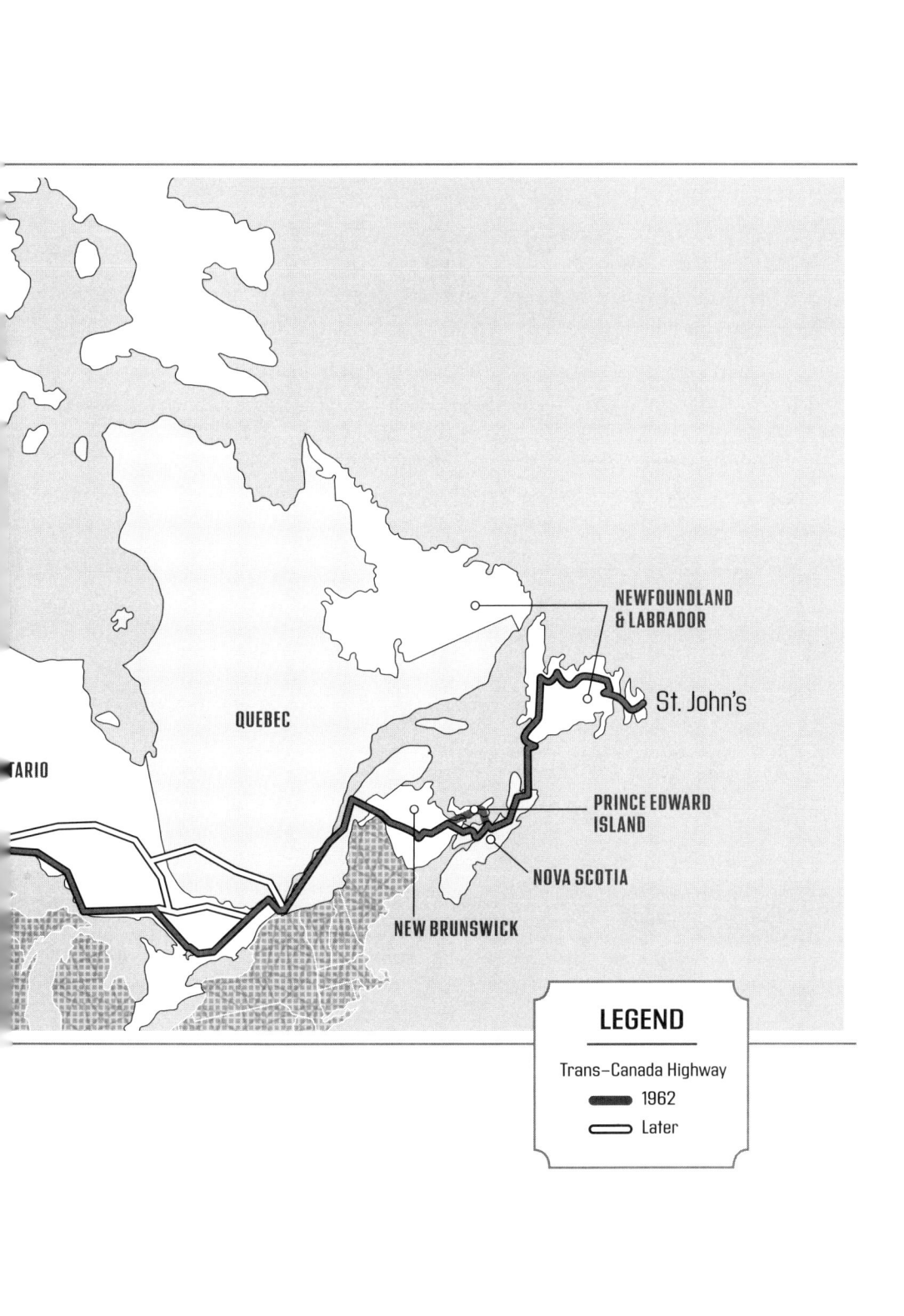

NEWFOUNDLAND & LABRADOR

St. John's

QUEBEC

PRINCE EDWARD ISLAND

NOVA SCOTIA

NEW BRUNSWICK

LEGEND

Trans-Canada Highway
- 1962
- Later

Prologue

It's easy to drive across Canada. If you have a reliable car, you can do it in a week. Over six time zones, it's 7,700 kilometres that blend and blur across the landscape on smooth asphalt curving through fields and trees, arrow-straight on the Prairies, punching over the mountains.

That's not the way to do it, though. You should take your time to appreciate the country and meet the people while experiencing some of the natural and cultural wealth of Canada. You don't need to do it all at once: just a few days at a time if that's all you can manage. The road is here now and it didn't come easy, so make the most of it.

□

The first drive across North America from ocean to ocean in a motorcar was completed in 1903 by Horatio Nelson Jackson, a Canadian-born doctor who'd married one of the wealthiest women in Vermont, and his mechanic, Sewall Crocker. It took 64 days to travel from San Francisco to New York City in their Winton car and included countless misdirections, breakdowns, rebuilds, and second guesses. Certainly, it was a rigorous challenge, but the landscape was well documented and there was already a path worn down by the stagecoach. A Californian named George Wyman completed the same journey three weeks earlier on a motorized bicycle, often bumping along on the railway ties of train tracks, though its engine eventually failed and Wyman had to pedal beside the Hudson River for the final 250 kilometres into Manhattan. In the following five years, at least 10 more cross-country road trips were completed as pioneering pairs of drivers pushed their way in rickety roadsters from one coast to the other.

Canadian drivers, all wealthy with varying spirits of adventure, read in their newspapers of the American exploits with a certain envy. Nobody followed the progress of the automobile more closely than Albert "Bert" E. Todd, who'd inherited his father's wholesale grocery and salmon-canning business in Victoria, British Columbia. Less than a week after Jackson and Crocker began their successful American drive, 24-year-old Bert Todd took delivery of a two-seater car built by the White Sewing Machine Company of Cleveland, Ohio. He paid $1,800 for it but had no experience of driving, so as a test run, he set off with the dealer's rep for Shawnigan Lake, 70 kilometres away. "They made the distance in the fast time of 2 hours and 53 minutes," reported the *Victoria Daily Times* later in the week. "Near Whiskey Swamp they encountered a black bear, and tried to run it down, but the beast got out of the way too quickly."

Todd was hooked! In the first decade of the last century, cars were a curiosity and much scorned by cynics who saw them as dangerous and expensive playthings, but Todd recognized their potential for personal transport. He was an advocate for building better roads, which would attract visitors in their motorcars. He became known as "Good Roads Todd" and organized the Pacific Highway Association in Seattle, which lobbied for a paved road to connect the entire west coast from Vancouver to Tijuana. In 1910, he married the daughter of the dealer who'd sold him his White Steamer car, and they spent their honeymoon driving home from Los Angeles through the dust and mud in a new Cadillac. As vice-president of the Victoria Automobile Association, and always looking to boost roads to his city, he commissioned a gold medal to be awarded to the first motorist to drive from Winnipeg to Victoria. When he was elected as the association's president the following

PROLOGUE

Dozens of motorists — affluent and optimistic — met at Alberni in 1912 to call for a Canadian Highway.

year, he commissioned another gold medal for the first motorist to drive right across Canada, staying within the country, from Louisbourg, Nova Scotia — about as far east as you could get before Newfoundland joined Canada in 1949 — to Victoria, to bring home the dream of a national highway. He put $500 of his own money into a bank account to pay for the awards dinner.

Todd was in Alberni on Vancouver Island on May 4, 1912, when the Canadian Highway Association gathered hundreds of enthusiasts from as far as Seattle to declare the need for a cross-country highway. The mayor of Victoria told the crowd that such a road "would arouse the whole dominion," and Todd helped dig a hole to plant a signpost that declared itself the western end of the "Canadian Highway." At the time, Alberni was one of the farthest-west communities in Canada and the town was keen to link itself to the national highway; its upstart neighbour, Port Alberni, was the western terminus of the Canadian Pacific Railway (CPR), and the two towns were rivals. Nobody from Port Alberni attended the motorists' gathering because, somebody told the newspaper, "they were too busy making money," though they found time a few days later to steal the signpost. It was returned the next morning by Port Alberni's apologetic mayor and re-erected, this time with a fierce-looking bull terrier, borrowed from the local doctor, chained to it for protection.

Back then, the railway was always considered superior to the highway. If you wanted to travel any distance in any kind of comfort, you took a ship or a train; roads were for delivering goods to market with a horse and cart, and most people never travelled much more than 20 kilometres from home. Not ever. That was about the comfortable distance a horse could pull a buggy in a day. So railways were the responsibility of the federal government and roads were just a provincial issue. Outside the cities, roads were usually mud tracks that led to the train station. In 1912, the only paved road in Canada was a 16-kilometre length of concrete outside Montreal.

That didn't deter Thomas Wilby, a 45-year-old English journalist living in New York City who had already driven twice across the United States. He

Thomas Wilby, left, and Jack Haney, at the end of their journey across Canada in 1912, with their Reo car festooned with pennants.

heard of the two medals being offered in Victoria and persuaded the Reo car company of St. Catharines, Ontario, to provide him with a new touring car and full sponsorship. More than that, he heard the call from the gathering in Alberni for a Canadian Highway and resolved to make the drive from coast to coast, if he could find the roads. There were no reliable maps to confirm it would be impossible. Jackson and Crocker had taken the prize for the United States; Wilby wanted Canada.

There was a challenge, though: Wilby didn't drive. It wasn't that he couldn't drive, but he believed a properly bred Englishman should leave such menial work to the chauffeur, as he and his wife had done on their road trip from New York City to San Diego and back. He persuaded the Reo company to also provide a driver so that he could sit in the deep leather of the rear seat and peruse the finer points of life on the road as the countryside rolled past, scribbling in his notebook and typing reports at rest stops for his eventual book, *A Motor Tour Through Canada*. Reo sent him the company's head mechanic, Fonce Val Haney, from Indiana. "You can call me Jack," said the 23-year-old Haney when they met in Halifax. "You will call me sir," said Wilby. The relationship went down from there. When his book was published in 1914, Wilby mentioned "the chauffeur" only rarely and never once referred to him by name.

Somehow, the two men not only survived their 53 days of travel together but actually made it to Victoria, where Wilby was feted by Bert Todd and the good roads dignitaries while Haney was all but ignored. They didn't win the medals, though. There was no road north of Lake Superior, where they took a steamer and then a train through to Manitoba. And in British Columbia, despite picking their way through the mountains as best they could, they were forced to detour briefly into the United States to find their way west. At one point, they even drove on the narrow road beside the Fraser Canyon where the car's gas-fired lights failed in pitch-dark, with a guide lying on the fender holding a lamp while all three men prepared to leap for their lives if the wheels slipped over the edge. But the rules held that the journey had to be made entirely in Canada.

A photographer named Ed Flickenger did complete the Canadian drive in 1925, with help from Dr. Perry Doolittle, but they took a different approach:

The Ford Model T that crossed Canada with Ed Flickenger in 1925 had its wheels changed to drive on railway tracks where there were no roads.

the Ford Motor Company supplied a Model T and they registered it as a train, switching over to flanged wheels so it could drive on railway tracks where there was no road. The car covered more than 1,300 kilometres like that, the first motorized vehicle to drive along the north shore of Lake Superior, and through the mountains from Golden to Revelstoke. Flickenger, who worked for Ford of Canada, didn't win the medal because the car didn't stay on roads, something Doolittle wasn't concerned about. He was the long-serving president of the Canadian Automobile Association (CAA), and the trip was publicity to press for the Canadian Highway that still didn't exist.

As an aside, it's been generally reported until now, by me and others, that Doolittle and Flickenger drove together for the whole distance, probably because this was what Ford's public-relations department announced in 1973 when it re-created the trip to publicize the new Mustang and Cougar models. But Doolittle was just an organizer based in Toronto, Flickenger was in charge of the car, and local Ford executives did most of the driving.

In fact, the first person to drive across Canada without changing his wheels was J. "Jimmy" Graham Oates in 1928. He was from Britain's Isle of Man and had been a military dispatch rider in the First World War, when he lost an eye in a gas attack and came home to start his own, unsuccessful motorcycle company. As a stunt to promote Castrol Oil, he rode a 500 cc

PROLOGUE

Jimmy Oates and his Ariel motorcycle, seen here with a young passenger in the Sturgess sidecar.

Ariel from Halifax to Vancouver, sleeping in its sidecar and bumping along between the railway tracks for the long roadless stretches in Ontario and British Columbia. But Jimmy Oates didn't win the Todd Medal, either, because the rules didn't allow using the railway in any form; they also held that the vehicle should be a car. He ended at Vancouver and never met Todd, who had become mayor of Victoria and then an alderman and literally worked himself to death that October.

It took the Second World War for Canada to finally build the last stretch of highway that would link east and west. The remaining 250 kilometres of gravel road through the endless trees of Northern Ontario was completed in 1943 between the logging towns of Hearst and Geraldton, so military supplies could be moved without relying on American support. And three years later, once gasoline rationing eased, Brigadier (Retired) Alex Macfarlane of St. Catharines drove in a sponsored Chevrolet from Louisbourg to Victoria in nine days with his friend Ken MacGillivray, the former city editor of the *Globe and Mail*. It was an uneventful drive with just two flat tires.

The road that would be the Trans-Canada Highway was finally declared open in 1962, 50 years after those motorists planted their signpost in Alberni. It had been a half century of political brawling and backroom deals. The problem was, while the federal government wanted the road built, it wasn't a federal responsibility. The Feds handled trains and ships, and more recently, aircraft, but highways were still a provincial matter. No prime minister could get away with telling a provincial premier what to do with the roads, and the Trans-Canada was no different.

Interest in a Canadian Highway had grown in the 1920s with the popularity, and affordability, of personal cars, spurred further by the constant promotion of people like Doolittle and Todd. It waned in the 1930s as the Great Depression dug in and car ownership declined, and then the Second World War took priority over everything. In 1949, as a recession loomed, the Liberal Party government of William Lyon Mackenzie King saw a way to put the country back to work. "The Trans-Canada Highway was built to provide employment, pure and simple," says David Monaghan. His 1996 thesis, *Canada's "New Main Street,"* is considered the definitive explanation of the highway's many political challenges. "The federal government had it as a 'shelf project,' and when they finally pulled it off the shelf, it was to create employment after the Second World War."

As with everything, money talked. In the United States, when President Dwight Eisenhower's government committed to build its interstate highway system in the 1950s and 1960s, it agreed right off the top to pay 90 percent of the cost of construction to be financed through a gasoline tax. Young Lieutenant Colonel Eisenhower had driven in a coast-to-coast military convoy in 1919 that convinced him of the need for a system of dependable roads that could help defend the country. Canada wasn't so concerned about defending itself and was more fiscally cautious, so offered its provinces just half the cost of upgrading existing roads or building new ones. Only six of the 10 provinces agreed at first. Prince Edward Island knew the Feds would build a bridge or a tunnel to finally replace the overworked ferry and was the first to sign on, but Nova Scotia and New Brunswick balked at the proposed route that would bypass Halifax and Saint John. Newfoundland balked at the cost. Quebec — well, Quebec really didn't care about linking itself to English-speaking Canada.

There were exceptions to the 50/50 deal, of course. The federal government had responsibility for national parks, and the roads in those parks were built to a high national standard, based on the construction standards for the new U.S. interstate system. The roads leading to them were another matter entirely. "You knew as soon as you were in the park," a Newfoundlander once told me about Terra Nova National Park in the early days. "Miles of dust and crap to get there, but inside the park itself, it was smooth sailing from one end to the other. It was all a tease for the miles of dust and crap on the other side when you left."

It was more than a decade before all the special deals were signed to make the Trans-Canada a reality. Saskatchewan was the first to complete its share of the highway, in 1957, but it had only 650 kilometres of flat roadway to widen and pave. Quebec was the last to agree, under the new premiership of Jean Lesage and with the promise from the Feds to build an ambitious — and expensive — bridge or tunnel across the St. Lawrence into Montreal.

The final stretch to be opened was a glorious 150 kilometres over the risky Rogers Pass between Revelstoke and Golden in British Columbia. The mountains were beautiful but prone to avalanches, and a series of snowsheds had to be built to carry falling snow and debris over the highway. It passed through Glacier and Mount Revelstoke National Parks and so the federal government paid for almost all of it, but that wasn't enough for B.C. premier W.A.C. Bennett. He'd wanted the Feds to pay for everything. So while Prime Minister John Diefenbaker was due to lead a convoy to Rogers Pass to formally open the Trans-Canada Highway in September, Bennett set up his own ribbon-cutting event for "B.C. Highway 1" five weeks earlier. He declared the road open in front of several thousand onlookers, allowing an estimated 347,000 people to drive through the national park before the prime minister's ceremony. "There was one of the most peculiar, self-centred actions that I've ever known," Diefenbaker reportedly said later.

That was at 3:00 p.m. on July 30, 1962 — the day I was born.

I first travelled the entire length of the Trans-Canada Highway in 2012, driving a yellow Chevrolet Camaro convertible borrowed from General Motors and blogging about the journey for *Maclean's* magazine. Again, in the summer of 2023, I drove the highway, this time in a borrowed Lexus SUV and writing for the *Globe and Mail*. Both times, I drove from east to west, from St. John's to Victoria. The first time, I brought my then-12-year-old son with me for the second half of the trip, and more recently, I travelled with my old friend, Peter, who I've known since we failed most of our exams together at college in the United Kingdom, before I moved to Canada in 1980.

Peter flew in from his home in Gloucestershire to meet me at my house in Cobourg, Ontario, and the two of us drove east a couple of days later in the Lexus RX 500h. The SUV was a hybrid prototype, and I chose it because it was built in Canada at Toyota's assembly plant in Cambridge, Ontario, just as the Camaro before it was built at the General Motors plant in Oshawa. Both makers were happy to lend me their vehicles for the publicity it would bring, though I warned them I'd be critical in any appraisal. Eleven years apart, they both shrugged. "Bring it on," they said.

Aside from clothes, notebooks, cameras, and all the other paraphernalia of a road trip, both times I carried three unique souvenirs. One was a horseshoe, found beside the road in British Columbia by Jack Haney during the 1912 drive with Wilby and then carried in his toolbox until his death. It was mounted on a small wooden shield and lent to me by the St. Catharines Museum. Another was a tin CAA grille badge from 1925 — the same year Ed Flickenger's car drove across the country on road and rail — given to me by the CAA. And the third was the Todd Medal itself, lent to me in 2012 by Alex Macfarlane's grandson, Jim, and in 2023 by Jim's widow, Nancy. "Take good care of it," they both said, "and we'll see you when you get back. It should be quite the journey."

PROLOGUE

It took Peter and me four days to drive the 3,000 kilometres to St. John's from my home near Toronto. It wasn't an auspicious drive because, like most travellers these days, we just wanted to get to the other end. The road through to Nova Scotia was four lanes and divided by a wide median with controlled access junctions, designed for fast and effective trucking. Very different from the days of the old pathfinders, and not very interesting at all.

Our golden rule was that we had to drive the entire length of the Trans-Canada on its traditional route across the country. If we left the highway to explore the countryside, we had to rejoin it at the exact same place to not miss anything. The rule could be stretched, though, because it was okay to miss a section heading west if we had already driven that same one headed east; we took advantage of this later to leave the monotony of the blacktop in Quebec and New Brunswick to explore the scenic roads beside the St. Lawrence and Saint John Rivers. And, after all, those older roads had been the original Trans-Canada in the 1960s before it was widened and improved.

The Trans-Canada Highway network diversified over the years and now officially accounts for about 13,000 kilometres of roads, including a long stretch of highway north of Montreal in Quebec that leads up to Val-d'Or before crossing into Ontario, where it follows the same road through the northern woods that Macfarlane took in 1946. The Yellowhead Highway in the Prairies is also officially Trans-Canada, though nobody ever thinks of it as such: it splits away just west of Winnipeg and travels through the more northerly cities of Saskatoon and Edmonton until it reaches Prince Rupert on the Pacific coast. In Ontario, an alternate route leads west from Thunder Bay to Rainy River and then north to Kenora, and another travels directly northwest from Ottawa to North Bay before reaching the Great Lakes. Peter and I would stick to the traditional route that was intended to cross the country in as short a distance as possible. That 1962 designation already included a split that gave a choice of driving through northern Nova Scotia or Prince Edward Island, so we drove east through Nova Scotia and would return west through the island province.

We shared the driving, roughly a couple of hours behind the wheel before pulling over for coffee, or gas, or just a pee, or all three, and then swapping places. That was the same arrangement Jackson and Crocker agreed on when they drove across the United States in 1903 — though they'd stop far more frequently for repairs and digging out — and very different from Wilby and Haney nine years later, when Wilby never once took the wheel or even assisted with maintaining the Reo. In truth, both Peter and I would have been quite happy to have not had the other person drive at all. Our styles at the wheel were very different, and neither of us ever quite got used to the foibles of the other, but that's a tale for another chapter and we pressed on regardless.

It was early June, and the 18-hour ferry that links Nova Scotia with eastern Newfoundland wasn't open yet for the season. That meant we had to take the six-hour ferry across to the southwestern point of the island at Port aux Basques and then drive the 900-kilometre length of the Trans-Canada across the province to St. John's. There's no other route over The Rock. We made it, stayed with some friends and explored the area, then, on a foggy Tuesday morning, drove to the Atlantic Ocean to begin our drive across Canada.

Map

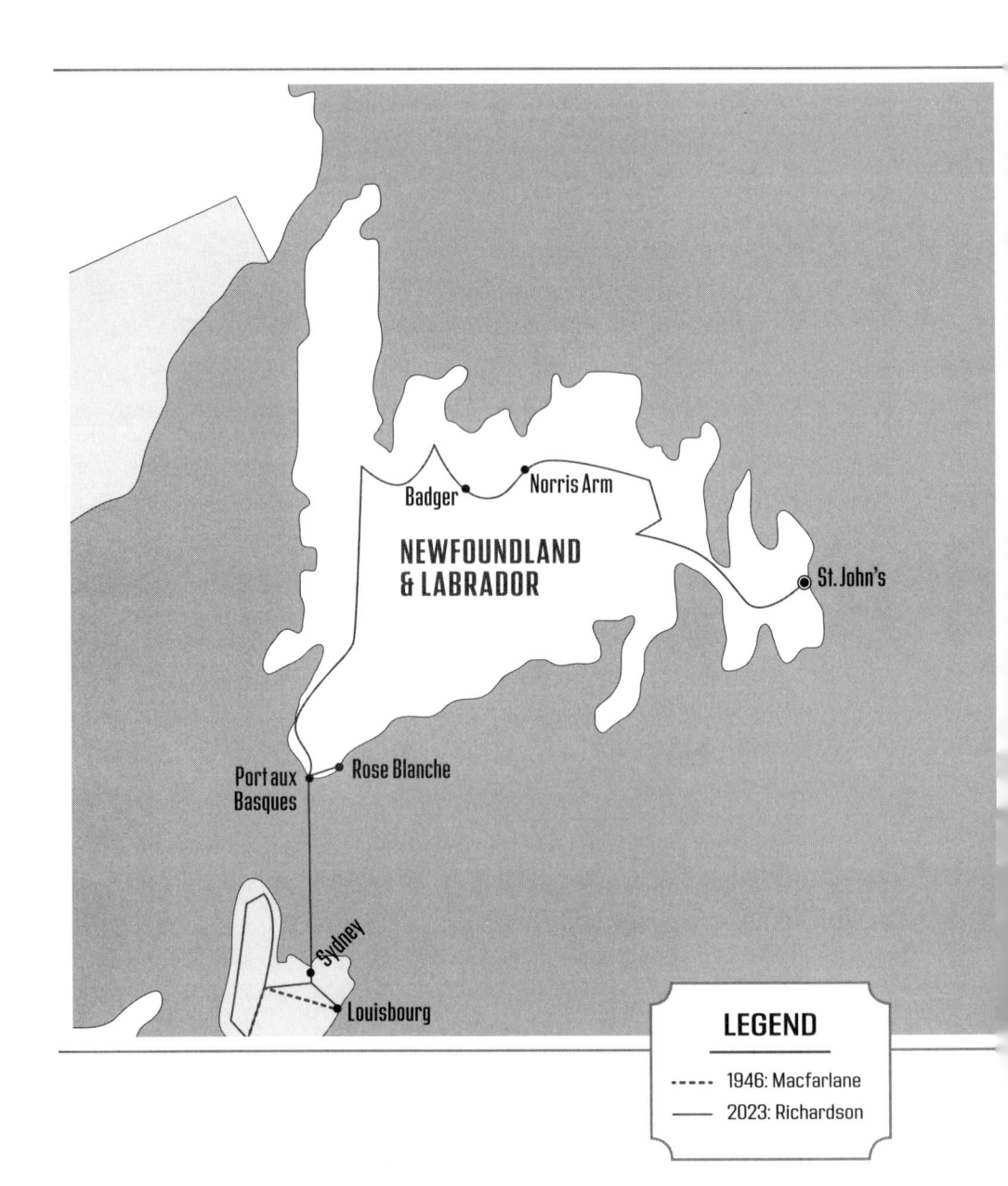

NEWFOUNDLAND & LABRADOR

- Badger
- Norris Arm
- St. John's
- Port aux Basques
- Rose Blanche
- Sydney
- Louisbourg

LEGEND
- ----- 1946: Macfarlane
- ——— 2023: Richardson

1
Newfoundland and Labrador

There's no sign on the Trans-Canada Highway that marks its start, or its end, in Newfoundland. Sure, there's a sign and a stylized map on the sidewalk outside St. John's City Hall that calls itself "Km 0," but the Trans-Canada itself was moved away years ago. When the highway was opened in 1962, it was routed through the downtowns of many of the cities it connected because merchants wanted the business from the visitors it would bring. Heavy trucks started using the wider, better-built road, and those local merchants quickly changed their minds. Now, the official highway usually bypasses the city and St. John's is no different. That's why, today, the Trans-Canada officially begins beside the municipal dump on the outskirts of town. Maybe that's also why there's no sign.

Peter and I drove to a boat ramp that drops into Quidi Vidi Gut, the harbour on the north edge of St. John's, and jostled with too many tourists at the wharf for too few parking spaces. There's a craft brewery there and a few souvenir stores and the whole area is very quaint, with brightly coloured wooden buildings at the base of the low cliffs. Fortunately, nobody had a boat or wanted to park in the ocean itself, so I backed the Lexus into the cold water for the official start of our long journey west. It

Mark in the Lexus, with its wheels dipped in the Atlantic Ocean at Quidi Vidi.

was early June, and we were wearing sweaters and jackets for the single-digit chill. At the last minute, I scooped some salt water into a plastic bottle to carry to the Pacific and then we drove into the mist to nearby Quidi Vidi Lake.

This seemed the right place to begin the actual highway drive. The official Trans-Canada was moved out to the ring road in the 1990s and that four-lane highway was extended east to the edge of the Robin Hood Bay Regional Waste Management Facility in 1999. There, the 7,700-kilometre national icon ends without notice under a bridge. A regular two-lane industrial road continues on for four dismal kilometres to a hard stop at the lake.

I would be writing stories along the way for the *Globe and Mail*, and shot a phone video at the lake decrying the lack of a sign. I'm not alone. On Google Maps, there's a locator pin and a few reviews that feel the same way. "Put up a sign please would like the satisfaction of acknowledging I came to the end of the road lol," wrote A Maze the previous year. The eloquently named arseface2k wrote that "they have a whole park set up for where Terry Fox started his run and not even a measly sign for this, which you could argue is more important." And a guy named Joe Caines wrote: "Am I there?? Did I make it?? Guess we will never know. Over 7000 km. Nothing. So much history of our country is connected to this hiway. Well, when I get there again, in June, I'm bringing my own spray paint, make my own plaque."

He's right that a huge part of Canada's history is tied in some way to the Trans-Canada Highway. For postwar Newfoundlanders, the federal government used the promise of a highway as an enticement for Confederation: it agreed to pay the costs of the Newfoundland Railway that already crossed the island, and to pay the entire cost of a reliable, regular ferry route to link the island at Port aux Basques with the mainland. More important, Newfoundlanders knew that if and when a Trans-Canada Highway should be built, the Feds would pay for a significant portion of its construction. This was a big deal: at almost 1,000 kilometres, it would be the second-longest stretch of any province, after Ontario. Not that Newfoundlanders really cared about the rest of Canada.

"The majority of people here in Newfoundland just think of it as a road across the island," Lloyd Adams told me at his home in Whitbourne. "But I would think that those people have probably never been off the island."

I met Lloyd in 2012 and sat down with him and his wife, Audrey, on their 48th wedding anniversary to talk about the Trans-Canada. He was fresh out of high school in 1953 when he landed a job as a surveyor's assistant for the new highway, earning $105 per month for holding a tape measure and plotting points on rudimentary maps. His team of a half-dozen men slept in tents and were in the bush for weeks at a time with no generators, no ATVs, no power saws. They worked from a camp, and when they completed five kilometres of surveying, they broke camp and moved it to the next new start, pressing across the island. They had the better job too. Another team of a half-dozen men swung the axes that cleared the way.

The beginning of the new road to be constructed was at the corner of Stamps Lane and Freshwater Road in St. John's, about three kilometres from the city hall, back when there was just a farm and a couple of houses at the intersection. They headed west from there. "Back then, what we were really doing was pioneering," said Lloyd. "I don't think I realized the challenges of the things we did, because it was just a job. We were in canvas tents, and the bathroom was a two-holer in the back."

They pushed on, five kilometres at a time, one of a number of crews doing the same job across the new province. Ponds were drained and muskegs filled for the road to run across, and more often than not, all the heavy work was done with picks and spades for the extra employment it created. Gravel trucks backed into a quarry to be hand-loaded by pairs of men with shovels. And when they were done in the late 1950s, and the road was finally complete from St. John's to Port aux Basques — avoiding out-of-the-way Labrador, of course — few people appreciated the physical effort it took.

Edward McCourt, an author and professor at the University of Saskatchewan, drove the length of the highway with his wife, Margaret, in 1963, the year after the Trans-Canada Highway was declared fully open. In Newfoundland, two-thirds of it was still unpaved.

"A wonderful road," he was told by a truck driver at a coffee stop. "The lots in St. John's is full of cars folks like you drove over from Port aux Basques and didn't figure was worth driving back. A wonderful, wonderful road."

McCourt's account of the journey in his book *The Road Across Canada* is perceptive and graphic and hard to imagine today:

> Rock-fills lightly coated with sand or gravel (the kind of road bed that keeps a man vibrating steadily for hours after he has stopped driving); dense clouds of dust hanging over the road for miles, through which monstrous trucks and cats (lights ablaze and visible through the dust for ten feet) bore down upon us with terrifying speed; roller-coaster forest trails hardly more than one-way tracks; blind hills and paralyzing right-angle curves — these were the orthodox hazards of the unpaved sections of the Trans-Canada Highway in Newfoundland.

Premier Joey Smallwood, who had brought the province into Confederation in 1949 and negotiated every facet of its integration within Canada, was well aware of the embarrassment of the Trans-Canada Highway and in no hurry to improve it. There was now a ferry service paid for by the Feds to bring goods to and from the island, and a railway bankrolled by the

Feds to carry them wherever they needed to go. If any improvements were made to the Trans-Canada, the province would have to pay half the cost, and canny Joey just pleaded poverty. Schools were more important, he said. Hospitals were more important. Prime Minister John Diefenbaker would just have to wait for his glorious highway while everything else took priority. When the Trans-Canada was declared open in 1962 at Rogers Pass — at the national ceremony, not the cheeky B.C. one — there was a convoy of politicians from across the country but no one from Newfoundland. Joey didn't want to pay 50/50 for the highway, and neither he nor Diefenbaker would blink.

It took a new governing party and a new prime minister to get things moving again, with a new deal in which Ottawa agreed to pay 90 percent of the cost of completing the highway to a high-quality, national standard. The country would mark its centenary in 1967, and Prime Minister Lester Pearson wanted everything ready for that showcase to the world. McCourt saw regular road signs that declared: WE'LL FINISH THE DRIVE IN '65, PORT AUX BASQUES TO ST. JOHN'S, THANKS TO LESTER B. PEARSON, and when the money started flowing in soon after, the curves were straightened, the road was widened, and the asphalt went down. It took a couple of years, but the Trans-Canada Highway would finally be complete.

◻

The road was wide and smooth for Peter and me as we drove west. The landscape seemed empty, with low trees and pond-spattered fields all the more desolate for the low-lying cloud that kept obscuring the horizon. There was rock right beneath the stubby grass, and erratic boulders were scattered about where they'd been moved by ancient ice. Quarries scraped out hillsides beside the road. You could graze sheep here, but that's about it. There were rarely houses, except in the few communities down by the coast. Sometimes, you could see the ocean off to the left or right — St. John's is on a large peninsula attached to the bulk of the island by a strip of land less than 10 kilometres wide — but the sea was grey that day, the wind cruel.

I remembered a comment Lloyd Adams had made just before I left his house in Whitbourne. "It was tough land to work on," he said as I'd put on my shoes, ready to head out to drive to the other side of the country. "These days, you don't even notice when you're speeding past. Now we have a four-lane highway and it only takes 45 minutes to get to Walmart. I guess that's progress."

The highway is constantly upgraded, and the government announced a $306 million project in 2023 to add lanes to it at some of its narrower points. Much of the Trans-Canada on the island is still just one lane in each direction, with roads and driveways leading off it, and the ultimate plan is to make it two lanes in each direction with a wide centre median. This is known as "twinning," and it's the safest kind of road because it's almost impossible for vehicles to drive head-on into each other. If they lose control and leave the road, they have to make it across the centre median before they can smash into oncoming traffic, which is the deadliest of crashes. Or, in government-speak in its press release, "Twinning the Trans-Canada here will lead to safer communities and better movement of goods across the island. That means spending less time on the road, and more time with your family."

I was spending less time with my family and more time with Peter, and now that we were headed west, we were starting to bug each other. I like to drive at the speed of traffic, which in most of Canada means about 10 or even 20 percent above the speed limit, but Peter was used to driving in the United Kingdom where enforcement is much stricter and speed cameras are everywhere. When I drove, he constantly flexed his right foot against an imaginary brake; when he drove, I regularly nodded for him to get a move on. I was, at least, bringing him around to the idea of sipping coffee from a cup while driving — or a tea in his case, which he was used to drinking before setting out to keep both hands free for the wheel. That's a good idea in crowded London or Liverpool, but irrelevant on the Trans-Canada and only wastes time skulking over tables at coffee shops.

Actually, I think he was also a little nervous for all the signs that put the fear of God into drivers about moose on the roads. They're a very real danger in Newfoundland where people are killed every year in collisions.

A standard greeting after any arrival on the highway is: "See any moose?" Back in 2012, the province spent $1.5 million on a couple of sections of "moose radar" that used roadside infrared sensor beams to detect large animals wandering onto the highway, then flashed warning lights at motorists for three minutes over a sign that read: MOOSE ON HIGHWAY WHEN LIGHTS ARE FLASHING. It didn't work, of course, and was pulled down after a few years. Sometimes, moose wandered back into the woods, and drivers didn't see them and assumed the lights were faulty; other times, moose grazed beside the road longer than three minutes and the lights went out while they were still there; most of the time, the sensors couldn't cope with the weather. In Newfoundland, the climate gets blamed for many things. Drivers learned to never believe the lights.

However, if the sensors had been installed on the central stretch of the Trans-Canada between Gander and Norris Arm, it might have helped Michelle Higgins when she drove to work on the morning of May 7, 2012. She hit and killed a full-grown moose that crushed her car with the impact and rolled its roof off as if it were a sardine tin, but she carried on driving in such shock that her brain didn't register the collision. It wasn't until she reached her workplace in Gander, 40 kilometres away, that she realized what had happened.

"I remember getting out of the car," she told me a month later when I stopped at her home on my first Trans-Canada drive. "I remember my co-worker coming up and putting her arm around me, and asked me if I was okay, and I kind of looked at her and asked, 'Well, why wouldn't I be?' And she said, 'Michelle, you're bleeding.' She said, 'Look at your car — were you in an accident?' I said, 'No, I wasn't in an accident.' And she asked, 'Did you hit a moose?' I said, 'No, I never even seen a moose, let alone hit one.' She said, 'Look at your car,' and when I turned around and looked at my car, I couldn't believe it."

I stopped at her home again in the Lexus, just to check in. She was on her back deck and told me she still had no recollection of the collision that broke two bones in her neck. She'd been worried back then that when she next saw a moose, the memories might return and overwhelm her, but she'd seen moose since and — nothing.

Michelle Higgins on the deck behind her house in Norris Arm.

Michelle wanted to tell me, though, that she wasn't alone. Three years after her collision, on a road on Newfoundland's northern peninsula near the tiny community of Conche, a man hit a moose while driving his son's car and carried on driving home without realizing what had happened.

"The moose come out of nowhere, quick — I never even had time hardly to see him, and next thing I know he was on top of the car," Stephen Bromley told the CBC later that week. "I didn't know nothing after that and just kept on driving, kept on going, and I figured I found it a bit cold, like, getting cool, so I figured the air-conditioning was on, so I turned that down, so I kept on going."

Another driver saw him and flagged him down. "I said, 'Stop! Stop!'" Tom Canning told the same CBC journalist. "He pulled over, and I said, 'My lord, Skipper — what happened to you?' He said, 'I don't know.' I didn't know who the man was, but when he spoke, I knew it was Steve because I liked to buy fish from him. I said, 'Steve! Man, you've got no roof on your car! And the windshield is gone!' He was in one terrible mess. He was buried in moose manure and his face was covered totally by blood."

The CBC contacted Michelle that week to tell her of the second collision and asked for a comment. "They said, 'We interviewed him, and he said that he never, ever believed your story,'" she told me. "Him and his dad were sitting out on the front porch when the story was aired and they said, 'That's crazy. There's no way that happened.' And I said, 'Well, I'm glad he finally believed me, but it was a hard way to learn.'"

A few months later, he contacted her to ask for advice about the dizziness he was still feeling, and they became friends on Facebook; several years after that, they arranged to meet for a coffee when they were both visiting Deer Lake. "Him and I met, we talked, and we've been together now three years," she told me. "I said, 'It's a hard way for God to bring us together, isn't it?'"

It wasn't love at first sight — Conche is a very small community, and "I didn't expect him to look the way he looked," she said, "but then I realized, this was the Conche look, and I finally got him wearing normal clothes now. He wore all these baggy pants. I says to him, 'You walk around a corner, your pants is going that way and you're going this way.'"

She still lived at Norris Arm and he still lived 400 kilometres away at Conche, but the plan was to spend winters together at her home and summers at his. "It's a beautiful spot," she said, and showed me photos on her phone. One was of the view across the bay in an evening, with multicoloured lights from the fish plant reflected in the water. "I says, this is my retirement spot. When you sit in his living room and you're looking at the fish plant, it's just unreal. Down there, it's a whole new world."

◻

The first cars to officially drive across Newfoundland were in a posse of five Land Rovers in 1958; they made the journey from St. John's to Port aux Basques on Lloyd Adams's new highway, with Premier Joey Smallwood himself at the wheel of the lead vehicle. Their four-wheel drive was handy on what McCourt later described as "an endless succession of iron-surfaced washboard, gaping potholes, and naked rock — a shoulder-twisting, neck-snapping, dust-shrouded horror." That was five years later, when the circus had to cancel its planned visit to St. John's because the highway bridges couldn't support the weight of the elephants in their trailers; they would have had to walk separately across the dozens of river crossings.

THE DRIVE ACROSS CANADA

It took until November 27, 1965, for the final stretch of highway to be paved in Newfoundland, and to celebrate, Joey Smallwood arranged another official drive for the following summer. This time, it was two separate convoys, one leaving St. John's with Premier Smallwood and the other leaving Port aux Basques with Prime Minister Pearson, and they met in the centre of the island at the road's halfway point near Grand Falls. Along the route, signs declared: WE FINISHED THIS DRIVE IN '65, THANKS TO MR. PEARSON. A 20-metre column was built on a hill overlooking the highway, made of red granite brought in from Smallwood's hometown of Gambo and fashioned by stonemasons from Quebec. An air show flew overhead, and the two politicians shook hands and congratulated each other on a job well done. The hollow pillar was named "Pearson's Peak," and a granite plaque on it let everyone know that "this shaft was unveiled by the Prime Minister Rt. Hon. Lester B. Pearson on July 12, 1966, to mark the official opening of the Trans-Canada Highway in Newfoundland." And then everyone went home and that was that.

The monument was spruced up the next year with lights and an illuminated maple leaf plaque to mark Canada's centenary, but there was nothing

Pearson's Peak had an illuminated maple leaf added in 1967 to mark Canada's centenary.

else there and it became just a place for young people to park their cars and drink beer and make out. Pieces of rock started falling off, and it was closed to the public with a heavy steel gate across its access road. Finally, in 1997, it was pulled down. The plaque and the maple leaf disappeared. I went looking for it in 2012 and eventually found an empty, unheralded site surrounded by trees with a driveway of cracked pavement leading up from the road.

"It seemed to me to be a waste of money," Ron Barrington told me at his home in Badger when I searched for it again in 2023. He'd been a labourer on the project, pouring the concrete and managing the scaffolding for the stonemasons. "It was probably only a couple of hundred thousand dollars, but that was a lot of money at the time. I finished work the day before it was opened, but I never went back on the day. Afterward, we used to hang out there and drink beer and stuff, but it was a garbage dump, people bringing in beer and leaving a mess. When they pulled it down, nobody really missed it."

That wasn't quite true. Terry Best missed it.

"As young kids, because so many older kids drank there, we would collect beer bottles thrown over the bank," he told me over the phone from his home in Windsor, Ontario. "My fondest memories were getting to hang with some of the older kids there, and because it was a free space, a public space, it didn't matter what your age was. You couldn't be excluded at Pearson's Peak."

Terry was from down the road at Buchans Junction, and in 2002, he bought the empty site of Pearson's Peak from the government. "It was just there for the taking, and I don't think anybody else ever considered it haveable. It was considered valueless." His plan was to build a four-bedroom lodge on the property that would have a huge chimney that mimicked the original monument, but then his health deteriorated and his children had no interest in the place, so he put it up for sale two weeks before I drove by in 2023. He was asking $29,000.

His realtor, Darryl Butt, met us there and showed me the land. A Skamper trailer was parked at the top, used by a friend of Terry's, but no one was home. Blackflies swarmed everywhere. A battered lawn chair sat next to a makeshift table outside the trailer door, looking across at a low stub of concrete in the centre of a gravel circle overrun by twiggy bushes. This was the concrete base that once supported the mighty pillar, 65 feet of granite to mark the 65th year of the century when the highway was completed. Now, there was just a red birdhouse sitting on it, the only splash of colour aside from the green of the fir trees. Darryl pushed his way through the branches and sat on the stub for a photo, smiling for the camera, while I swatted at bugs and Peter escaped to the closed-window sanctuary of the Lexus.

"It's zoned commercial, so whatever goes here's got to be something tourist-related," said Darryl. "You've got the location and you've got the view, and the Trail is just down by the Trans-Canada." The former railway line, decommissioned after the construction of the highway, is now a hiking and cycling trail that runs across the island. "And normally, we've got the best weather in Newfoundland."

It was probably going to be a tough sell because of the requirement for tourism, he acknowledged, though an Airbnb might get around it. So far nobody had shown an interest because of its connection to the monument. Ron's cynical words seemed to ring true, that it had been a political glad-hander and a waste of money. When Darryl left, I joined Peter in the filtered air of the Lexus, and we drove away without looking back.

◻

It took another couple of days to reach Port aux Basques. We could have made it in five hours if we'd driven like truckers, but we wanted to take our time and appreciate the scenery of the low mountains and occasional broad lakes. The trees seemed to grow taller as we headed west, with wide swathes cleared beside the highway so drivers would have more warning if a moose should emerge from the forest, though we never saw any. The road was under construction near Deer Lake, and we were diverted onto a small residential road beside the lake for a few kilometres but soon rejoined and continued south past Corner Brook and Stephenville. There were patches of June snow on top of the flat peaks of the dark Table Mountains to the east, and as we followed the two- and three-lane road down its final stretch toward Port aux Basques, we entered the Wreckhouse region, home to some of the highest winds on the island. Some of the highest winds in the world, for that matter.

Ferocious gusts from the mountains can hit 200 kilometres an hour, enough to roll trucks onto their sides. Back when the train was running, the railway company installed a phone at the home of a local farmer and paid him $20 per month to warn the dispatcher if he felt the wind was too dangerous for the trains. Lauchie McDougall was known as the "human wind gauge" because he could "smell" the strength and character of the coming wind. He did this for more than 35 years before he died in 1965, the year the highway across Newfoundland was finished.

We stayed with friends in the nearby Codroy Valley and made a side trip to Rose Blanche, an hour out along the south coast, which I'd visited on my 2012 drive. Edward McCourt also visited Rose Blanche back in 1963 and wrote in *The Road Across Canada*:

> Rose Blanche more than fulfills our dreams of what a Newfoundland village ought to look like.... Houses perch on the point and the off-shore rocks and cling to the cliff-faces rising from the water's edge. The parts of the village are bound together by elevated wooden sidewalks snaking over water and rock and occasionally a substance that might pass for land. Since most places in the village are accessible mostly by boat, Rose Blanche suggests a Venice in miniature — if you can accept a fish-packing plant for a doge's palace and a rowboat for a gondola.

The wooden sidewalks were long gone when I visited in 2012, but I'd stayed then at the only guest house in town, newly opened by a retired couple from Ontario who'd seen the beauty of the small community and wanted to help it prosper. There was an abandoned outport across the bay, Petites, and I went there for an afternoon and wandered its empty houses. I met a couple of summertime fishers who'd been born in the village and left when its 11 families were resettled by the provincial government in 2003; they'd taken the money and bought houses in Rose Blanche but maintained their old homes as best they could. They were now connected to the world by the highway, and on that day, they wanted no part of it.

"I had the opportunity to move to an outport — my husband's from one — but I was never going to go," Mandy Francis told me when we met for lunch during my drive with Peter. She's a freelance journalist who now lives in Port aux Basques. "What do people do? When you're there, everybody goes to bed the same time, 9:30, and the lights are out everywhere. If somebody's lights are still on, you know somebody's not well and you're going to start checking in on them. Everybody is up at five o'clock — that's just the way it is — and your clothes are out on the clothesline by 6:30 for sure. But what do you do in your spare time? There is no spare time, because everything else is harder. So if you're going to kill a caribou or a moose or whatever for the winter, you've got to cut, butcher, and pack that. You've got to hang it, you've got to dress it, you've got to do all the things. That takes work. If you have a wood stove, you've got to cut your wood because there's nowhere to buy it. It's a lot of work. People can't imagine how laborious it is. However, there's no gym there because you don't damn well need one. By nine o'clock, you're beat to a snot and you're ready to go to bed."

The construction of the Trans-Canada Highway helped spur Newfoundland's Resettlement Act of 1965 for its isolated outport communities; towns and villages linked by the road were more economically viable than fishing ports bonded only by sea. Nearly 300 communities with almost 30,000 people were resettled between 1954 and 1975, and more than half of those were moved in the five years after 1965. Even today, remote, isolated communities are still eligible for resettlement if at least 75 percent of their residents request it. These days, it's not the asphalt highway that threatens them — it's the information highway.

"When the internet came, all of a sudden people got connected and the social structure was kind of damaged," said Mandy. "People can order stuff in, and that was just not as easily accessible before. Every week, the supply ferry is piled high with Amazon boxes."

By 2023, the retired couple with the guest house had both died and Rose Blanche was a little busier, with its restored lighthouse as the main attraction. Peter and I parked near the Lightkeeper's Inn bed and breakfast and started walking on the pathway to the lighthouse, but a woman called to us from the other side of the fence to come back and pay admission. When we returned to the car and found some money and went to where she'd been at the ticket hut, she was gone on some errand and was nowhere to be found. We walked out to the lighthouse anyway, and it was easy to imagine both the loneliness and the clarity of life there a hundred years ago. The sea still beat against the rocks in the exact same way it must have done a century before. When we came back to the parking lot, the woman who'd called to us to pay was still nowhere to be found. There wasn't even a sign stating the cost, or a box in which to place payment, which I would have gladly given, for the lighthouse was a superb restoration. So we left Rose Blanche and returned along the coast to Port aux Basques, feeling a little less welcome than when we'd arrived.

I was sad not just for the sense of losing a small community that was slowly merging into the modern day, which I recognize as a simplistic viewpoint. I was also sad for finally reaching Port aux Basques, where I would drive down to the harbour to see the utter devastation wrought upon it by Hurricane Fiona the previous September.

☐

Thrusting my hands deep into the pockets of my down jacket for warmth in the thin mist, I strode down to the water with René Roy. He's the editor-in-chief of Wreckhouse Press, and one-quarter of the staff of the *Wreckhouse Weekly*. The newspaper has won regional awards for its coverage of the hurricane; his sister, who's the senior reporter, wrote a piece for the *National Post* that won a National Newspaper Award. René led the way, talking about the house that once stood here, the trees that were once there, the person who died, and the people who lost everything.

"We knew it was coming, but I don't think the gravity hit a lot of people," he said. "At six o'clock in the morning, I heard every single siren in town coming down the road. When I got up, the wind was unreal, the rain was incredible, and you could feel the salt. You could taste the salt. I've been through several hurricanes, but this was unlike any other. There were no gusts — the wind was constant. I equated it to a bomb that went off for 20 hours."

René Roy beside the washed-away beach at Port aux Basques.

We paused on Water Street. A slope of gravel led down to the rocks beside the calm bay, but this was no beach — it was the filled-in land where homes had stood until the storm surge hit.

"There was an orange house here," René said, pointing to the right, "and there was a two-storey apartment building with 10 units here." He pointed to the left. "There was a house here where we're standing, and these were all crushed by Fiona. The surge will come in and it stays, and then the next wave comes in and it stays, and the next and it stays, and it will eventually crest. And then eventually it will move out and take everything with it. There was a gentleman here named Smoky, got swept under his house, and it was only when the water backed off for a quick second that he was able to come out and run for his life."

There were some white-siding bungalows, and they seemed fine until I looked more closely and saw walls and windows missing. A length of white picket fence ran beside the road, and René strode up to it. "This woman had just started a home business, a massage and wellness spa, and the water just came in and took it out. Took the oil tank and put it across the road. Right here on the road, I was in probably two and a half feet of water. There was a smell of fuel oil. If there'd been a spark, with the fuel in the air, everything would be gone, so I got out of there."

Fiona lasted all day, affecting much of Nova Scotia and Prince Edward Island, but striking hard right here at Port aux Basques. It was a category 4 hurricane that became the costliest weather event ever to hit Atlantic Canada. More than 100 homes were condemned in the community of 4,000 people. A woman died when she and her husband ran out from their home to their car to drive away to safety — at the last moment, she went back to her house to retrieve something and was swept out to sea by the surge.

I'd seen the footage on TV, and it had seemed like just another awful weather event, daily occurrences in the end-of-days television montage of storms and fires and tornadoes and floods. But here at the site, where residents in the summer calm of previous years had relaxed in deck chairs and cut their lawns and drank tea, it felt real and dreadful.

"You can build for wind, and you can build for snow, and you can build for earthquakes, but there's nothing you can do to build against the ocean," said René. "One cubic metre of water weighs one tonne. You have a thousand cubic metres and there's no chance at all. No chance."

We knocked on the door of a house that seemed intact, surrounded by derelict wrecks of homes and empty lots. Elias Osmond came to the door.

"We always felt safe here," Elias said, "but we had five houses around us and now they're all gone. I'd like to sell, but who's going to buy?" He's lived in the neat and tidy two-storey house with his wife, Margaret, for the past 54 years while working a lifetime at the ferry terminal. Damage to their home was minimal, just the luck of the draw, but like everyone else, they were denied coverage by their insurance company because the water damage came from a storm surge, not "overland water."

"I can't even think of us staying here for another winter," said Margaret. "The waves is going higher, it seems like the water is getting higher, and the wind's getting stronger and more often. For sure there'll be another. When the wind's up, I don't feel safe. I don't sleep and I just goes from window to window. I can't handle it. It's taking a toll on us for sure."

I took some photos of Elias on his deck, with a fresh-painted fishing-boat weathervane behind him and the shell of his neighbour's washed-out home just beyond that, then René and I walked back to the warmth of the newspaper office two streets away.

"There's scars on the community and there's scars on the people, too, eh?" said René. "Everything's different now about Port aux Basques. Everything. You used to be able to go to the grocery store and say, 'How you doing?' But now you go to the grocery store and people just move along. The scars are still there. That home on Water Street that was left dangling over the water? The woman who lived there used to go down there and have a cup of tea and look at her house, because that's where she used to have her cup of tea before. Every day, she's reminded that her house is destroyed, because it sat there for six months. There's weight to that — that's heavy on you."

René was born here but moved away as a boy, and only came back eight years ago after a short career with Canada Post in Halifax. He founded his newspaper after the previous local paper was sold and closed down, which had put his sister out of a job. I asked how important the ferry was for the town's existence — after all, Port aux Basques is an intrinsic part of the Trans-Canada itself. The highway enters the island here and leaves here to connect the province.

"The only reason Port aux Basques is here is because that ferry's here," said René. "There's no fishery anymore — the odd crab boat, the odd lobsterman, but that's just sustainability fishing. There used to be hundreds of boats in the harbour here, but now you get just a rowboat or two. It's the only thing keeping this community going. I'd say 60 percent of the people in town work for the ferry, at least."

And the benefits for the town? Aside from the ferry, the recent streamlining of the highway means there are few passengers who stop for anything more than gas or a coffee at the Tim Hortons. "People get off the boat and they're gone," he said. "It used to be that you'd get off the boat and be in town, but they've bypassed the town now."

So I asked him the big question, just before heading out myself and lining up in the Lexus with Peter to catch the daily crossing over to the mainland: Why on earth would he want to live in Port aux Basques?

"This is home. It's familiar, it's peaceful, there's no crime," he said. "You can leave here, walk five minutes away, and be completely alone in the middle of nowhere, and that's very therapeutic. You're not overwhelmed with people, not inundated all the time."

I must have looked unconvinced.

He leaned closer across his desk. "There are people here that are still resilient and say, 'I lived here my whole life — I'm not leaving,'" he said. "When I went to the Salvation Army, they had a giveaway of materials that had been donated, and somebody had donated pins — you know, like the ones that say PORT AUX BASQUES STRONG or BOSTON STRONG and so on? Our pins said FUCK FIONA. And I thought that was so much more perfect. The Salvation Army had these pins out, going 'Yup.' I thought it was beautiful. That's Port aux Basques."

LEGEND

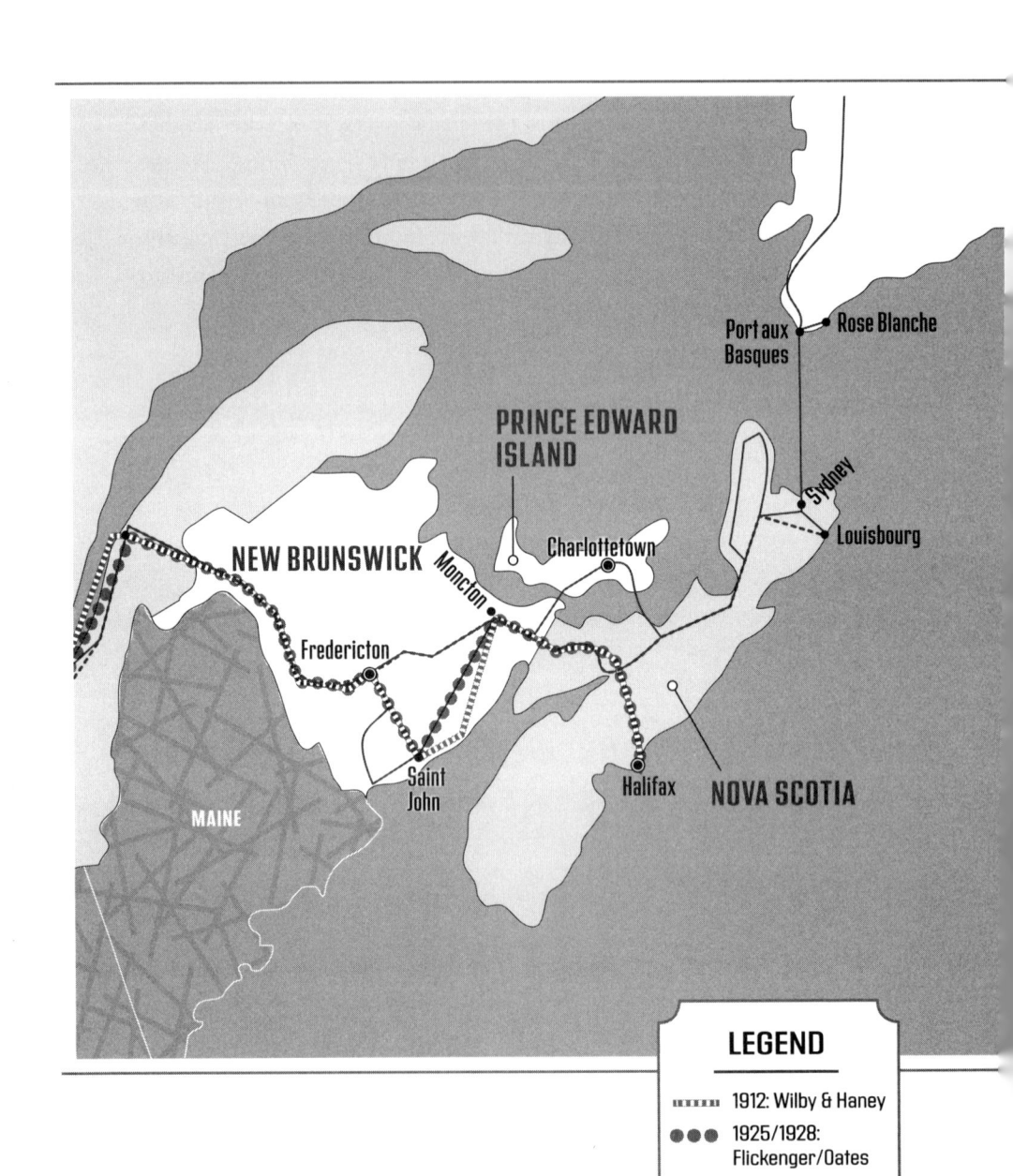

- ▪▪▪▪▪ 1912: Wilby & Haney
- ●●● 1925/1928: Flickenger/Oates
- ----- 1946: Macfarlane
- ——— 2023: Richardson

2
Nova Scotia

Louisbourg is about an hour's drive in the wrong direction from North Sydney where the ferry empties its vehicles to head southwest through Cape Breton on the Trans-Canada Highway. Peter and I took a detour to Louisbourg anyway, speeding along roads not yet slowed by tourist traffic. I was driving, and we stayed a depressing night in a motel that should have cost $100 but charged us twice that. There are nice places to stay in the town, but this motel wasn't one of them. We ate chicken fingers and fries out of plastic baskets and swigged long-neck Schooner beer while we played unimpressive pool in a cavernous, almost deserted bar. Three or four locals watched from the other end of the room, but none of us felt much like talking.

We wanted to come to Louisbourg because this was where Brigadier (Retired) Alex Macfarlane and Squadron Leader (Retired) Ken MacGillivray began their drive to earn the Todd Medal in 1946. The rules for the medal originally stipulated Louisbourg as the starting point because it was about the most easterly place in Canada — at least before Newfoundland joined the country in 1949. That requirement was quickly lifted, since there were enough challenges with the rest of the roads that a start from the Atlantic

Ocean at Halifax was deemed fine. Even so, Macfarlane and MacGillivray decided to damn it all and do it properly and left from Louisbourg on May 9, 1946.

Actually, MacGillivray probably had little say in the decision. He never drove the car, and because of that, his name isn't on the medal. Macfarlane was happy to take full credit. Sound familiar?

"I am and always have been an active rather than a bookish person," Macfarlane wrote for the medal committee in a brief account of the journey once it was complete. "I would always rather see things and have a small part in them than read about them. That is one reason why when I heard that in 1912 Victoria's ex-Mayor Albert E. Todd had offered a gold medal for the first motorist to cross Canada from coast to coast without going beyond the

Brigadier (Retired) Alex Macfarlane was awarded the Todd Medal for being the first person to drive across Canada on Canadian roads.

borders of the country, I became interested in making the trip. It wasn't the medal, but the thought of it lying unclaimed for a matter of thirty-four years was, in itself, a challenge."

The Brig, as most everyone called him, was a larger-than-life man who loved a challenge. He was born into a comfortable home in Montreal in 1890, but his father made some bad investments in the railway and lost most of the family money. When his parents moved to the Niagara area to start again with a fruit farm, young Alex went to Wyoming to be a cowboy, and then, the year after war broke out in Europe, he joined the Canadian Army as a private. He enrolled in officer training and became a lieutenant in charge of transport for Canada's 58th Battalion, but this was no cushy headquarters position — he earned a reputation in the French trenches as a sniper. "A German would light up a cigarette and that was it," his grandson, Jim, told me. He was shot and wounded three separate times in action, earning three Distinguished Service Orders and France's Croix de Guerre for his courage.

Macfarlane was promoted to lieutenant colonel in charge of his battalion and returned to Canada a hero. He joined the Ford Motor Company and moved for a while to Australia to set up its production facilities and then, that done, came back to Canada, became a stockbroker, made a fortune, then lost a fortune in the Wall Street crash of 1929.

Jim told me his grandfather was a natural salesman and started making money selling liquor out of the back of his car — presumably taking it over the border to nearby Americans while Prohibition made it lucrative. When the Second World War began, Macfarlane rejoined the army as a colonel director of mechanization in Ottawa, then was posted to Winnipeg where he earned a U.S. Army Silver Star for his part in training paratroopers at Camp Shilo. He resigned the post in 1944 as a protest against forced conscription.

And then there was MacGillivray, the newspaperman with "a quiet but forceful personality," according to his obituary in the *Globe and Mail*. He'd been the youngest-ever city editor of Toronto's *Globe* at 26 years old, but eventually left in 1938 to become an advertising man. His military career in the Second World War sent him around the Mediterranean as a press liaison officer for the Royal Air Force and ultimately to handle public relations for the Royal Canadian Air Force in London. When he returned to Canada, he went back to advertising but took time out to drive across the country with Macfarlane, who shared his love for horses.

MacGillivray was 18 years younger than Macfarlane and was described in the journey's account as "my associate and co-pilot." "Really, the other guy that was there didn't do anything," said Jim, all those years later. "He was probably just confirmation that it was done."

For some reason, Macfarlane seemed to think of the drive as a race, even though the rules for the medal were clear: "Tour is to be in no sense either a speed or reliability trial." Macfarlane was never much for following rules he disagreed with, and so everything was a rush.

He'd wired the Victoria Automobile Club on May 6 to say he'd make the attempt to earn the Todd Medal, and the club wired him back the next day to accept the attempt. He'd already used his considerable contacts to persuade General Motors to provide a car. "We picked on the sort of car that anyone could see himself driving," he wrote in his account. "It happened to be a standard model Chevrolet 4-door Sedan and the only special equipment was an extra spare tire." Two days later, under the watchful eye of the mayor of Louisbourg, they backed their rear wheels into the Atlantic and then sped off through the rain toward the Pacific. The maritime roads were paved all the way, and they wasted no time. That night, they reached Edmundston in New Brunswick, just shy of the Quebec border, "after what seemed a fairly good day's run of 681 miles." That's almost 1,100 kilometres, which is quite an achievement even today, let alone in a 1946 Chevy Stylemaster.

I can only imagine the stiff-upper-lipped conversation, or lack of it, in that car as the two drove west and north on "long straight stretches that make for both comfort and safety and, perhaps behind our hand, we might add the word, speed."

◻

Peter and I didn't bother trying to dip our wheels into the ocean at Louisbourg — we'd already done that in St. John's, the only place where it now matters — but we did take a short drive to the huge fortress. It was closed to visitors and wouldn't open for another hour. We didn't stick around because the fortress, and the reconstructed town alongside, deserves at least a day of exploration.

If we'd stayed, we'd have seen guides in period costumes wandering the houses and offices of what had once been the pride of France. The fortress was built after the Treaty of Utrecht in 1713 to protect the approach into the St. Lawrence River, with its access to Quebec City and Montreal, and the town and deep-water port it stood over became one of the largest European fortifications in North America. It took only three decades before the English and French started fighting again, when a militia force of New Englanders grabbed the opportunity to come up and lay siege. The undermanned French surrendered after seven weeks, but dysentery and typhoid moved in with the occupiers and claimed almost 1,000 of the young militiamen over the next two winters. In 1748, worn out from the ravages of sickness and surrounded by shallow graves, the disease-ridden men gave the fortress back to France. Then 10 years later, the English decided they wanted to get rid of the fortress after all and laid siege again, this time with 12,000 Regulars who died by the hundreds on the beaches and in the swamps behind. When the French finally surrendered for the second time, after holding out for five months of carnage, Vice-Admiral "Foulweather Jack" Byron razed the place to the ground. All that was left were scattered stones, foundations, and the maps, plans, and books Parks Canada used in the 1960s to reconstruct about a quarter of the town.

We missed all of that. After all, Peter lives in a country where such history lurks beneath every rock, and our real journey was only just beginning.

◻

We were grateful for the GPS that guided us around the bypasses of Sydney and North Sydney, where the ferry leaves for Newfoundland and the Trans-Canada Highway resumes its way west. Once we were beyond the big-box stores and coffee shops, and loaded up on caffeine and bacon, the distance began to tick along on course as it had on The Rock.

This is a peculiar stretch of highway across Cape Breton, however, because it's the only section of the Trans-Canada's direct route that isn't part of the National Highway System. It's one of the strange exceptions that have mired the highway in political squabbling since its inception. It seems everywhere you go in Canada, more so than in most other countries, if there's any doubt whatsoever on who's responsible for something political, then it's automatically the problem of somebody else. To their credit, transport ministers at all levels of Canadian governments tried to fix this for the country's roads in 1988 with the creation of the National Highway System, which designated 24,500 kilometres of existing highways as being of national importance, so the federal government would assist with their maintenance or improvement if needed. Another 14,000 kilometres were added in 2004.

Not this stretch, though. The Trans-Canada through Cape Breton isn't part of the national system. That designation goes to Highways 104 and 4, which run between Port Hawkesbury and Sydney on the other side of Bras d'Or Lake. How come? Nobody seemed to know, so I called up a retired planner for the Ministry of Transportation, and his answer was simple: the Trans-Canada didn't need improving in 1988, but Highway 4 did. It required some major investment to smooth out its corners and hills, and it was a slightly shorter route too. Either road qualified because they linked the same two important ports, so it would have been an easy choice for the province to tap the federal coffers. Then why wasn't Highway 4 designated as the original Trans-Canada Highway? "I heard a rumour that a federal politician lived in Baddeck and he said the road had to go by his place," the retired planner told me. In Nova Scotia, rumours are rife.

◻

The impact of Hurricane Fiona wasn't confined to Port aux Basques — far from it. We saw whole stands of slender trees pushed over to obscene angles beside the road from Louisbourg, and it was no different on the dull stretch of highway out of North Sydney. Trees were about all we could see beside the two- and three-lane road until it curved to the right, the horizon opened up, and we began to drive across the slim, blue channel that connects the ocean with Bras d'Or Lake. Ahead of us was the Seal Island arched bridge, built in 1961 for $4.5 million. Edward McCourt described it two years later in *The Road Across Canada* as "one of the most beautiful bridges in Canada, a slender green filament suspended between water and sky.... The hills rise up abruptly from the water's edge, and hills and water and sky combine to form a flawlessly balanced pastoral."

The bridge is indeed beautiful, with an elegant green arch that swoops across the deepest section of the channel, but it's falling apart. You can't see the crumbling concrete in the trusses below, or the rust in the metal spars. Engineers say it has another 15 years of safe use and then something must be done, except nobody can agree on what exactly that should be. Repair the bridge for maybe another 50 years of use? That could cost 100 times the original price. Build another bridge alongside? That could be even more expensive still.

One thing the politicians agree on is that nobody wants to move the bridge. Before it was built, the channel was crossed by a pair of ferries, one 20 kilometres to the north and the other 20 kilometres to the south. The bridge put both those small communities out of business. It's generally held that it was placed squarely in the middle of the crossings to placate the ferry operators, but local lore has it that a provincial politician pushed for the placement to make money from selling his land. What is it with these rumours about Nova Scotia politicians?

The bridge crosses west to the base of Kellys Mountain, which rises rapidly in that flawlessly balanced pastoral to some 240 metres above the water. This means there's a hairpin on the Trans-Canada with flashing warning signs and a recommended speed of 40 kilometres per hour. It's the only sharp curve on the highway outside British Columbia, and it pushes the original standard that drivers should always be able to see 600 feet ahead, or at least 182 metres. The province has no plans to change it, however. Right now, they're still trying to figure out how to pay for the bridge.

□

The road continues on to Baddeck, but we'd travelled through that town on our drive east to Newfoundland and knew the highway to be monotonous for drivers: spruce and birch and maple trees are cut well back from the two-lane road, with the occasional farm or lumberyard to one side. The community itself is blessed with laid-back charm — there are no traffic lights, and plenty of restaurants offer lobster suppers and craft beer. In summer, pleasure boats fill the harbour on the saltwater lake, which is actually so large that it's a tidal estuary. As such, Baddeck is popular with tourists who come to visit the museum dedicated to Alexander Graham Bell, its most famous resident.

In fact, Bell and his family split their time between their townhouse in Washington, D.C., and their large property across the sound from Baddeck, which he bought as a summer home after becoming wealthy from the invention of the telephone. The museum sells newly printed copies of *Baddeck, and That Sort of Thing*, written by the American novelist Charles Dudley Warner after he visited in 1873, and which claims to be "the book that brought Alexander Graham Bell to Baddeck." Warner extolled: "The most electric American, heir of all the nervous diseases of the ages could not but find peace in this scene of tranquil beauty."

The hills and lakes reminded The Great Man of his native Scotland, and they were a welcome break from the humidity of the American capital. "[We] had already spent several summers seeking a place of salt water, mountains and valleys and cool climate, far enough from fashionable centres to put our little girls in trousers, and live a simple, free and unconventional life," wrote Bell's wife, Mabel. "We had found it at last." The Bells built a number of houses on the peninsula, and Alexander appreciated the peace and quiet for being able to think through the many projects and experiments he conducted over the next 37 years. The most notable were with hydrofoils and seaplanes on the lake, where he sponsored the first powered flight in the British Empire.

Instead of revisiting Baddeck, Peter and I took a sharp turn after crossing Kellys Mountain and drove to the short chain ferry at Englishtown to make a detour around the island. For the 28 kilometres that pass Baddeck, the Trans-Canada Highway is also part of the Cabot Trail, a 300-kilometre loop that twists and turns through the wooded slopes of Cape Breton Highlands

National Park and dips to run past the Acadian harbours and sandy beaches of the Gulf of St. Lawrence. It's considered one of the world's great drives, and I wanted to show it to Peter, but in the end, all we saw for most of it was dense fog and occasional brake lights ahead. The breathtaking scenery and inspiring vistas were lost in the late-spring mist. We returned to the Trans-Canada to travel the last hour of Cape Breton Island and finally cross over to Canada's true mainland.

□

Cape Bretoners were mixed in their feelings toward the Canso Causeway when it was built in the 1950s. They knew it would only boost the economy of the island, but they didn't want to lose their independence. Most traced their ancestry directly to Scotland where the English *sassenachs* had evicted them from their land in the Highland clearances, and they didn't want a

Some 40,000 people attended the opening of the Canso Causeway in 1955, linking Cape Breton Island to the Nova Scotia mainland.

permanent connection to the mainland to do the same thing. Gaelic was still spoken widely. Many were quick to quote an apocryphal prayer, attributed to an unnamed 19th-century Presbyterian minister on the island: "And more especially do we thank thee, O Lord, for the Gut of Canso, thine own body of water, which separates us from the wickedness that lieth on the other side thereof."

For its part, Nova Scotia had held out against agreeing to the Trans-Canada Highway because the route wouldn't go through Halifax, its largest city — it was directed by the federal government to take the most direct route across the country, and that didn't allow dipping back down to the ocean. If the province was to consent to such a concession, it would need something to make up for it, and that was a fixed road to Cape Breton. After all, the railcars of island coal and steel had to be ferried across the swift-running strait in all weathers, and the proposed highway to Newfoundland would only increase traffic.

When the federal government finally agreed in 1952 to pay for a causeway, Angus L. Macdonald, Nova Scotia's proud small-town Cape Bretoner premier, recognized the good deal and wasted no time. On September 16, 1952, he was there to help dump the first load of rock into the strait. Over the next 27 months, it was followed by more than nine million tonnes of granite.

Engineers had considered building a bridge but ruled it out because of the potential pressure of winter ice on its foundations. A causeway, however, would need to be the deepest in the world, built up from 65 metres below the water's surface. The rock was right there at nearby Cape Porcupine, and it was dropped into the water, truckload after truckload, until it formed a pyramid that twists gently in an S-shape for more than 1,300 metres through the strait. At its base, the causeway is 262 metres wide, rising to a tenth of that above the surface, where the two traffic lanes are protected from sea waves by short walls of rock. A quarter-kilometre canal with a swing bridge was built at the north end to allow small ships through, and the water on its eastern side now remains ice-free throughout the winter. No one expected that. It was called the eighth wonder of the world.

Not everyone was impressed, of course. When the causeway was formally opened in August 1955, at a ceremony in front of an estimated 40,000 people, 100 invited pipers marched across from the mainland playing "The Road to the Isles" on pipes and drums, followed by 500 more who weren't invited but joined in anyway. The story goes that one of them, Roderick MacPherson — Big Rod the Piper — refused to blow into his bagpipes in silent protest. Like the location of the Seal Island Bridge, it's a story that only grows in the telling.

When Peter and I reached Port Hastings at the Cape Breton end of the causeway, we paused at the little park that looks south across the strait. I could imagine the granite highway packed with visitors, and over on the mainland, the dignitaries gathered on a stage to impart the importance of the day upon the people. Many politicians spoke then, but not the man most instrumental in pressing for the link: Premier Angus L. Macdonald had died the previous year. The late premier's brother, Father Stanley Macdonald, was at the podium, though, and when he spoke in Gaelic, the crowd listened closely to his words.

Journalist and author Linden MacIntyre was a 12-year-old boy on the day of the festivities, watching from near his home in Port Hastings, though he didn't hear any of the speeches for himself. He writes in his poignant memoir, *Causeway: A Passage from Innocence*, that Father Stanley was originally given just one minute to speak in Gaelic, but he complained and they gave him two minutes. "And from what I hear," wrote MacIntyre, "he used the whole two minutes to talk about how ignorant the people from Ottawa were, trying to limit the one speech of the day in the language of Adam and Eve to a minute or even two minutes. But how he forgave them because you had to remember that Ottawa was still a young and unsophisticated place compared to here."

Most of the assembled people understood Gaelic, and they laughed and applauded, so the politicians, who hadn't followed a word, all laughed and applauded too, which made the people laugh and applaud even more. Then C.D. Howe, the federal minister of trade and commerce, swung a Scottish claymore from the Battle of Culloden through the tartan ribbon across the road and declared the causeway open. Out on the water among the pleasure boats, the guns on HMCS *Quebec* thundered in salute, Royal Canadian Air Force jets roared overhead, the pipers began piping and marching across the causeway, and Cape Breton was an island no more.

◻

It took less than a minute for us to cross the causeway in the Lexus and continue through to the mainland. We barely noticed the deep water to either side before the smooth road carried us to Antigonish County, and the hills lessened to caress the sky instead of bumping against it. The highway itself was mostly just one lane in each direction with the occasional passing lane, slowing our speed to the pace of whatever was the slowest vehicle at the front of a long line of traffic. When Peter took on the driving, that was us, and I just watched the green fields and well-kept farms slide by to either side of the highway. It was relaxing, I must admit.

We stayed the night in Antigonish at a pleasant bed and breakfast and resumed west the next day. The highway finally expanded into four lanes, divided by a wide central median and hemmed in on both sides by shallow gravel slopes. This was the newest stretch of opened Trans-Canada, so recent that our GPS showed us driving through green swathes of roadless countryside. In the next few years, the provincial government plans to widen and twin the highway like this all the way through to the causeway. The drive will be quick, safe, and almost as monotonous as staring at trees.

Just west of New Glasgow, the Trans-Canada splits away from the conventional Highway 104, which stays on the mainland to skirt past Truro and then head north to New Brunswick. It divides into a second road, Highway 106, that travels directly north for 10 minutes or so until it butts up against the water again at the Caribou ferry terminal. This is the shortcut to Prince Edward Island, Canada's smallest and most overlooked province, and we lined up there with the other cars and trucks and waited our turn to board.

◻

But before we cross, let's back up. Not to 1946, when Macfarlane and MacGillivray are speeding along old Highway 4 with nary a backward glance, but to 1928, with Jimmy Oates on his motorcycle, and to 1925, with Ed Flickenger in his Ford Model T. And the first of them all, 1912, with Thomas Wilby, Jack Haney, and the Reo. Everyone is backing into the ocean at Halifax, ready to drive to the Pacific.

Wilby told the local newspaper he expected the journey to take 35 days, though it ended up consuming 53. He knew it would probably be impossible to drive across the roadless north shore of Lake Superior, but he held out hope that a guide would help him pick his way through British Columbia's mountains. If he succeeded in this, he would at least qualify to win Todd's second medal for the Winnipeg to Victoria run, entirely in Canada. This would just be gravy, however. He was both an author and a journalist and not entirely successful at either, but he had the full sponsorship of the Reo Motor Car Company and he intended to write a book about his pioneering drive across Canada. He was freshly inspired from his journey the year before, when he'd persuaded the Ohio Motor Car Company to provide a car and chauffeur for himself and his wife to drive from New York City to San Francisco and San Diego and then back to New York. It was a three-month journey on rudimentary but established roads, which he used as the basis for a romantic novel, *On the Trail to Sunset*. Trust me — you don't need to read it.

This time around, Reo supplied him with a special touring car, the same 30-horsepower model that in 1905 had been the first automobile to complete a round trip across North America. It had even won the speed record five years later when it was driven from New York City to San Francisco in 10 days. Wilby's car was assembled at the company's Canadian factory in St. Catharines, fitted with boxes on the running boards to carry chains, pulleys, and spare gasoline tanks, and then sent by rail to Halifax where, somewhere along the way, it was promptly lost.

That wasn't a good start to the trip. Several days passed before it was found in a Quebec shipping yard and sent on to the East Coast, during which time, Wilby and the driver, Jack Haney, got to know each other a little better. It didn't help that Haney was half the age of Wilby, but it was a downright insult to the journalist that Haney was an American from Indiana. He'd already written to Reo to demand his chauffeur should be either Canadian or English, who would presumably be suitably deferential, but the Reo manager insisted it must be Haney or nothing. After all, Jack Haney was the company's head mechanic in Canada, a proven troubleshooter, and well travelled from being dispatched to repair cars across the country.

When Haney and Wilby finally met, the latter's opinion was already firmly decided. "He was a young expert driver, very much like those whom I had seen in the States," Wilby wrote in *A Motor Tour Through Canada*, "sturdy, independent, self-contained fellows, with the sense of relationship to their fellow-men hopelessly confused by their own interpretation of democracy and equality." He promptly sent Haney off to buy him some clothes; the British author believed in packing light, and his only luggage, aside from the clothes on his back and his trademark battered fedora, was a shaving kit, his writing materials, and a change of socks. Haney bit his tongue and lent him two of his own suitcases, then purchased a change of clothes for him, charged to expenses, of course.

Thomas Wilby collects some salt water from the Atlantic Ocean at Halifax in 1912, while Jack Haney waits to start their drive across Canada.

On August 27, 1912, after a suitable lunch, Haney drove Wilby to the stony beach in Halifax and backed the Reo into the ocean. Wilby gathered some salt water into a bottle, called "All on board for Vancouver!" and then they drove to the city hall where there were speeches and the deputy mayor gave him a letter of greeting for the mayor of Vancouver. It was raining, and they headed north on the red clay highway with an escort of a half-dozen local cars. "We reached Truro that night over wet, muddy roads with no trouble," wrote Haney later in his diary.

The weather was better for Ed Flickenger on September 8, 1925. He was a staff photographer and "movie man" for the Ford Motor Company; while he filmed everything, somebody — probably the local Ford dealer — backed the car into the water and collected a letter for the mayor of Vancouver. The Model T at least had a permanent roof, and the drive would have been amiable and comparatively comfortable; the wheels wouldn't be changed for travelling on railway tracks until they reached Quebec.

The drive was organized by Perry Doolittle, a family doctor and former competitive cyclist who formed the Toronto Automobile Club in 1903, and who then became president of the Ontario Motor League and then the Canadian Automobile Association until his death in 1933. He'd spent a lifetime advocating for better roads, and most of all, for a coast-to-coast highway across the Dominion. As he told an American journalist in 1921, "I don't want an up-and-down tombstone. They can lay me away with a smile on my face if they will put mine flat on the ground — a ribbon stretching for 4,000 miles."

Doolittle had driven to Vancouver many times, always ducking into the United States where there were no roads in Canada. He'd recently returned home to Toronto from a drive to Halifax and back, which he spoke about that month at the annual meeting of the CAA, calling the Maritimes "a veritable motor tourists' paradise." For the Ford's cross-country drive, he designed a route that would allow the Model T to travel by its own power entirely north of the border. It was to be a high-profile demonstration of the need for Canadian roads, and Flickenger filmed a movie to be shown in theatres.

A second passenger, J.L. Scrymgeour, a former newspaperman, came along for much of the journey to handle the many ceremonies at cities along the way, while the actual driving was entrusted to local Ford executives and dealers. It would take them 40 days to reach Victoria, where the *Daily Times* newspaper explained that "no one driver had piloted the car across the Dominion, but as each one of the eleven branches of the Ford Company in Canada was reached a new driver would take the wheel. Mr. Flickenger is the only one of the original party which left Halifax to make the whole trip." Like Wilby and Haney, Flickenger and the Ford officials headed north on dirt roads and stayed the night in Truro.

It was Jimmy Oates in 1928 who had the rough deal. He was a British adventurer who happened to wander into a motorcycle shop in Toronto the previous year, where he was introduced to the Canadian representative for Castrol Oil. The Castrol rep turned out to be an old wartime chum, and they ended up drinking at a local hotel. Maybe it was the whiskey talking, but when the rep confessed that Castrol wasn't selling well in Canada, Oates suggested it needed a publicity stunt to prove itself — and he was the guy for it! A coast-to-coast drive would demonstrate reliability, and a smaller motorcycle would be more capable than any clunky car. Astonishingly, it still seemed a good idea the next morning.

The Ariel Motorcycle Company agreed to provide him with a new 500 cc "two-port" model, and the Sturgess company of Hamilton fitted it with an extra-long sidecar that could be used for a bed. Oates called the bike "Toby." He met many times with Perry Doolittle to plan for the journey, though there would be no swapping of his wheels to ride on the rails themselves, just a bumpy trip on the ties between the tracks. He even rode the train on the route beforehand to figure out where to leave fuel and oil supplies, because unlike everyone before him, he'd be alone on this venture. He persuaded the CPR to register Toby as an "unscheduled freight train," and he learned how to climb telegraph poles to use field telephones. However, his sponsorship didn't extend to shipping the bike to Halifax by rail, and on the ride east from Toronto, the journey almost ended before it began.

"Driving downhill on a narrow road when I was suddenly confronted with a nasty looking corner," Oates wrote in his journal. "It was impossible to get round in safety, so I ran across someone's front garden where three children were playing. Their surprise at seeing me was unbounded and one little fellow did his utmost to imitate a monkey by attempting to climb the nearest apple tree! Roads unsafe for fast travel on high averages."

Oates slowed down, made it to Halifax, and on the morning of July 21, 1928, backed Toby down a slipway into the ocean for the gathered photographers. The mayor was there and gave him a bottle of water and the obligatory greeting for the mayor of Vancouver — how many greetings does a mayor need? — and Oates headed off. It's not known where he spent that night, but at least it wasn't raining. "Had pictures taken," he wrote. "Bid Halifax bye bye and started kicking the gravel again. The roads were terrible and many times I had to lift my feet to prevent their being injured whilst crashing through the loose stones."

◻

There were no loose stones for Peter and me when we drove east through Nova Scotia on the Trans-Canada a couple of weeks earlier on our way to Newfoundland. The road from the New Brunswick border was fast and smooth all the way, as it should be: we were non-residents of the province and paid a $4 toll to drive the highway. This is the only toll still left on the Trans-Canada, unless you include the cost of ferries and crossing the Confederation Bridge out of Prince Edward Island, and it's been a political hot potato for years. It was only in 2021 that the newly elected Progressive Conservatives made good on that year's election promise and announced the highway was free to use for all Nova Scotia residents.

It wasn't always to be this way. In the 1990s, the provincial government expected to widen the existing Trans-Canada that threaded its way in two and sometimes three lanes through the sleepy and scenic Wentworth Valley, 15 minutes to the east. The concrete highway was built there in 1957 to replace the dirt and gravel roads, part of the provincial commitment to the Trans-Canada, but it had become dangerous with greatly increased traffic. Additional land was already expropriated for inevitable expansion, and the plans for the valley route were good to go. The only problem was the local residents, who most definitely didn't want it in their backyards.

"Traffic was terrible," said Carol Hyslop, a retired elementary schoolteacher from Wentworth, when I met her in 2012. "Fumes from the traffic were terrible — children were getting asthma. You couldn't cross the road. There were always accidents, but that was the only route they'd thought of to develop. They hadn't considered any alternatives. So we got a petition going. We didn't want it to go through the valley, period."

Carol and her husband, Bob, helped form the Wentworth Valley Environmental Protection Association and began a letter-writing campaign to develop an alternate route for the Trans-Canada. The 40 or so local property owners were well educated and well organized and they never let up. Eventually, the provincial government agreed to avoid the valley completely and built the new highway on top of Cobequid Pass alongside. In winter, the weather up there can be fierce and motorists are sometimes stranded in the snow for hours, but the rest of the time, it's swift and safe and bothers no one. The mountain construction cost much more than the original sheltered route, so the toll was introduced to cover the extra expense.

Carol and Bob Hyslop, seen here at their home in the Wentworth Valley in 2012.

"She had the most powerful computer in the world," former MP Bill Casey told me in 2012. "It was only a Commodore 64, with a dot-matrix printer, but it got a highway moved to the top of a mountain."

Peter and I doubled back from the toll road to drive through the Wentworth Valley and meet up again with Carol. We found her at the same home where I'd sat on her porch and chatted with her and Bob, swatting at bugs and enjoying the clean air. She seemed as well and feisty as ever. Bob died a few years ago, but I reminded her of what he'd told me back then. "I'm proud of her," he'd said. "She took on the government and won. She proved that you really can make a difference, you know."

It took only a leisurely day for us to then run the length of the Trans-Canada through Nova Scotia: 460 easy kilometres from the New Brunswick border at Amherst to the ferry at North Sydney. Now, it was time to return, and when the ferry to Prince Edward Island opened its cavernous hull at Caribou, we drove on board with the other tourists and soon watched the green shores of Nova Scotia slip away beyond the horizon.

3
Prince Edward Island

The first car ever to be driven in Canada was a steam-powered contraption that took to the roads of Prince Edward Island in 1866. Well, it sort of took to the roads. It was bought in New Jersey by a P.E.I. priest and shipped to the island in December that year, but it took a team of horses to drag it from the Charlottetown dock to its new home in Rustico. Nobody had ever seen a car before, let alone knew how to drive one.

It was built five years previously by a railway engineer named Elijah Ware, who liked tinkering with steam engines and probably created it as a home project in his company's machine shop. It was basically a platform between four huge, thin wheels, which were connected to the engine by a chain. The wood-fired boiler sat behind a pair of seats and a steering wheel, and the driver used ropes to pull the car into either forward or reverse gear. It was capable of 50 kilometres per hour, but Ware drove slowly on the streets. The brakes were rudimentary at best. The *Boston Globe* later reported that "the people under stovepipe hats and poke bonnets must have been surprised when the glittering engine came whistling along the peaceful roads without tracks, kicking up dust and vomiting smoke wherever it went."

Ware didn't always drive slowly, though. He took his car to New Jersey to race against some horses on a wooden-plank road, and perhaps it was seen there by Father Georges-Antoine Belcourt, a priest visiting from Rustico, Prince Edward Island. Belcourt had a reputation for being bloody-minded and for getting his way, and he bought the steam car for $300. That was a lot of money in those days, and it's possible that some newly arrived parish funds were diverted to cover the cost. Nobody really knows for sure. What we do know is that it was shipped from Philadelphia, and its arrival on Prince Edward Island was reported in Charlottetown's *Herald* on December 19, 1866. That date is important: the first Canadian-built car, another steam buggy powered by coal, made its debut on September 24 the following year at the Stanstead Fair in Quebec, but we know that Belcourt drove his new car at the local Saint-Jean-Baptiste parade on June 24, 1867.

That drive, in front of 900 people, didn't go well. "Its trial trip, made on the occasion of a picnic held near the Church at Rustico, proved a dismal failure," reported an account in a later history of Prince Edward Island's Catholic Church.

> It contributed no doubt to the amusement and hilarity of those who were present, but it demonstrated beyond all cavil the utter unfitness of the machine as a means of conveyance. The starting point was near the church, and for a short distance, the machine moved in an orderly and well-behaved manner but soon manifested a spirit of independence quite unusual in mechanical appliances, putting on a burst of speed without let or hinderance on the part of the driver or chauffeur. Presently, it became altogether unmanageable, left the beaten track of its own accord, and finally became entangled in a fence by the wayside where it came to a sudden and inglorious halt.

The contraption's end was an ignominious beginning — Canada's first car crash. "The God-fearing Acadians of Prince Edward Island had never seen anything like it," wrote the automotive historians Hugh Durnford and

Glenn Baechler in their book *Cars of Canada*. "Many might have called it a contraption of the devil had it not been brought into their midst by their own parish priest."

Belcourt continued to drive his car, mostly as a community curiosity, until he moved to New Brunswick a couple of years later. It's unclear what happened to it then. One story says it was sold to a local blacksmith who used its engine in his shop, another that it was peddled to someone in Nova Scotia and its engine used for either a tugboat or a threshing machine. A third says it was just parked and its metal eventually melted down for bullets in the First World War. Maybe all three stories have some truth to them. What we do know is there wouldn't be another car on the island until 1900.

It's ironic that the first Canadian car should have been in Prince Edward Island, because the province banned all cars from island roads in 1908. Local historian Rudy Croken says the heavy-handed move was unprecedented anywhere in the world — plenty of places didn't like cars, mostly because of their unmuffled noise and boisterous drivers, but they were still at least tolerated, or only partially prohibited. "Why they were only banned in little P.E.I., I don't know," he told me, "but in the newspapers, there were a lot of letters from outside P.E.I. praising the island for their foresight in banning these terrible vehicles. There was a guy in Calgary who wrote and said: 'I wish it was like that here because they're racing up and down the roads, these autojockeys, these cowboys.' It created interest all over the world."

The government's motion to ban cars was passed unanimously, and all seven of the island's vehicles became illegal to drive. "There will be no hardship inflicted by suppressing them," said D.P. Irving, who seconded the motion. "They are owned by men of wealth and leisure who force the public off the road." More worrisome was their cacophonous noise, which was frightening to horses. As one resident wrote in a letter to Charlottetown's *Guardian*: "Many farmers refuse to let their wives and daughters drive on the roads unless accompanied and the pleasure of a quiet ride on our country roads will be rare if those vehicles are allowed to travel as they are now."

Not everyone agreed, though. As islanders travelled more widely over the next few years, they became more accustomed to cars and their benefits. Henry Ford's Model T of 1908 made such vehicles more affordable and quieter, and a group of local businessmen lobbied for the ban to be rescinded. In 1913, the government relented and allowed the use of cars on Mondays, Wednesdays, and Thursdays; they were still forbidden on market days, the Saturday shopping day, and the Sunday church day. Even then, though, a plebiscite gave the final decision to the province's individual districts, and many voted to continue the ban. Islanders who wanted to drive into town might do so through one district, then have horses tow their cars through the next district, or perhaps load them onto railway carts. This gradually relaxed as various authorities softened their stance, until 1919, when the ban was finally lifted completely. Even then, however, there was still animosity from some of the peace-and-quiet-loving islanders. One lifelong resident, Cyril MacFarlane, was wistful in his thoughts when he spoke to local historian Deborah Stewart of *Island* magazine in 1978:

> "When I was a teenager, neighbours were visiting each other probably, well, quite often. Now we go in the car and go perhaps to Summerside, but it used to be that there was more neighbourliness somehow," he recalled. "But I don't know if we're better off or worse. Lots of times, I'd probably just harness the horse and go to one of the neighbours for, well, just a little drive out in the evening or something like that. Now they drive into town, or go to Florida. Sure don't stop in town."

☐

Peter and I had our sights set on much farther than Florida, and it was convenient that we could travel to the island on the seasonal ferry. We were lucky too. The MV *Confederation* broke down five days later and was out of commission for a month; its drive coupling failed in the engine room and a new part had to be manufactured and tested and shipped from Germany. While the ferry was sidelined, the only way to drive onto the island was over the Confederation Bridge from New Brunswick, just as it is in the winter months. That's a 300-kilometre detour, but on our pleasant Monday morning booking, we had no inkling of the straining mechanicals beneath us and cruised serenely across the Northumberland Strait in just over an hour.

My friend Simon made this same crossing 22 years earlier with his new wife, Nicole, at the start of their honeymoon. Once out on the open water, however, there was confusion on the ship with patchy news reports being shown on the deck televisions; something had happened somewhere in the world and nobody was quite sure what. It wasn't until they reached the dock at Wood Islands that the signal strengthened enough for the passengers to learn of planes crashing into New York City's Twin Towers. Simon and Nicole tried to maintain an idyllic, romantic honeymoon, but it was a losing battle. They separated several years later. I made a point of not watching the TV on the passenger deck just in case.

Like the ferry to Newfoundland and the ferry to Vancouver Island, the privately run P.E.I. ferry is officially part of the Trans-Canada Highway, and the federal government contributes nearly $14 million per year to subsidize its operation. There are supposed to be two ships that run the 25-kilometre route from May to December, but neither have had an easy run of it lately. The engine of the MV *Holiday Island* caught fire in 2022, and the 52-year-old vessel had to be scrapped. A temporary ferry was found in Quebec to fill the gap, but it wasn't yet ready for the year when the MV *Confederation* broke down. Now, a new Norwegian ferry that can carry more than 200 cars has been bought for nearly $40 million — well, new to us, anyway, since it took to the European water in 2007 — and a Quebec shipyard will build a replacement for the 30-year-old MV *Confederation*, but that won't be ready until at least 2028. So, for now, we muddle along.

There's actually no cost to enter Prince Edward Island, but you have to pay a toll on the bridge or the ferry to leave. You can just turn up at Caribou without a booking, and if there's space on the ferry, you can travel without having to pay the $86 round-trip fare for a car with two people. But if you want to be sure and make a reservation, like most travellers on a schedule, you must pay the full return fare. And since the ferry people and bridge people don't talk to each other, your ferry ticket doesn't get you a crossing on the bridge, and vice versa. That's private enterprise for you. It'll get you both coming and going. These islanders are smart.

THE DRIVE ACROSS CANADA

□

The Trans-Canada Highway covers barely 120 kilometres in Prince Edward Island, but none of it was cheap to construct. The entire province rests on sandstone and clay, and that's far too soft a base for good roads. Crews need gravel to lay below the asphalt, and aggregate for mixing into the asphalt, and it all has to be trucked in from New Brunswick or Nova Scotia, sometimes even Newfoundland. Still, once it's there, the road settles nicely into place between the farms with their lined-up furrows and neat-as-a-pin hedgerows. As Edward McCourt observed back in 1963, all the fields look as if they're waiting to have their pictures taken. On a previous visit to Prince Edward Island, I did take a photograph of a vast but tidy potato field, and it's still the wallpaper on my laptop, even as I type this. The image just settles the busy mind into an orderly calm, knowing that at least for that moment, at that confluence of brown ridged earth and blue sky, with a gentle separating ribbon of green woodland along the horizon, all is right with that perfect piece of the world.

In Prince Edward Island, the potato fields are picture-perfect and help settle the busy mind.

All wasn't quite right with the highway leaving Wood Islands, however. Great swathes of trees lay wrecked beside the road: birch and maple and hemlock and red oak heaved from the ground, crashed into one another, still waiting nine months after Hurricane Fiona to be cleared and hewed and burned. One government report estimated about 34,000 hectares of the island's forests lost more than 70 percent of their trees. It takes at least 40 years to grow such trees to maturity, to a point where they can reach their full potential to clean the air and fully house birds and animals, and yet Fiona took less than a day to ruin it all.

The two-lane Trans-Canada follows close to the coast on its way up to Charlottetown, but the water can rarely be seen. Instead, there are green fields to each side, with prosperous, cared-for farms, their names hand-painted on folksy wooden signs. Strictly speaking, the highway shouldn't even take this route because there's another paved road that runs in a straight line from Wood Islands through to Orwell Cove, which shaves fully 10 kilometres off the curvaceous Trans-Canada, but the surveyors went with the longer route anyway. This was in direct contravention of their instructions to place the highway on the shortest route across the country, which caused such dissent from both Nova Scotia and New Brunswick. The next morning, in an interview with the minister of transportation and his chief engineer, I asked why this longer route was taken and how come it was accepted. Both men shrugged as if it was news to them, which it likely was. "You'd have to ask somebody back in the 1950s," said Ernie Hudson, the minister. "That's before even my time."

I'm sure I know, though. I can imagine the chief engineer of the day reading the directive that landed on his oak desk, saying the highway should be as direct as possible between the dock at Wood Islands and the capital, Charlottetown. "No — expand the road that takes the coast through Flat River," he'd have been told by somebody from an Important Island Family. "It's in better shape than that direct one, and it takes the tourists to their rooms down by the water. And do it swiftly and cheerfully. We want them to give us that fixed link to the mainland." And in Ottawa, where somebody would have to approve the 50 percent federal payment to the province, the planned route would have passed with barely any notice. Those bureaucrats who rejected the highway detouring 100 kilometres to Halifax and Saint John probably just shrugged — it was only quiet little Prince Edward Island, after all, and they had bigger fights to come.

There was no question the Trans-Canada would pass directly through the provincial capital. The island was already connected by mainland ferries at both Wood Islands and Borden, with Charlottetown halfway between the two. The highway ran along both the main downtown roads of University Avenue and Grafton Street, turning directly in front of Province House, Prince Edward Island's second-most famous building. This was the site of the 1864 Charlottetown Conference, which led to the signing of Confederation in 1867. It took until 1999 before the highway was eventually rerouted to a far more efficient, far less interesting, big-box bypass that runs to the north of town.

For all its neoclassical grandeur, Province House still lies in the shadow of a much smaller building an hour away on the north coast near Cavendish. Far more tourists come to visit the home of Lucy Maud Montgomery, and after a leisurely half-hour of taking in all the sights of Charlottetown, Peter and I left the Trans-Canada to follow the trail to Green Gables. When we arrived, we didn't go in — neither of us have read *Anne of Green Gables*, and the many comparisons with the fictional Avonlea would have been lost on us. Besides, the place was crowded, especially with visitors from Japan, many of whom wandered, looking slightly confused, around the house of Montgomery's birthplace where she lived until she was two years old ($6 for entry), Green Gables Park ($8.50), and the homestead ($6) where the renowned author actually lived as an adult and wrote the first of her many books. They're all National Historic Sites. You can, at least, visit Montgomery's grave in the local churchyard for no charge, though she had to be brought home to her final resting place after dying in Ontario where she'd lived her last three decades.

I still have a straw hat with sewn-in red pigtails and a fringe that I bought when I first came through in 2012. Peter resisted the temptation to add to the L.M. Montgomery coffers, and good for him, since he's the father of a 20-something daughter who loves all things Disney. When journalist Walter Stewart visited Cavendish in 1999, he was astonished by the plethora of Anne products, everything from an Anne raspberry cordial to an Anne rocking horse, counting 269 of them in just one catalogue. Pretty much everything you can think of was available with an Anne tag, though he wrote that "we have been able to avoid Anne vibrators and Green Gables garbage bags." These islanders may be quiet, but they're still smart.

□

The quiet islanders were about to wake up, however, when I first drove through in 2012. Heavier traffic from the bridge meant the Trans-Canada needed to be fixed and repaved west of Charlottetown, and the Ministry of Transportation had found a way to save some provincial money. Fixing would cost $9 million, but if the highway was moved and improved, half the $16 million price tag would be paid by Ottawa. That would cost the island $8 million instead, and the highway could also be levelled out and straightened to remove steep slopes and several below-standard curves. The original plan was to route the new highway directly through the top of a provincial park. That didn't go down well.

"From an engineering and safety perspective, that was the line to take," Robert Vessey, the minister of transportation at the time, told me that summer. "But people came out to support the park, let's say that. They didn't always support it by visiting, but they supported it at the public meetings, and the outcry was phenomenal."

That was Plan A. The ministry quickly cancelled it and moved to Plan B, which meant buying up property and paving over woodland, including the last stand of old-growth hemlocks on the island. Streams would need to be diverted and culverts built. I drove through while the government was still negotiating with landowners and trying, unsuccessfully, to avoid the expropriation of any land. One man, who would lose some of his lawn, told me, "Water drains down the road here and then freezes on the curve, where it's in shadow, and cars, trucks hit the glare ice and that's it for them." Another man, whose home of 47 years would be demolished, told me, "There's at least two, three, four times a year that people come knocking on my door and say they've put a car in the ditch."

But the Plan B Protesters, as they came to be known, had their own reports that showed the road wasn't unsafe at all. They believed the entire purpose of constructing the new road was so the province would pay $8 million for the needed repairs, not $9 million. In early fall that year, they moved in and set up camp in a field at the site, dozens of them with placards and loud voices. Some slept in the trees themselves in their efforts to stall the clearing of the land. An Indigenous group that called itself the Hemlock Warriors lit a sacred fire in a clearing and prepared to wait out the road-builders. The fire burned day and night to unify the people, but it didn't stop construction. Protesters started getting arrested and being charged with trespassing. The interim leader of the Green Party, Darcie Lanthier, was arrested and charged with mischief when police said she lay down in front of a tractor, dressed in camouflage gear.

"I was wearing my ski jacket and pants purchased at Sears," Darcie told me when I called her up this time around. "It is a kind of brown camo print. We were all standing in front of equipment — excavators, feller-bunchers, dozers — in an attempt to stop or delay the destruction. Not lying down, even near a tractor. Guilty of the crime of tree-hugging."

Three days later, the RCMP moved in and cleared the camp. The sacred fire was disturbed — an RCMP officer "picked up a log and he chucked it in the mud, just on the edge of the stream," one of the protesters told the CBC — and the bulldozers knocked down the hemlocks and the other trees and that was that. Some protesters stayed near the site for months, monitoring progress and reporting transgressions to the Ministry of the Environment, but the new road went through and was opened a year later. Was it all worth it? Darcie told me both yes and no.

"People don't come to Prince Edward Island to speed through as fast as they can to get to Charlottetown," she said. "People come to Prince Edward Island to do exactly the opposite of that. People come to Prince Edward Island to slow down. Our pace is slower. They come to stop and smell the flowers, to look at the vistas, to pull off and enjoy the views, and to walk down those clay roads that you didn't like in your sports car. There are more accidents now because people drive faster. If it saves 12 seconds to cost $16 million and cut up the environment and kill the fish, then I don't think that's a fair trade-off."

On the other hand, Plan B was definitely the start of something. The influential Citizens' Alliance of PEI environmental group was formed from the protesters, and its influence helped enough Green Party candidates get elected in 2019 to become the official opposition on the island — the first time anywhere in Canada. "It was a huge community builder," said Darcie. "The end result was a hugely more aware citizenry that doesn't just take everything that's said at face value anymore. We just don't buy the spin."

I didn't even notice the changes in the highway when I drove through with Peter in the Lexus. It was just a wide, smooth road that curved gently past fields and woods. We paused to find a go-cart track that I'd stopped at in 2012, when the owner told me that losing his frontage onto the highway would mean the end of the business. It took a while, but eventually we discovered the abandoned track, overgrown now with weeds in the cracked pavement, beside a dead-end side road that was once the Trans-Canada. It was a hot Tuesday afternoon, and nobody was around to ask what happened. I left a note at a nearby house, but no one ever responded. A local grocery store manager told me the track owner had left the island, and Darcie said she heard he'd gone bankrupt. I kicked some stones around on the remains of the cracked asphalt while Peter had a smoke, and then we got back into the cool air-conditioning of the Lexus and sped north to the bridge.

"Climate change is going to make our grandchildren miserable," Darcie told me. "It's going to destroy their lives. There's almost zero chance that a child born today is going to have what we look at as a normal life. So if we're not prepared to do everything we can to bring some sense and order to this, then how can we ever look them in the eye? I will do anything I can to ensure a better future for the babies being born today and the ones who aren't born yet. And making roads bigger and faster through pristine areas is not a step on the right path."

☐

One of the conditions of Prince Edward Island joining the path to become part of Canada was that the federal government would provide "Efficient Steam Service … Winter and Summer" to the island from the mainland.

Prince Edward Island had held out against joining Canada in 1867, despite hosting the conference that began it all three years earlier, because it considered itself fiercely British and saw no advantage to being Canadian. But then it got into huge debt with constructing a railway and changed its mind five years later. Ottawa seduced it with an offer to take over all the debt and provide the steamship service, and when island residents were asked to vote between joining Canada or paying higher taxes, the choice was clear. Prince Edward Island became Canadian exactly six years after Confederation on July 1, 1873.

The steamships ran for several decades, though they weren't exactly efficient, nor were they "continuous" — another stipulation of the agreement. Shipping to and from the island was laid up during winter storms, or when the ice was too thick on the Northumberland Strait to push through a channel of open water. When that happened, iceboats with metal runners to slide over the frozen surface could carry a few people at a time — they cost $2 dollars for each passenger, or 50 cents less if the passenger got out to help push. The first proper ice-breaking ferry arrived in 1917 on the shortest route over, 13 kilometres from New Brunswick's Cape Tormentine to Prince Edward Island's Borden, and the service continued with a variety of different ships for the next 80 years. When the Trans-Canada was declared open in 1962, the MV *Abegweit* was plying the route and became an official part of the highway.

Three years later, Lester Pearson's government — probably in a good mood for seeing the road paved through Newfoundland — agreed to build a combined causeway, bridge, and tunnel that would cost $148 million. The ground was broken for the highway on the island side at Borden, but the price rapidly doubled and the project was shelved and finally cancelled in 1969. A writer to a Charlottetown newspaper in the early 1960s proposed a free alternative in which there should be an island-wide bottle drive and all the whiskey and beer bottles should be thrown into the strait, which would surely create a causeway within a year. For some reason, nobody seemed to take this seriously.

The original MV *Abegweit* ferry was retired in 1982 after 35 years of faithful service; it found a home in Chicago where it's much loved and permanently moored as the home of the swanky Columbia Yacht Club. The ferry was replaced on the crossing by a new one, also called the *Abegweit*, which comes from the Mi'kmaq name for the island, *Epekwitk*, meaning "Cradled on the Waves." Ferry users, however, normally called it the "Big Wait." Ernie Hudson, the P.E.I. transportation minister, said, "I remember times when the ferry was the connecting link, traffic would be backed up to Albany sometimes, backed up miles waiting to get across." Albany Corner is seven kilometres from the old dock, and even when traffic wasn't backed up, it was common to wait several hours for the ferry in the peak season or during bad weather.

It came down to Brian Mulroney's federal Progressive Conservatives in the 1980s to press for the "fixed link," this time to be paid for entirely through private financing. Federal submissions to build the bridge were requested in 1987, and the project immediately separated the island into two divided camps of opinion. The following January, Premier Joe Ghiz called for a plebiscite among residents to settle the issue. Environmentalists, fishers, and sentimentalists opposed the bridge, creating the Friends of the Island lobby group that said the lobster breeding grounds would be ruined, and it would attract prostitutes and drug dealers and other nefarious types from the mainland, while business, tourism, and labour groups supported it and organized themselves into the Islanders for a Better Tomorrow lobby group. The two sides fanned out to take the podiums at standing-room-only meetings in schools and community halls across the province. "One of the best lines I heard," the president of Islanders for a Better Tomorrow told *Maclean's* magazine, "was when a guy stood up at one meeting and said, 'Look, there aren't people lurking in the bushes in New Brunswick waiting to come over to rape and pillage.'"

The plebiscite voted almost 60 percent in favour of building the bridge. Premier Ghiz, *Maclean's* reported later, voted against it, as did his wife, but the people had spoken. Work began five years later and took another four years, constructing each of the 62 piers on dry land and placing them separately in water as deep as 35 metres. That's almost as far beneath the surface as the curved bridge is high, and there's a graceful arch in the centre that rises to clear 60 metres for ships to pass underneath. Its biggest physical challenge is the pressure of ice in the wintertime, and the piers have reinforced cones at their base to deflect icebergs. It's by far the longest bridge in Canada and the longest bridge over ice-covered water in the world, and it's designed to last more than 100 years.

All that and it's privately owned by a consortium set up especially for the job. It was paid for entirely with commercial funds and cost more than a billion dollars by the time it was opened in 1997; the consortium gets its money back with 35 annual payments from the federal government of almost $42 million. That's how much Ottawa was paying for the ferry service, and ownership will be transferred to Canada in 2032. It also makes money from tolls, of course. It cost $50.25 for Peter and me to leave the island in the Lexus. "Why the 25 cents?" I asked when I rolled up to the booth. The ticket-seller just shrugged. I tapped my credit card, and the two of us were across in less than 15 minutes.

There's no doubt Prince Edward Island has profited from the Confederation Bridge, for better or worse. The island had 1.6 million visitors in 2019, the year before Covid-19 shut everything down, most of who drove in over the bridge. It's still a sore point for some, though, and its name is

The bridge that links Prince Edward Island with the New Brunswick mainland was built entirely with private funding and is the longest bridge over ice-covered water in the world.

also a source of contention. It's not so much that there's anything wrong with "Confederation," as much as the word is everywhere on the island: Confederation Court Mall, Confederation Centre of the Arts, Confederation Landing, Confederation Trail, Confederation Realty, Confederation Construction — you get the idea. I never found Confederation Vapes and Smokes or Confederation Exotic Massage and Spa, but I'm sure they would have popped up on one of Peter's Google searches.

"Confederation Bridge" was the most popular name when the P.E.I. government asked for suggestions in a 1996 Canada-wide appeal, but it wasn't the name recommended to the public works minister. More than 2,200 submissions were received from Canadians everywhere, and 300 of them suggested Confederation Bridge, but the second choice was Abegweit Crossing, with 89 votes. That's the name the provincial panel recommended, because it "resulted from the understanding of the unique relationships and feelings of each of the names to this world-class project and not simply from an analysis of the numbers." The panel was bound to present the three most popular names to Ottawa, and Ottawa said, "Nah, we like Confederation," and that was it. Neither side was too taken with the third most popular name — "Northumberland Strait Bridge." Of course, this was all long before internet campaigns; these days, the most popular choice would surely be "Bridgy McBridgeface."

In 2022, the provincial legislature voted unanimously to rename the bridge "Epekwitk Crossing" and forwarded that request to Ottawa for approval, with a copy to New Brunswick. A year later, when we drove through and finally left the island, the federal government was still thinking about it. Bureaucracy moves slowly, especially when it's being second-guessed.

4

New Brunswick

For anyone who's ever looked at a map of Canada, there's a certain sense of solidity when driving into New Brunswick. The province is part of the central core of mainland, not some limb hanging off it, like Nova Scotia, or even some island, be it near or distant. No — New Brunswick is right there in the continental landmass and nothing can now stop the determined driver from reaching the other side.

This is a rosy-hued viewpoint, of course. As one person told me, a true map of Canada seen through its population is far more like a shoestring, draped thinly over the top of the United States. Fly for an hour away from the American border at almost any point and Canada will be a sparsely populated wilderness of forest or prairie or tundra. There are exceptions, of course, as any resident of Newfoundland or Edmonton will be quick to protest, but the rule generally holds true, and it's a guideline mostly followed by the original planners of the Trans-Canada Highway. Now that Peter and I were in New Brunswick, we would stay within a couple of hundred kilometres from the United States all the way through to the highway's western end in Victoria. Never once, however, did we feel we were in any place other than Canada.

For a driver hell-bent on crossing between the East and West Coasts, it's still quicker to travel on mostly American highways — you can cut two sides off a triangle if you don't take the route over the top of Lake Superior, and the speed limits in the western states are often higher. Peter and I were reminded of this now that my feature stories of the journey were being published in the *Globe and Mail*, and readers were enthusiastic to comment that the American interstate system is faster and much superior.

"I've driven most countries in Europe, only to have it reinforce what a disgrace our TCH really is. Shocking that Canada sees fit to distribute international foreign aid when the underdevelopment of our road system demonstrates its dangers to our population," wrote one online commenter named kidspeed. That commentator continued: "Poor politicians, in a country dominated by regionalism. Unable to bring it up to an international standard." And "Compared to US interstates, the transcanada is pathetic," wrote Len F2, while IanT49 added, "Imagine if they tried to build it now … hopeless."

My favourite comment came as a reaction to the final story published by the *Globe and Mail*. "And how did the environment hold up?" asked rharder. "I don't want to do the calculation on how much CO_2 was put into the air by a car that probably gets somewhere around 20 miles per gallon, on a very long, and totally unnecessary trip. Now that we no better, without any doubt, such trips should be deemed illegal, and the perpators arrested." Fortunately for me, another less spelling-afflicted reader pointed out that the fuel consumption of the hybrid Lexus, as mentioned in the story, was 33.4 miles per gallon, and a third reader defended me, saying, "The CO_2 from one dump truck or one highway (class 8) dwarves the CO_2 from this car. Suggest you tilt at other windmills. As for the making such trips illegal and arresting drivers, how ludicrous can one be?"

Some readers were incensed that Peter and I were driving a borrowed press vehicle and not a car paid for by the *Globe and Mail*, or preferably, by me personally, as they would have to do. I was careful to only include mention of the Lexus in a few self-contained paragraphs at the end of each article, which ran in the "Driving" section of the *Globe*'s website, but that was still too much for some. "The blatant promotion of Lexus and the car's features is inappropriate and unnecessary in a travelogue," wrote app_75792508. "Is this the only way the *Globe* can pay its bills?"

I read that, and I wondered what those safely anonymous critics would have thought about Thomas Wilby, Ed Flickenger, and Jimmy Oates pushing their ways across the country with borrowed vehicles, each of them with large signs on the side promoting the manufacturer. Would any commenters stand up and look Brigadier (Retired) Alex Macfarlane in the eye and accuse him, in his borrowed Chevrolet, of "smarmy promotion," as C. Parsons commented about me? I think they'd light up a cigarette and that would be it. And whatever would they have said to the three CBC journalists who drove the length of the unopened highway in 1960 in a borrowed Chevrolet Impala?

I've not yet mentioned the epic drive of Ron Hunka and Doug Brophy, with technician Ken Frost, because although they broadcast live almost every weekday evening for five weeks, the recordings from the first and last weeks have been lost. We do know their Chevrolet was fitted with an oversized battery to power their Magnecorder tape-editing machine. The car also had special heavy-duty shock absorbers because parts of the highway weren't finished yet — they were given permission to drive with an escort through the Wawa Gap in Ontario, and Hunka was driven through British Columbia's Rogers Pass by a highway engineer in a Jeep.

I did get to listen to the broadcasts made from Nova Scotia to Alberta, however, and they're fascinating, with interviews of merchants and residents and highway engineers all along the way. The CBC carried advertising until 1975, and the reporters were shameless in their promotion of the car.

From Charlottetown, Hunka reported:

> Most of our drive through Nova Scotia was quite an easy one, though we did hit a couple of fairly long gravel sections that haven't been paved to the Trans-Canada standards as yet, and there were quite a few miles of twists and turns, too.
>
> We really had to be on our toes, but you know, cornering was a cinch, because Chevrolet really sticks to the

curves. With a Chevy, you can take the corners with plenty of confidence, and believe us, we took plenty of them this morning. We don't drive carelessly, of course, but with Chevrolet's wide tread and long wheelbase, you really get a grip on the ground. And naturally, Chevrolet's low silhouette helps, too. The weight is all low, so there's not any tendency to sway badly or to lean on the corners. No doubt about it — Chevrolet handles wonderfully for a car of its size.... Why not try a Chevrolet for smoothness today?

I was happy enough in the borrowed Chevrolet Camaro in 2012, but I had no hesitation about accepting the offer of the Canadian-made Lexus RX 500h this time around. It was comfortable, and I'm no spring chicken, so Peter and I drove off the bridge and onto Cape Tormentine, and after a flat drive across the low marsh, we swung the car north to rejoin the same section of Trans-Canada Highway that took us south a couple of weeks before.

□

In New Brunswick, the entire length of the Trans-Canada Highway is like an American interstate: two lanes in each direction, a wide central median for safety, and accessed only by ramps that merge traffic on and off. There are no traffic lights and no highway service centres, other than the giant truck stops and gas stations at the exits. This is one reason why New Brunswick is known as "The Drive-Through Province" — there's no reason to stop except for food and gas, or perhaps these days, to recharge your electric car.

The provincial tourism bureau does do its best to promote attractions off the highway, and possibly the best known is Magnetic Hill, well signed just to the north of Moncton. Peter and I had to try it out. Everyone does. In the summertime, the hill can get as many as 350 cars driving on it in a day, one or two at a time.

The road is an optical illusion, of course. You drive your car down a hill, and before the road rises again, you stop next to a white signpost and shift into neutral. Then you take your foot off the brake and your car will roll

Magnetic Hill was once the third most popular tourist attraction in Canada and still draws thousands of drivers every summer.

backward, back up the hill. At least that's what seems to happen. In truth, the upward slope behind you is really a downward slope — it just appears to be upward because you can't see the horizon on the rolling terrain.

People knew about the hill in the 1880s about as soon as the road was built and buggies started rolling backward on it. Carriage drivers would stay off the brakes when they thought their horses were climbing, but the wagons would run up and clip the horses' hooves. It was a strange phenomenon that no one could explain. Such places aren't alone in the world — there are many similar "gravity hills" — but Moncton's is probably the best-known. It made the headlines in 1933 when a trio of newspaper reporters from Saint John's *Telegraph-Journal* went in search of it in a car to check out the rumours. Apparently, they spent five hours asking around for its location and drove every slope in the Moncton area without success, until they stopped to stretch their legs and their car started rolling away from them uphill. Right. Again, it's a good story. They noticed a stream beside the road also appeared to flow uphill, so there wasn't any actual magnetism, but they couldn't figure out how it could be. When they wrote about the mystery of the place, everyone with a car wanted to try it for themselves.

Around this time, an enterprising local woman named Muriel Lutes opened a nearby canteen with a gas pump outside, and her business grew quickly with all the visitors. She moved the canteen closer to the actual short stretch of magnetic road and expanded to sell ice cream and souvenirs, and the business grew even more. In the 1950s, Muriel and her husband, Ludwig Sikorski, added a gift shop, dining rooms, and a motel, and Magnetic Hill became the third most popular tourist destination in Canada, after Niagara Falls and Banff National Park. After all, it was a place for drivers who wanted to play with their cars.

The CBC crew tried out the hill during their 1960 drive and spoke to a visitor who had just driven it for himself. Doug Brophy asked him to explain it. "I don't know," said the unnamed visitor, "but my gosh, I'll swear to gosh it was still going uphill.... It sure appears to be going down to me. It really is a puzzle." And this was an opportunity for Ron Hunka to speak up again in the broadcast. "I'd like to say here and now that this Chevrolet has the finest brakes. We have Chevrolet's Safety Master Powerbrakes on the Impala … and when you put your foot on that brake pedal, you stop — straight, clean, and fast," said Hunka. "And one other thing. Sometimes on these hills, we've been using Chevy's Powerglide low gear, and there is a mighty smooth way to brake on hills."

Muriel and Ludwig sold up, and eventually the City of Moncton took over the site. Now there's a small zoo and the Magic Mountain amusement park, as well as a collection of gift stores and restaurants. The season hadn't quite begun when Peter and I rolled through, so there was no charge to drive on the hill. We shared it with an unimpressed cyclist named Mustafa on his electric bicycle, but in another couple of weeks, there would be toll booths in service and summer students would charge visitors $7 per carload to try it out. Its popularity "just exploded to another level when the Trans-Canada Highway came through," the zoo's director told me. "People used to come from all over Canada, but now they come from all over the world."

□

The highway brought visitors to New Brunswick, but back in 1949, the provincial government still needed persuading to join the project and pay the 50/50 cost of construction. The Feds insisted the route should be the most direct across the country and that would mean completely bypassing Saint John on the Bay of Fundy, the province's major port and centre of finance. There was arguing back and forth, but New Brunswick knew it needed the road link and didn't have any extra cards to play, so it caved and signed up the following year. Its existing roads were improved to the basic Trans-Canada standard at the time: three inches of asphalt on a gravel base, at least 22 feet wide for two lanes and with 10-foot unpaved shoulders. Slopes could have no more than a 6 percent grade; fortunately, Magnetic Hill was left well out of the plans.

Visitors came, trucks rolled through, and traffic grew and grew, and the pavement itself began to deteriorate under the stress of the congestion. The Trans-Canada may have been the link to the Atlantic, but through the 1970s and 1980s it became just a twisting, patched-up, two-lane road with traffic lights and driveways. Not only that, it was downright dangerous, especially on the busiest section between Fredericton and Moncton. "It's a highway designed in the '50s, unable to cope with the traffic of the '80s," reported CBC journalist Kevin Evans in 1988. The dean of engineering at the University of New Brunswick who had studied the highway told him, "It is the weak link of the entire system. From a safety point of view, it is by far the worst situation."

The cost to fix it was astronomical, estimated at $1.5 billion, but the province's Liberal government eventually came up with a plan to pay for it — tolls. They'd seen the examples of the Confederation Bridge and Cobequid Pass. So, contract a private consortium to build the four-lane divided highway, get the Feds to pay half, then get the road users themselves to pay the provincial half through tolls. If drivers don't use it, they don't have to pay for it. Genius! The contract was awarded in 1997, the same year the privately financed bridge to Prince Edward Island was so successfully completed, and the same year the Cobequid Pass toll highway opened to Nova Scotia drivers. The deal was done: it would be built by the private Maritime Road Development Corporation (with a former federal minister of transport, Doug Young, as one of its executives), which would then charge tolls for 25 years to recover its costs before handing the highway over to the province.

This wasn't popular among New Brunswick drivers, however, who felt their taxes were already high enough. Still, the new highway between Moncton and Fredericton was built on time and under budget, four divided lanes safe and fast, and the first of four toll booth stations was constructed where the westbound road splits to head either down to Saint John or across to Fredericton. On opening day in 1999, it charged cars 75 cents per trip, with the eventual cost planned to be almost $7 once all the stations were built. Trucks would pay $30. But unlike the bridge and Cobequid Pass, the highway had been free to drive on for the past year and motorists saw the new toll as no more than a government cash grab. Furious drivers created lengthy lineups at the booths by writing cheques to pay the 75 cent toll, or using pennies, or $100 bills. What's more, other politicians agreed with them. "Any toll on any highway between the major marketplace and Newfoundland and Labrador is a toll on the cost of moving goods and services to this province," said Brian Tobin, Newfoundland's premier. "We can be tolled out of existence." Prince Edward Island's premier went a step further and threatened to sue: "The toll roads really are an inhibitor to the easy movement of goods and people through the region," said Pat Binns, a bit cheeky considering the much higher cost of using his bridge.

The politician who benefitted most from the tolls was Bernard Lord, the 33-year-old leader of New Brunswick's Progressive Conservative opposition. He made it an election issue, promising to end the highway tolls within 200 days if he should be elected premier. The money owed to the private consortium would still need to be paid, but he told voters it would cost about $30 million over four years, while his critics suggested it would surely be 10 times that. Didn't matter. He was voted in, and 200 days later, he shuttered the toll booths. The New Brunswick government has been paying for them through higher taxes ever since.

"Now we have what they call shadow tolls" of about $30 million each year, Jeff Carr told me. He was New Brunswick's minister of transportation and infrastructure when I drove through with Peter. The consortium will transfer responsibility for the highway to the province in 2028, he explained, but "I'm not sure if a highway is ever paid for. It's an ongoing process. I equate it to somebody who has a mortgage on their home that's due to expire, and maybe they decide to do a kitchen or bathroom renovation and redo their mortgage to pay for that."

I say Carr *was* the minister because the following week he had a falling-out with his premier and was fired from the Cabinet. It's a dirty game, politics.

□

The Trans-Canada Highway between Moncton and Fredericton may be fast and safe, but it's dull as ditchwater for a motorist. There's one stretch of almost 50 kilometres between controlled junctions that has nothing to look at for the entire distance except trees and rocks — no houses, no rivers, not even any moose, which are all safely behind the wire moose fencing well back in the woods. Peter and I drove it two weeks before, headed east, so this time we skipped it and followed the original route of the early pathfinders down to Saint John. This road was almost as dull — more trees — but it took us somewhere new and I wanted us to stay that night with a friend who lives on the other side of the port city.

If we'd had more time, we would have driven the new parkway that follows more closely to the coastline of the Bay of Fundy. This is a freshly built, meandering tourist route, with well-kept picnic areas overlooking the water to the south. It wiggles visitors down to the quaint village of St. Martins, and it might have been closer to the original routes of Wilby, Flickenger, and Oates. In the early years of the past century, roads stuck near to the water; there was rarely good reason to head too far into the woods.

Wilby and Haney didn't have reliable maps in 1912 and had to count on local residents to either guide the way or point them in the right direction. They made good time from Moncton, travelling the 150 kilometres to Saint John in just over six hours with a stop for lunch. In his book *A Motor Tour Through Canada*, Wilby makes fun of the names of the local towns, "a choice collection of impossible Indian words.… It seemed impossible to believe that men had actually thought of naming villages Plumweseep,

Apohaqui, Passakeag, Nanwigeauk, Quispamsis and Scoudouc, and had escaped lynching." And, of course, he managed to get a dig in at Jack Haney in one of his rare references to the man who'd gotten him this far: "To make matters worse, I was impelled to inquire my way. Pronunciation of names was out of the question, and the chauffeur was no help since he knew only American English." They made it, though, and he collected a letter from the mayor of Saint John, James H. Frink, to be delivered to the mayor of Vancouver, though in his book, the Great Journalist misspelled the local mayor's name as Fink.

They wouldn't have made it if not for Haney, who kept a diary of his own. He said they reached Moncton the night before at 7:30 p.m. after 12 hours where "roads were bad. Had much trouble with poor gas and spark plugs, motor missed all day. Done some cussing." I'll bet that annoyed his English passenger, who checked in at the hotel and then went for an evening stroll to look at the tidal bore. The twice-a-day tide runs up from the Bay of Fundy and fills the shallow riverbed before draining it again each time. Wilby was unimpressed. Meanwhile, "Worked on car at Moncton until 11:30 p.m.," wrote Haney. "Clutch knocked, took out universal, it had no grease. Filled the cups with dope. Put 'Rajah Plugs' in, and they have been doing fine. 133 miles."

It was hard work, for Haney at least, but they still had an easier time of it than Jimmy Oates with his motorcycle. On that second day of the journey in 1928, on the way to Fredericton,

> the day was very hot and the roads owing to lack of rain were very dusty. Passing cars was a positive nightmare and in order to keep my average speed I was called upon to take many long chances. Where I saw a straight road ahead and free from traffic, I let Toby go as fast as possible. During one of these fast interludes I saw a line of stones laid carelessly across the road about twelve inches apart. I attempted to use the brakes to pull up and the machine commenced to skid broadside. The road being narrow and high in the centre caused the outfit to make for the left

hand ditch which certainly did not look exciting. It quickly occurred to me that it was impossible to prevent a crash and so I turned sharp left and hoped for the best. To my great surprise the machine cleared the ditch and landed in a field. Not being satisfied with this it continued its mad plunge onwards, carrying down four fence posts and many feet of wire. I by this time was out of harm's way lying between the machine and sidecar and calculating how long it would take before we came to rest.

The damage to Toby wasn't too bad, thanks to staying mostly upright during the whole incident, and Oates found some passing motorists to help him get the bike and sidecar back on the road. He was uninjured from the detour through the field, but in dire need of some sunscreen. "My face was giving me a great deal of pain, it having been blistered and peeled by the combined efforts of sun, wind, and rain," he wrote. "It ached and I almost felt like taking a rest instead of a contemplated all night ride." Unfortunately for Jimmy Oates, it would be another couple of decades before modern sunscreen was developed. That July, with his face constantly exposed to the elements on the motorcycle, his best skincare option really was to ride at night.

☐

The next morning, waking at my friend's home, the sun was nowhere to be seen; fog was thick against the shore, and it was my turn to drive first. We were close to the water — don't worry, Zac told me, the mist will disappear once you start to drive inland. He recommended a road we could take to Fredericton that would avoid doubling back to Saint John. The story goes that the little-used Highway 785 from Pennfield to Fredericton Junction was built solely because a local politician wanted a shortcut to get to the legislature in Fredericton. "It's a fun road to drive," he said. "Watch for moose — always watch for moose — but make the most of it."

I didn't mention this to Peter, who was still waking up in the passenger seat. Instead, we drove a short distance to Pennfield and then headed north on Highway 785. When the mist cleared and the residential driveways ended, I pressed a little harder on the throttle, and then a little harder still. Peter pushed his feet against the floor at the first corner, but I didn't lift off — the Lexus was a performance edition vehicle and I wanted to see how it could handle on the roads it was built for. Peter began moaning in the passenger seat, but I didn't let up.

"The empty country road was bumpy and often off-cambered, but to its credit, the RX 500h never put a tire wrong and allowed for a swift, smooth, and very satisfying drive," I wrote as part of my later account in the *Globe and Mail*. "My loaner car is equipped with the adaptive variable suspension that continuously and instantly adjusts the shock absorbers for such variations, as well as an advanced all-wheel drive system that constantly assesses the best distribution of power between the axles."

Perhaps I should have added that the Lexus really stuck to the curves. With a Lexus, you can take the corners with plenty of confidence, and believe me, I took plenty of them this morning. Why not try a Lexus for smoothness today?

Wilby and Haney stayed the night in Fredericton Junction after leaving Saint John two and a half hours before. They'd been delayed there, Haney wrote, by "some fool doings," which was presumably the schmoozing with the mayor and his entourage. They found an inn where they ate in a small backroom "where a big stove strove vainly to counteract the chilly effect of the linoleum-covered floor," wrote Wilby. "Tea and Canadian steak, of doubtful cut, but usually served under the imposing name of 'tenderloin' or 'sirloin,' followed by cake and canned fruit, proved to be the staples of the meal."

Peter and I, however, travelled considerably more swiftly and continued on to Fredericton where we went to a Starbucks and had it out.

I wasn't driving dangerously, I told him. I could always see far enough up the highway to stop for any obstacle, and I wasn't speeding excessively.

Peter stayed quiet. He was still shaken. Eventually, after some more sips of tea, he said he'd kept his eyes shut almost the entire way. He said he was not used to taking risks, as he felt I had done with driving at the higher speed.

But I never took a risk, I said. I always kept back plenty in reserve. If I'd taken risks, we'd have driven significantly faster. Peter clearly didn't agree, but after more tea, it all started to come out.

In the United Kingdom, Peter owns an older Porsche 968 that's kept for lapping days at the racetrack. He'd not driven it for three years, since it blew up at speed at Brands Hatch and laid a streak of oil down the straight. He'd fixed it, but then Covid happened and he suddenly stopped driving anywhere. And his marriage deteriorated and his children left home and now he'd left home too, living in a rented house in a new town an hour away. His work, as a commercial property manager, was stressful and unrelenting. All of it had taken a toll on his nerves, and he'd gone from driving nowhere to driving one of the longest roads in the world and it was taking a while to adjust.

I already knew about the Porsche and the work and the separation — I'd been his best man at the wedding almost 30 years earlier. I really hadn't cut him any slack for it, though, and now that he opened up, I realized this was a joint venture. We had to be equals in this journey, even if he was, in his own words, just along for the ride.

"Don't worry," I told him. "There are no more roads like Highway 785 — at least, not for a while yet."

□

The original roads to Quebec followed the Saint John River Valley for close to 300 kilometres between Fredericton and Edmundston and then up to the provincial border. They crossed back and forth over the river, including on the covered bridge at Hartland, famous for being the longest covered bridge in the world. When the Trans-Canada began to come through in the 1950s, it followed some of those same roads, even using the single-lane covered bridge until a wider and stronger concrete bridge was built alongside in 1960. The highway twisted in from Moncton and then crossed the river near the centre of Fredericton before looping north to Hartland. Then, when the modern highway was built in the early 2000s, its four lanes blew through fields and woods, high above the western bank of the river, crossing over at Grand Falls with nary a thought for existing routes.

This means that west of Fredericton, near the town of Pokiok, you can drive on three parallel roads beside the river from three different times. The Trans-Canada blasts past to the south, and it'll get you to either Quebec or Nova Scotia in about three hours if you just hang on to the wheel. Then the Pokiok Road sits down in the valley alongside, and this was the original Trans-Canada. There's not much there now, though, and it fades out after a few kilometres of servicing a handful of houses among the trees. Just before it does, however, you can turn right onto the Lower Shogomoc Road. This is the original route that the first pathfinders were sure to have taken.

That road is still paved and painted in some spots along its remaining two kilometres, but it's barely wide enough for two vehicles to pass and it's overhung by leafy trees. It ends now at Shogomoc Cove where there's a sturdy walking bridge for hikers, and it's a quiet and peaceful place. We skipped stones on the water there for a while and tried to imagine how it would have looked 100 years before when Wilby described the gentle river where "every island was duplicated with photographic fidelity in the limpid

The original road across New Brunswick can still be seen at Shogomoc, where it soon becomes submerged under a flooded reservoir.

waters; and the fresh revelation at each bend of the great stream would have perfectly reproduced the green hills and deep blue waters of its beautiful predecessor had it not surpassed it in dignified grandeur." Even so, it was difficult to picture. The cove was created in 1967 when the Mactaquac Dam was built downriver and the road here was flooded out. We could see the asphalt dropping away under the water, so we turned around and retraced our drive to Pokiok.

There's nothing much in the half-flooded town anymore. The pretty little waterfall that emptied the Pokiok Stream is long gone, submerged under the new reservoir. There's the Pokiok Motel beside the old Trans-Canada, but it's empty and abandoned. An auto shop nearby seemed the only inhabited place, and I asked the owner if he knew when the motel closed. He shrugged and suggested I speak with Gerald Stone, who lived down the road. When I knocked on the door and Gerald answered, he was happy to talk of how his town had been before the new highway went through.

"Over there," he said, pointing with a crooked finger from his porch at a paved-over field on the other side of the road, "there was an Irving restaurant and a gas bar and truck stop. The tire place where they sent you over here, that was a Shell gas bar and it also had a restaurant. My mother worked there one time. They've all gone now, took them out when the new highway went in. Nothing left except the tire place."

Gerald said he'd lived in the area all his life, "and I'll be 83 on Saturday!" He missed the business of the community when the main highway drove right through the town, but he was philosophical about its replacement by the bypassing blacktop up on the hill.

"Look at it this way," he said. "I never was for something like this, but my mother and father were killed on this road, head-on collision. If the four-lane had been in there, that may never have happened."

Half a century later, he was able to tell me the story matter-of-factly without shedding a tear, but obviously it had been rough. Harold and Frederica Stone had been out to the local Legion on a Saturday night in 1971, visiting for a dance or a darts night, and afterwards they went for dinner in Meductic, the next community upriver. "Murray Grant had a restaurant there at the garage," said Gerald. "It was a good place to eat, and they was up there, having something to eat, and when they left, they didn't make it no further."

Their friend Irene Stairs was in the car with them, and they headed back for Pokiok. Also out on the road were two young local men, Perry Knox and Clair Gullison. "They'd been all over to different garages for their alternator they had on the car, and they were drunk," said Gerald. "Nobody would fix them because they didn't want them on the road, and they were headed up to the garage up at Meductic, that would be Murray Grant's, used to be there, and they met my father and my mother right there. They hit head-on. Them two burned, and somebody came along and hauled the three out of the other car before they burned."

The crash was reported the next day on the front page of the *Daily Gleaner*, confirming that "the car carrying Mr. Knox and Mr. Gullison burst into flames and the identity of the two was not confirmed until late Sunday evening." There was no more information than that, though, except to say, "Police investigating the accident said it was unlikely an inquest would be held. There were no eyewitnesses to the accident."

There were no later reports, or at least none that I could find. Gerald's allegation of the two young men's drunkenness is his own, but it seems the police thought this an open-and-shut case. Head-on collisions are the most fatal of car crashes because of the combined speed of the two vehicles, and especially back in the early 1970s before seat belts began to be fitted to cars. It's why the original Trans-Canada between Moncton and Fredericton was so dangerous, because impatient drivers would pull out to pass slower trucks and smash head-on into oncoming traffic. And it's why "twinned" highways like the present-day Trans-Canada in New Brunswick are so much safer. If an incapacitated driver hits a vehicle in the lane alongside, then both vehicles are already driving in the same direction, probably at similar speeds. And if that driver leaves the lane to the left, the out-of-control vehicle almost certainly goes into a wide ditch or grassy median, not into an oncoming truck.

"If the four-lane was built and they was on it, they'd have made it home that night," said Gerald. "My brother's daughter, Katie, was born that morning they died. If they'd driven on a four-lane, they'd have met their granddaughter, but they never did. I had to go identify their bodies instead."

Twinning the Trans-Canada has undoubtedly made it safer, but there are still inherent risks to highway travel. The next day, in Carberry, Manitoba, 17 people would be killed on the Trans-Canada when their bus was T-boned by a transport truck. It would be one of the worst collisions in the highway's history, and when we heard of it on the evening news, Peter and I knew we would pass the charred site just a week later, with Harold and Frederica and Irene and Perry and Clair still fresh in our minds.

◻

And so we were finally on the last stretch across the Atlantic provinces, about to reach Edmundston almost at the border of Quebec. If this was about speed, then Brigadier (Retired) Alex Macfarlane and Squadron Leader (Retired) Ken MacGillivray are the clear winners, taking just a single day in 1946 to reach the town from Louisbourg. They took the causeway ferry and a detour around the Sussex woods because the river was flooded, but even so, they covered almost 1,100 kilometres, slept the night, and then shaved, breakfasted, and were rolling by seven thirty the next morning. "Note to other travellers," wrote Macfarlane, "remember the substantial breakfast, porridge, bacon and eggs, etc., if you won't want to be hankering to stop two hours after you get started." *Sir yes sir!*

Everyone else took two or three days to make it from Halifax. Edward and Margaret McCourt probably had the most pleasant journey in 1963, ambling along the original route that hugged the Saint John River before parts of it were flooded out, and before the tragic death of Gerald Stone's parents. As he wrote: "Most visitors to the province are agreed, I think, that of all possible drives in New Brunswick, the one up the Saint John via the Trans-Canada Highway is the loveliest and most relaxing." The CBC crew agreed when they took the same route three years earlier. "If we'd only had the time, we'd probably have loaded the Chevy down with flowers because I don't think I've seen as many flowers in one short space of time before in my life, all wild ones. There were daisies and goldenrod, buttercups, iris," said Ron Hunka before continuing. "I'm sure glad that we're driving a Chevrolet. This car has all kinds of entrance room. You can step in or out without having to wind your head up and down into your neck like the proverbial turtle.... There's room for three of us to travel comfortably all day in the front seat.... So why not try on a Chevy for size very soon?"

Ed Flickenger and the local Ford executives would have chatted away amiably in 1925 as they manoeuvred the Model T along the narrow road to the area of the Shogomoc Cove, but as usual, Jimmy Oates had the greatest challenge riding through the night on his motorcycle three years later. He hit thick fog that slowed his speed to 15 kilometres an hour — just as well, since he fell asleep after a short while and rode into a fence post — and then it started to rain, hard. "I am getting tired, my arms ache, my eyes are feeling the strain of the constant watch on the road ahead, and my face surely must be bleeding after having the rain smashing on it, every raindrop feels like a knife thrust." At one point, he gave up and tried to get some sleep lying in his sidecar, but that really didn't work. "Why did I ever think of this confounded across Canada trip?" he lamented. "My neck feels as if the hangman has been putting in a little practice on me. My spine I swear will never be the same again and I am cold as ... well, never mind, I am." Even so, he pressed on with true British pluck, the sun came out, and he made it to Quebec the next day.

Thinking of true British pluck, Thomas Wilby and his American driver, Jack Haney, found their way along the unmapped roads beside the river but were challenged by the fuel consumption of the Reo. It had a 60-litre gravity-fed gas tank, but in those days, gasoline was often sold in bottles and jugs and not easily available, especially in the wilds of Canada. The Reo sucked back fuel at about one litre for every five kilometres, or 13 miles per gallon in the old measure, and seemed in perpetual danger of running dry. To Wilby, this was obviously Haney's fault: "Sometimes," he wrote, "owing to the ineradicable instinct of chauffeurs to economize on petrol, we were held up trying to convince the remaining drop of 'gas' that it was capable of doing the work of a couple of gallons, and reached our hotel long after the dining-room had closed its doors for the night." This was apparent when the fuel line ran dry on the final after-dark approach to Grand Falls on an uphill slope just after they'd driven through a swamp. "Men from a neighbouring farmhouse emerged from the shadows and silhouetted themselves in helpless curiosity in the strong rays of the lamps," recalled Wilby. "After some time, by dint of blowing into the tank to gain pressure, the car was started again.... It was a miracle! It was a miracle, too, that the unfortunate chauffeur did not burst his cheeks or succumb to asphyxia, for it fell to his lot to blow into the petrol tank every few moments of the remaining journey."

The main difference between Wilby and Haney and all the other drivers I've mentioned so far (and yes, there will be more — wait till you meet Percy Gomery in Montreal, with his hapless wife, the Skipper) is that Wilby and Haney were driving through Nova Scotia and New Brunswick on the left side of the road. Well, mostly they were, when they weren't in the centre or dodging rocks and holes in their way. Unlike the entire United States, all three Maritime provinces drove on the left, like the British, until the 1920s, and Newfoundland too. Haney would have to move the Reo to the right when they crossed into Quebec, and stay on the right until they reached British Columbia, when he'd move it back to the left.

It took another decade before New Brunswick became the first of the eastern provinces to change to the right, switching over at the stroke of midnight on December 1, 1922, with surprisingly little damage to show for it. Nova Scotia followed four months later, and Prince Edward Island a couple of years after that. Newfoundland, as it likes to do, held out many years more, switching to the right only in 1947, two years before turning away from the British Empire and becoming the 10th Canadian province.

Peter and I didn't think of any of this, of course, as we sped north on perfect, safe asphalt, the river almost entirely hidden from view beyond the wide potato fields, holding to a safe and legal 110 kilometres per hour on laser-guided active cruise control, cameras aligned to keep the Lexus in the centre of its lane, straight into the perpetual construction of Quebec.

LEGEND

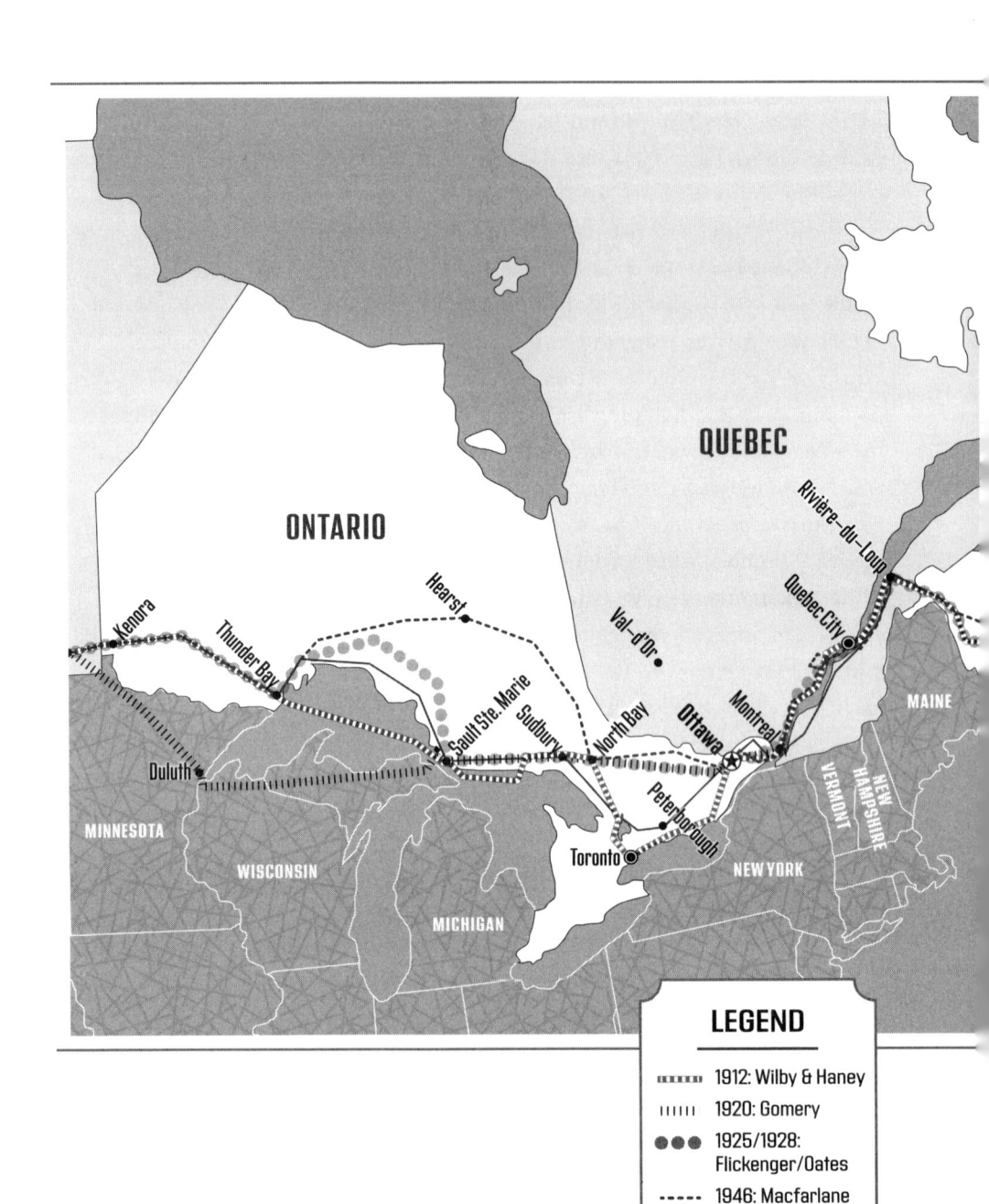

- ▦▦▦ 1912: Wilby & Haney
- ||||| 1920: Gomery
- ●●● 1925/1928: Flickenger/Oates
- ---- 1946: Macfarlane
- —— 2023: Richardson

5

Quebec

The road restrictions began within just a few minutes of entering Quebec. We gained an extra hour with the change in time zones, which helped make up for the slower pace. Traffic was relatively light, and we held at the speed of the heaviest trucks on what became a two-lane road, separated in the middle by only a pair of painted solid-yellow lines.

It's almost 100 kilometres northwest from New Brunswick to the St. Lawrence River, where Autoroute 85 meets the fast Autoroute 20 that travels west to Montreal and the Ontario border. There was construction here when I drove through in 2012, but everything was still on schedule and the end was finally in sight. There were just 40 more kilometres to be twinned in 2023 to turn Autoroute 85 into a full-fledged four-lane divided highway, just like in New Brunswick. This is the last bottleneck for trucks on their way to and from the Atlantic ports, and when it's finished in 2026, the route will be twinned all the way from Windsor, Ontario, through Toronto and Montreal, to Halifax.

The $1.7 billion project began in 2002, a few months after eight people were killed in a ghastly crash here on the two-lane highway. For some reason, a minivan carrying a family of three from suburban Montreal drifted over

Construction seems permanent in Quebec, but Autoroute 85, seen here near Lake Témiscouata, is scheduled to be fully widened to four twinning lanes by 2026.

the line and smashed into a car carrying five young men from Edmundston. Just the same as the crash that killed Gerald Stone's parents, there was nothing to prevent the head-on collision and the car erupted into flames. Two of the young men were identified only by their dental records. "There are at least 14 people who've died on that stretch of highway [in] the last year and a half," said Jacques Martin, Edmundston's mayor, talking to a newspaper reporter a couple of days afterward on New Year's Eve. He added that plans to twin the highway were stalled because of a lack of funding. The money was found soon after, and the memories would have been fresh for the workers when they began the mammoth 25-year project.

We passed a sign that announced potential dynamite explosions, though the warning was entirely in French; fortunately, there's not much doubt what *Zone de Dynamitage* means. Construction is all the more challenging because the easiest route is already taken, where the existing Trans-Canada runs between the hills and Lake Témiscouata; the second pair of lanes under construction seemed to curve, rise, and fall quite separately from the original lanes we were driving on, slow and steady beside an unending string of orange barrels. Huge interchanges were being built, and bridges and culverts constructed, and more than 30 dedicated crossings for wildlife prepared beneath those bridges and between the new moose fencing. Animals are plentiful in the woods alongside the road, protected now more responsibly than 100 years ago, and much of their survival is thanks to a mysterious man who made his home here in 1928.

◻

The highway hugs the shoreline of Lake Témiscouata for about half the water's curving 40-kilometre length. There's a national park on the other side of the slim lake, and the green-treed landscape seems little spoiled by time. It was here, a couple of months after Jimmy Oates roared through on his motorcycle, that the English conservationist and writer (and fraud and bigamist) Archie Belaney built a cabin and planned to establish a beaver colony; at the time, beavers were hunted almost to extinction. His first article about the Canadian wilderness, "The Passing of the Last Frontier," was published in Britain's *Country Life* magazine in 1929, using his name A.S. Belaney. When his second article, "The Vanishing Life of the Wild," was published the following year in the Canadian magazine *Forest and Outdoors*, he used Grey Owl, his adopted name and persona. The aristocratic young man from Hastings, England, had completed his transformation in that cabin where "the great pines still stood towering, mighty in their silence; and standing there immoveable in their impenetrable reticence, they seemed to meditate, and brood upon the past." He had become an Indigenous spokesperson for the environment, the supposedly Mexican-born son of a Scottish settler father and Apache mother. His fluency in the Ojibwe language, honed while living with his first wife even as his second wife waited in England to join him, helped the facade.

Grey Owl fooled everyone, and maybe even came to believe it himself. As a boy in England, abandoned by his deadbeat father who was preoccupied with squandering the family fortune, young Archie would play in the woods, pretending to be a "red Indian." He sailed for Canada at 17, and soon after, moved north to work at a resort deep in the Ontario woods beyond Sudbury. He met and married an Ojibwe woman and learned her culture, then disappeared for months, years at a time, living off the land and even signing up to fight as a Canadian sniper in France during the First World War. His fellow soldiers had no idea of his English upbringing. When he returned to Ontario's northland, after marrying a childhood friend and then leaving her behind to join him later, he lived as a trapper and hunter's guide, and then he fell in love with Gertrude Bernard, almost half his age at 19 years old. His English wife divorced him, but his Ojibwa wife never did. Let's just say, life was complicated.

Gertrude was of Kanien'keha:ka and Algonquin descent, and he called her Anahareo. She persuaded him that trapping beavers was unnecessarily cruel and that the endangered animals needed protection. One thing led to another and the two of them moved, in the fall of 1928, to the woods on the far shore of Lake Témiscouata in what would eventually become the national park, where they built a cabin beside another small lake, and Grey Owl began to write and even to lecture at a nearby resort. His writing was both captivating and poetic, and it was helped immeasurably by the illusion he fostered that he was Indigenous, though he had no papers to prove himself as such. In his first book, *The Men of the Last Frontier*, which he wrote in that hand-hewn cabin on Birch Lake, he described:

> A region of illimitable distance, unknown lakes, hidden rivers, and unrecorded happenings; and changed in no marked way since the white man discovered America.
>
> Here, even in these modern days, lies a land of Romance, gripping the imagination with its immensity, its boundless possibilities and its magic of untried adventure. Thus it has lain since the world was young, enveloped in a mystery beyond understanding, and immersed in silence, absolute, unbroken, and all-embracing; a silence intensified rather than relieved by the muted whisperings of occasional light forest airs in the treetops far overhead.

The two of them were deep enough in the woods to be sheltered from the noise of everything except the wind and the wildlife. Much of the land was logged, but they scraped by there for three years, nurturing and protecting a pair of beavers and then a second pair when the first pair was lost. Finally, Grey Owl's writings and lectures, and his appearances in several short films about beavers, were noticed by the Canadian government. He was offered a job as a conservationist in Manitoba and then Saskatchewan, which both came with a wilderness cabin and protection for his beavers and plenty of time to write and travel on the international lecture circuit. He spoke to packed theatres, dressed in the authentic regalia and full-feathered headpiece of an Indigenous chief, and captivated audiences with his pleas for environmental sustainability. Anahareo moved away, but Grey Owl became one of the most famous people in the world, and in November 1937, he even spoke for two hours in a performance at Buckingham Palace to King George VI and his 11-year-old daughter, Princess Elizabeth; when they met afterward, he apparently slapped the king on the back and said, "I'll be seeing you, brother!"

His schedule was relentless and his health suffered, made worse by his alcoholism. He married a French-Canadian woman, despite never divorcing his original Ojibwe wife, and she adopted the name Silver Moon and travelled with him on his lecture tours. The following March, Grey Owl spoke to 3,000 people at Massey Hall in Toronto and was given "the greatest ovation of his life," according to one of his biographers. Two weeks later, back at his cabin in the woods, he succumbed to pneumonia and exhaustion and died at 49 years old.

The story of his true ancestry came out that same day and made headlines around the world over the Easter weekend. The *North Bay Nugget* newspaper had apparently been sitting on it for three years, holding back because Grey Owl's powerful message of conservancy was considered more important than the scandal of his personal truth. As the *Saskatoon Star-Phoenix* reported in announcing his death, "Less than a year ago, Grey Owl wrote to a friend here: 'I am taking very seriously the responsibility that seems to have come to me as a connecting link, an intermediary between the white man and the Indian. I have an unparalleled opportunity with my Indian mind, training and experience, and my lucky entry into the public life of the civilized world to act as interpreter for both.'" And then on the Monday, the headlines changed: "Grey Owl Mask Gradually Being Lifted";

"Grey Owl Really an Englishman, Old Friends Insist"; and "Grey Owl Put Over Fast One." A white friend in Saskatchewan said he'd admitted the truth to her when she heard him play the piano at her home. He was "playing the sweetest music you ever heard," she recalled, "but before doing it, he would ask if there was anyone else in the house. He didn't like anyone to hear him play like that. If there was anyone else about, he would just sit down at the piano and bang away as though he were unable to play."

Most of the people closest to him were astonished and defended him as an Indigenous North American. His publisher defended his friend's claimed heritage, despite admitting puzzlement over Grey Owl's blue eyes and English accent. Anahareo, his partner for 11 years, swore she had never known.

In the end, for the time, it really didn't matter. Archie Belaney found a far more receptive audience for his environmental concerns through the persona of Grey Owl, and if the showmanship involved a white man speaking eloquently on behalf of supportive Indigenous people, was there really a difference? It wasn't exploitive, disrespectful, or even stereotypical. Today, his cultural appropriation would be a far greater scandal and deservedly so, but in the

Grey Owl was exposed as the Englishman Archie Belaney soon after his death.

1930s most of the Indigenous Peoples in North America didn't have his western education or communication style that helped non-Indigenous lawmakers and the general public be more receptive to his message of conservancy.

"What does it matter if he never was a red Indian but a paleface who persuaded the Indians to believe he was one of them?" asked the *Daily Express* in London, England. "You can forgive him the deception, for it hurt nobody." And Britain's *Daily Herald* took it a little further: "He preached a gospel of tolerance towards the animal world, not for sentimental reasons but because 'it is just sense.' He was a man who had the courage to tell the civilized world it still had much to learn."

□

The highway continued north past the woods and forest and onto the flat, cleared fields that mark the southern shore of the St. Lawrence. Peter and I stayed the night near Rivière-du-Loup at a near-anonymous hotel that required no knowledge of French with its online registration, though we shouldn't have worried about any lack of communication. People in this area are used to slightly confused-looking travellers who can't quite make it through Quebec in one silent hop, and they were entertained, rather than insulted, by our innocent slaughter of their language. On my previous Trans-Canada drive in 2012, I'd dragged along my French-speaking friend, Costa, for assistance with the more subtle intricacies of translation, and he proved his worth when we visited a nudist camp near Drummondville; this time around, I had enough confidence to go it alone with Peter. Besides, we had Google Translate.

The app came into its own the next day when we struck off the main highway to drive down by the river. We'd already travelled eastward on the Trans-Canada, Quebec's Autoroute 20, all the way through from south of Montreal, and we knew the scenery to be flat and monotonous, with narrow, far-reaching fields to each side and frequent road repairs that limited the highway to just one lane beside a line of cones. Every other interchange offered Tim Hortons, McDonald's, and Burger King, all looking exactly the same. As Edward McCourt wrote in 1963, the highway "runs arrow-straight mile after mile through dismal spruce forest, and the few villages it touches are without personality or interest. It is a road with a sinister reputation, for boredom and long, straight stretches of flawless asphalt invite high speeds and sudden death." The road down by the river, however — well, that was the road taken by the original pathfinders, and it could be in an entirely different region.

"When you reach the river you are in the country of the French villages, the small places with the big churches, so like one another that if you didn't catch a name over the Post Office you might think you were standing still," wrote Alex Macfarlane after he streaked through in 1946. I doubt his passenger, Ken MacGillivray, ever thought their car was standing still. Jimmy Oates and Ed Flickenger would both have pressed on beside the river to Quebec City, while before them, Thomas Wilby watched the river roll steadily past from his overstuffed leather seat in the back of the Reo. The road from Rivière-du-Loup was a grassy path in 1912, because most farmers still transported their goods from wharves on the St. Lawrence, but it was smooth going for a while. "Over its unconventional surface the car sped like an arrow," wrote Wilby. "The bigness and grandeur, the majesty and beauty of the St. Lawrence were such as to sweep away all other memories, while the mind dwelt upon all the wonders before it in mountain and sky, in water and in air." His driver, Jack Haney, was more succinct. "We had 25 miles of good road along the St. Lawrence River," he wrote in his diary. "Got picture of it. Some scenery all right."

I drove the Lexus along the gently curving road, sometimes just a stone's throw from the water, and Peter was happy for the frequent small towns that kept our speed in check. We could see small, dark islands out on the river, but the opposite shore was more than 20 kilometres away and hard to make out. Then, somewhere just outside the tidy village of Saint-Jean-Port-Joli, so well kept it seemed immediately familiar from real-estate calendars and tourist brochures, we paused at a strange metal tower that was just standing there beside the road, nestled against a cliff-face. It was an observation tower, five storeys of circular staircase leading to the top of the north-facing cliff, and Google Translate told us from its entrance sign it was called The Tower of Innovation, built to celebrate local businesses. I climbed to the top and walked over a short wooden footway to the cliff where a statue of the Madonna stood watch on a ledge. No one else was around and it all seemed very strange. I walked back and looked out at the river where the islands and their lighthouses could be seen more clearly, and then I glanced down, across the road, and saw a trim, green field, spackled with yellow dandelions, with a large house against the trees at its far end, closer to the water. There was a sign beside the house, and when I climbed down the tower and went across for a closer look, I saw this was the Museum of Living Memory. A small bronze plaque declared that it was built on the site of the Aubert de Gaspé manor, and it was where Philippe Aubert de Gaspé wrote *Les Anciens Canadiens*. This novel, declared another sign, was a landmark of Canadian literature. And I'd never heard of it.

The original English translation of Philippe Aubert de Gaspé's 1863 novel, *The Canadians of Old*, is convoluted and pretentious, which may explain why it was less popular outside Quebec. A second translation in 1890 is more readable but left out the notes and clarifications that helped explain its context. It was finally translated into engaging English in 1996, but I was unaware of it at the time. It's too bad. It's a rewarding read, telling the fictional tale of a Quebec family a century earlier in North America when France and Britain fought each other in the Seven Years' War.

Except the author's own story is far more interesting. Philippe Aubert de Gaspé was born as the seigneur of Saint-Jean-Port-Joli, the French-bestowed lord of the manor, but the manor itself had burned to the ground nearly three decades earlier during the Conquest of Quebec. There was still family money, and Aubert studied law in Quebec City, married an American woman who he named "Belle des Belles," and in true Catholic Quebec fashion, went on to have 13 children. At age 30, he was sheriff of the district, responsible for keeping the peace, collecting fines, and enforcing sentences. But he was a spender. He founded the Quebec Literary Society and helped found the Jockey Club and the Quebec Bank, and he held lavish parties, totally beyond his means. He incurred tremendous debt, and his father, who wanted to protect the seigneury for the future, disinherited him. In 1826, he was ordered to repay almost £2,000 to his creditors, which was quite beyond his income of £100 per year. He struggled on for a dozen more years, living more quietly and moving his family to his mother's home, before he was arrested and charged with embezzlement.

Philippe Aubert de Gaspé was imprisoned in the jail he used to run. As historian Claude La Charité of the University of Quebec in Rimouski has said, "Overnight, the man who had shone brightly in Quebec City's high society became an outlaw, practically a pariah." He was cut off entirely from his family, and his eldest son died during the incarceration. When he was released after three years, he returned to his mother's home to continue an even more restrained life. Twenty years later, at 76 years old and after decades of writing, his novel was published and was an immediate success. Much of it was based on his own memories and experiences: "There was just a street between us," writes the prisoner in *Les Anciens Canadiens*, looking out the window of his cell toward his family home, as Aubert had done from jail. "During long, sleepless nights, I saw the movements near their beds, the lights being turned on and off in one room and then another. I trembled each time I saw those signs of life disappear."

Philippe Aubert de Gaspé's life was everywhere at the Museum of Living Memory, which includes a faithful modern reconstruction of the seigneurial manor on its original site, where his story is told. There was no highway back then except for perhaps a grassy track that ended at the river, but decades later, all the pathfinders would have driven past the estate. Peter and I left to continue west, grateful we'd taken the detour from the new Trans-Canada to travel for a few hours on the old highway, where the memories and the stories are still fresh, where we could look out across the wide river and see it still as Wilby had seen it in 1912, and Aubert de Gaspé had seen it 50 years earlier, and as he remembered it through the hero of his novel, when fires burned on both shores 100 years before.

☐

The Trans-Canada Highway stays south of the St. Lawrence and never travels over the river to Quebec City, but all the earlier pathfinders made the crossing. Autoroute 40 on the north shore was the traditional road between the provincial capital and Montreal, travelling through Trois-Rivières along the way. Alex Macfarlane sped over the Quebec Bridge, still the longest cantilever bridge span in the world, and was happy the toll had ended a few years before. Jimmy Oates would have taken the ferry, looking up enviously at the railway bridge that didn't add its first highway lane until the following year, but Ed Flickenger wasn't deterred. For the first time since leaving Halifax, he changed over the rubber-tire wheels of the Ford Model T for flanged wheels, then gave the driver's seat to Perry Doolittle who had travelled in for the occasion. Doolittle drove across on the bridge's steel rails while Flickenger went ahead to film it driving across the bridge without incident. He mounted the camera on the back of a handcar just in front, and cyclists pedalled on the walkway alongside. On the north shore, Doolittle shook the hand of a local dignitary as "congratulations on driving the first automobile across the bridge since it was officially opened."

In fact, Doolittle may not have been the first to drive across the bridge, as the silent movie's title card claimed. The *Sault Daily Star* reported that month that Doolittle, "the veteran good roads champion of Canada, who had the honour of driving the car across the famous bridge, stated at a banquet given to the party at Quebec that a man by the name of Doyle had bumped his way across on the ties some years ago, in one of Henry's old reliables." But why let the facts get in the way of a good story?

The Quebec Bridge was controversial for years. Work had begun to build it in 1904, and the ambitious construction continued until 1907 when its poor design caused it to collapse under its own weight: the half-kilometre central span took just 15 seconds to twist and plunge into the water. Eighty-six workers were on the bridge that day and 75 of them were killed, making it still the worst bridge construction disaster anywhere in the world. Work resumed after a royal inquiry into the tragedy and a new design was commissioned, and then that bridge collapsed during construction in 1916, killing an additional 13 workers. The bridge was finally completed in 1917, five years after Thomas Wilby and Jack Haney came through and crossed on the ferry with the Reo.

Wilby wrote:

Quebec City is no place for a self-respecting motor car. On landing from the Lévis ferryboat, there is apparently no way of mounting to the Upper Town except by a steep ascent following a winding approach to the ancient gates. The "street" was paved with granite blocks, and in its upward progress described a huge "S." Had we been wise, we should have beaten a hasty retreat when retreat was still possible, or hitched our block and tackle to the University at the top and requisitioned a score of polite Frenchmen to haul us up....

The car, heavily loaded, realized by some mechanical instinct before we did the absurdity of the unequal contest. It showed the white feather, and half-way up tried to run down again backwards. What it actually succeeded in doing was to come to a full stop athwart the line of traffic, while all Gaul collected on the sidewalks. The situation was ludicrously humiliating. The delighted crowd did not scruple to point sarcastically to the inscription on the tire drum which flauntingly announced the Pacific as our destination....

I sprang out to lighten the load. "Turn her round and back her up! Quick!" I cried, and ingloriously sought self-effacement among the onlookers. Here we were undertaking the longest road tour ever attempted in Canada, and yet we were unable to climb a paved hill!

It got worse. "The car maneuvered for the right-about-turn while I glared into a shop-window with ostentatious indifference, and decided to go in and buy something for which I had no earthly need," admitted Wilby. "From the inside of the shop, I could see the car creeping laboriously backwards up the hill while the crowd panted along in its wake."

The problem was, once again, that the car's fuel was fed by gravity from the gas tank in the rear to the engine in the front, and on long uphill climbs, the gas wouldn't flow through the line. The solution was to drive backward, keeping the fuel tank higher than the engine and using the gear with the lowest ratio, but then most of the weight was on the front wheels and the rear-wheel-drive car would lose traction, especially on a slippery road paved with granite.

It was left to Haney to find the solution, of course, though he describes the situation differently. "Had trouble getting up a hill about 20 miles out of Quebec," he wrote in his diary, with no reference to driving in the city itself. "It was too steep for gas to feed with full tank so I tried backing up, but when about 100 ft. from top could not get traction. There were four French peasants standing along the hill. I got them in the rear seat to hold her down and was able to back up and over it."

It's possible this was an entirely separate incident — the pair was used to backing up hills and probably did so multiple times every day — but it's more likely that Wilby was using some artistic licence to spin out the story. It might also explain why Wilby had gotten out of the car: normally, his weight would be wanted over the back axle, but I'm sure he would have been horrified to share his leather seat with four French peasants. Whatever, the two of them pressed on and made it to Trois-Rivières for 10:00 p.m. "I will be glad when I get out of the cussed country," wrote Haney, "for I can't understand anything they say, everybody is French."

◻

Peter and I stayed south of the river and found our way back onto the Trans-Canada Highway where it travels through the northern region of the Eastern Townships. We wanted to cross Montreal before rush hour and stay with my cousin at her farm close to the Ontario border. It wasn't to be so straightforward, however. There were soon roadworks that shut down the pair of eastbound lanes for lengthy stretches, forcing all the traffic to share the two westbound lanes, with concrete dividers to protect from head-on collisions. Then somewhere near Saint-Hyacinthe, about 30 kilometres shy of the City of Montreal, traffic ground almost to a halt. It was due to repairs to the bridge-tunnel across the river and we should have taken a different crossing but we couldn't — this was the only route of the Trans-Canada and we'd avoided it heading east.

The Louis-Hippolyte-La Fontaine Bridge-Tunnel was the missing link that finally persuaded Quebec to commit to the Trans-Canada Highway. In the late 1950s, Montreal's existing three bridges across the St. Lawrence were beyond their capacity, carrying almost 10 times the vehicles they'd carried after the war, just 15 years earlier. A fourth bridge was under construction, the Champlain Bridge, but it wouldn't be completed until 1962, and even then, it still wouldn't be enough. Premier Maurice Duplessis had held out against agreeing to the Canadian Highway travelling through his province, but he died in 1959 and his Union Nationale government was replaced by the federalist Liberals. The new premier, Jean Lesage, signed on to the Trans-Canada Highway Act in 1960, making Quebec the last province to do so, with the promise from Ottawa that it would contribute to a fifth crossing over the St. Lawrence.

The Trans-Canada Highway could have continued along the north shore of the river, through Trois-Rivières, and crossed at Quebec City before the water widened, but the Quebec Bridge there that Macfarlane used wouldn't be adequate for the increased traffic. A new bridge would need to be built — and the larger Pierre Laporte Bridge was eventually finished alongside the original cantilever structure in 1970. The highway south of the river was in dire need of improvement, however, and the federal government would pay half the estimated cost of almost $300 million for rebuilding if it was considered to be Trans-Canada. That included a crossing for the city's underserved east end, which Lesage was happy to accept.

Quite what, and where, that crossing would be, no one was yet sure. Maybe a bridge, maybe a tunnel. Four places were considered for the site, and in the end, the most easterly was chosen between the small working-class village of Longue-Pointe and the growing suburb of Boucherville. Among other things, this route would need the least expropriation of land, but even so, 300 families lost their homes; some, like the Vinet and Robert families, had lived there for two centuries. Paul Robert's grocery store was razed and the Saint Francis of Assisi parish church was demolished, replaced by a more modest church nearby two years later. Probably no other portion of the Trans-Canada Highway required more expropriation of property and destruction of homes.

The most obvious crossing would be a suspension bridge, but it would need even more land for its long approaches at each end, not to mention an enormous amount of steel that would have to be imported from the United States. It would also need to be so high for ships to pass underneath that it would soar over the river's Boucherville islands and leave them unserviced. A tunnel was the other obvious choice, but it would have to be deeper than usual to accommodate the extra-hard bedrock of the riverbed. Also, there was no excavation equipment capable of boring a hole wide enough for six lanes of traffic.

In the end, an ideal compromise was reached: a low bridge from the south shore to the islands, and a tunnel from the islands to the north shore, created from seven prefabricated caissons, or concrete tubes, floated into place and then dropped into a trench across the bottom of the river and sealed together. It was an engineering tour de force designed and built in Quebec using local concrete. It was also the least expensive option and ended up costing $75 million when the bridge-tunnel was opened for traffic in 1967, of which 60 percent was paid by Ottawa. Ironically, that's the equivalent of $670 million today. The deadline for everything was always 1967: that was Canada's centenary and the year of Expo 67 in Montreal when the country — and Quebec — showed itself off to the world.

Now, however, the two-kilometre tunnel is showing its age. It needs "major structural rehabilitation," as well as upgrades and a redesign of its service corridors, and that means three of the six lanes will be shut off to make repairs for two years, and then the other three lanes for at least two years after that. The estimated price tag to shore it up for four more decades is a staggering $2.5 billion — far, far more than the original cost. The bridge-tunnel carried 120,000 vehicles a day before the reconstruction began in 2021 but carried about half that when Peter and I came through, with everyone else using a different crossing to get between Montreal and the south shore.

For us in the Lexus, this meant a three-hour crawl to travel about 80 kilometres into and through Montreal, and we arrived late at my cousin's farm south of Rigaud. She wasn't surprised. She's a Quebecker, and Quebeckers are used to construction. We left the next morning, returning to the Trans-Canada Highway at the junction where we'd left it. Most traffic here turns southwest to join Highway 401 toward Toronto, but Canada's national road doesn't go to Canada's largest city, so we turned northwest toward Ottawa and the political start of it all.

6
Ottawa

The federal government never really wanted to be in the roads business. After all, it built a railway across the country in 1885 and that connected all the provinces just fine. Trains could travel long distances with fast ease and in comfort, while horses and carts were only good for maybe 20 or 30 kilometres, and a stagecoach could manage perhaps 100 kilometres in a day. Then, in the first decade of the 20th century, along came cars.

At first, cars were a curiosity — toys for the rich and easy to dismiss. Roads were supposed to be the responsibility of the individual provinces, but those governments fobbed off the maintenance onto local municipalities, which in turn gave them over to property owners. "The trouble with us is that beggarly Statute Labour system which compels personal service on the roads, or accepts that service instead of a cash tax," complained a clearly transplanted Quebec acquaintance of Thomas Wilby in 1912. "Rose out of the Monarchical slave labour business in France of the Louis, you know. Wretched system from a business point of view, because we get no trained labour! The farmer knows more about his fields than he does about highways. He does his roadwork grudgingly and badly, and as he votes the road superintendent into power, discipline is out of all question. He is practically his own employer."

Cars changed all that as they became more affordable and grew exponentially in numbers, particularly so in the United States. Highways were more driveable south of the border where the federal Office of Public Roads had been established in 1905. Canadians realized that decent roads would attract those American visitors and their American dollars, and the first "modern" highway was completed in Quebec in 1912 to lure tourists to Montreal. The Canadian Good Roads Association was founded in 1914 when there were 74,000 vehicles registered in the country and almost one in every four drivers on Ontario roads was American. A year later, the province completed its first concrete highway, between Hamilton and Toronto. By 1918, there were 350,000 vehicle registrations in Canada. Cars and trucks were no longer a curiosity, and they needed roads.

In that second decade of the century, provinces began to form their own departments of highways, though they were still more concerned with connecting to American markets than with each other. They realized they could make a sizable revenue from licensing the vehicles, and in 1922, from taxing gasoline and then from licensing the drivers as well. Jackpot! This money helped finance road construction and improvements, which in turn encouraged more registrations.

Ottawa wasn't blind to this, but the Feds were now hamstrung by the terms of the British North America Act, accepted at Confederation, that made roads the responsibility of the provinces. As David Monaghan reports in his definitive historical thesis, *Canada's "New Main Street,"* the Conservative government tried to provide funds to the provinces in 1912 for building roads, but the Liberal opposition shot down the proposal. It tried again the next year, though J.A. Lougheed, a Conservative senator, admitted, "I doubt there is any subject that has received less attention at the hands of the provinces of the Dominion than the improvement of the highways." The Senate, dominated by the Liberals, blocked the move. "It is constitutionally beyond the function of the Dominion to make an appropriation of that kind," stated Sir George Ross, a Liberal senator.

Even so, under pressure from the influential Good Roads Association and the newly formed Canadian Automobile Association, the new Union Party government in Ottawa was able to pass the Canada Highways Act in 1919,

Tour guides at the House of Commons pose in 2012 with the Chevrolet Camaro that Mark drove across Canada that year.

providing $20 million over five years to the provinces for improvement of the roads, as long as those provinces paid 60 percent of the cost. It was a start, but the provinces weren't happy. As Monaghan reported, "the New Brunswick minister of public works demonstrated that the 40 percent subsidy was actually only 20 to 25 percent of road expenditures, once one accounted for such excluded items as preliminary engineering costs, rights of way, and bridges."

It was a beginning, though, since the act's purpose was to "form, as far as possible, a general system of interprovincial highways." Of course, a nation-building road network was really just a bonus. The true intention was to provide employment after the First World War for all those young men standing idle on street corners. And as Daniel Francis writes in his excellent illustrated book, *A Road for Canada*, "government money did not necessarily mean rapid construction. So long as the point of the highway project was to provide jobs, there was little incentive to finish it. Projects often were denied heavy equipment, including bulldozers, as efficiency took a back seat to the labour-intensive methods of the pick-and-shovel brigade."

The 1920s was a prosperous decade for Canada, and you'd think the road network would benefit from this; after all, highway spending was now the greatest expenditure in any provincial budget. But it was money out the door. The pick-and-shovel brigade wasn't very good at building roads. The newly formed highway departments knew there was money to be spent keeping themselves in business, and the standards for road construction changed frequently; when that happened, the roads had to be reconstructed to the new standard. As Monaghan writes, it was a cycle of obsolescence in which the highway departments were both instigator and victim. In 1930, the provinces spent more than $76 million on roads but brought in revenues from registrations and the gas tax of less than $43 million. And the Liberal politicians in Ottawa who opposed highway funding in 1913 were now in power under Prime Minister William Lyon Mackenzie King. Their government won a minority and was forced to accept and even extend the Canada Highways Act to 1928, but after they gained a majority at the next election, well, that was the end of it.

The Liberals lost the 1930 election, however, and the Conservatives were voted back into power, partly on a promise of building the Trans-Canada. "What Canada needs is a policy to provide jobs," stated their platform. "A policy that will build a national highway across Canada instead of forcing motorists to use American roads to get past the Great Lakes, with the result that they now leave in the United States the money which they spend by the way instead of spending it for supplies in Canada, as they would if Canada had a through road, and thus solve the unemployment situation." Another $20 million was allocated within the Unemployment Relief Act that year for projects, including the "Trans-Canada Highway" — its first mention by name in receiving federal funds — and Ottawa offered to pay 50 percent of its construction.

Still, however, the Trans-Canada was all about employment and had little to do with motorists' needs or national pride. As well, work camps for the highway had the added benefit of moving bored young men out of the cities and into the remote bush. Monaghan writes that "construction techniques regressed: the chief engineer overseeing work in Ontario proudly reported in 1933 to his colleagues at the Engineering Institute that 'the work was carried on as an Unemployment Relief measure without the assistance of any efficient machinery now used in road making. Every effort was made to use man power.'" Funding was more of an issue this time around, though, for the 1930s lacked the overall prosperity of the previous decade. The river of money became a trickle, and especially so when the Liberals regained power in 1935. And then the Second World War began, and Canada changed its priorities entirely.

☐

Highway 417 was smooth and swift for Peter and me between the Quebec border and Ottawa. This is the Trans-Canada Highway and has been since it was completed in 1975, just in time for Montreal's summer Olympics the following year. As Expo 67 proved, there's nothing like a major international showcase event for providing a deadline.

The original Trans-Canada ran along Highway 17 beside the gentle sweep of the Ottawa River and curved down through the rich Franco-Ontarian farmland of Plantagenet and Alfred, just as it ran beside the St. Lawrence in Quebec. That small Ontario road is a charming, relaxing, and scenic two-lane route that's lovely to drive. Of course, before the big 417 opened to carry the route's heavy passenger and freight traffic, Highway 17 was known as "the killer strip," where peak traffic averaged one vehicle every five seconds. "What do travellers find on the killer strip in 1970?" asked the *Ottawa Citizen*. "A lumbering pulp truck in such poor repair it snails along below the minimum speed limit. And toward suppertime, school buses trundle along, letting off students; farmers herd their cattle across the highway. The result: the death-defying passing along long lines of vehicles which makes Highway 17 such a thrill to drive on."

The intrepid CBC journalists took Highway 17 to Ottawa in 1960 and made time to see some of the sights in the city. Doug Brophy met with four Girl Guides who were visiting the Houses of Parliament, and the interview was awkward, to say the least. "Well now, what about this troop? Is this a summer camp for you?" Brophy asked, trying to make himself heard over the bells of the Peace Tower.

"Yes," answered a Girl Guide.

"Enjoying it?" he asked.

"Oh, yes," said the Girl Guide.

"Are there Girl Guides from other parts of Canada here at your camp?" he asked.

"Well, I don't know. I guess there must be," said the Girl Guide.

"Well, Doug," chimed in Ron Hunka, once the segment was thankfully over, "we've learned about a lot of things, including the Chevrolet we're driving. It's the finest, low-cost way of going from place to place."

Of course, back in 1946, Alex Macfarlane's sponsored Chevrolet was running like a top when he passed through Ottawa. He'd left his hotel in Montreal that morning in too much of a hurry to be introduced to his first grandchild, a baby boy named Alexander after him, the son of his own first-born son. He and Ken MacGillivray did find time in Ottawa, however, to meet a couple of old chums for lunch at the Rideau Club; they had their photos taken in front of the Parliament Buildings before speeding off up Highway 17 beside the river to North Bay. Macfarlane ran into some more friends there, including his younger son, Hugh, and no doubt regaled them with stories of speed and daring. "We were into North Bay by six o'clock," he wrote, "not having had a hint of trouble." Ron Hunka would have been proud.

Macfarlane would appreciate that today's Conservative provincial government recently increased the speed limit on Highway 417, though he'd probably advocate for no speed limits at all. This was part of a three-year trial on six provincial highways to raise the limit to 110 kilometres per hour, boosting it from the 100 kilometres-per-hour speed limit that was shared by both the new four-lane and the original Highway 17 two-lane back in 1965. In 2022, after finding operating speeds and collision trends were still pretty much the same as other highways with the lower, unaltered limit, the government made the change permanent and later raised the limits on many other stretches of the 400-series highways. I had to remind Peter of this as he drove us in the Lexus to the capital at the slower speed, pausing for a barbecue lunch at the home of David Monaghan, the historian author of *Canada's "New Main Street."*

"My thesis organizer told me, just keep digging and you'll find the smoking gun," said Dave, pressing the burgers against the grill to make them sizzle. "I'd go to work, I'd come home, I'd have dinner with my wife and the kids, then I'd say good-night to the kids and take the bus down to the National Archives and I'd go to the reading room." He did this, off and on, for four years before submitting his thesis and earning a master's degree in history from the University of Ottawa.

"One night, I was going through the microfilm of Cabinet decisions, reel upon reel, and there it was. It was a discussion of unemployment and the prime minister was absent, and a decision was made to recommend to the prime minister that they move ahead with the national highway to relieve unemployment, and that was it. I sat there and started whistling and made some notes, packed my bag, got on the bus, came home, and woke up Frances. I said, 'Fran! I've found the smoking gun!' She doesn't even remember that now, but that night, I had to share it with somebody."

At the time, Monaghan was a curator at the National Museum of Science and Technology, as it was called then, and he'd gone back to school part-time for his master's. He needed a subject that involved federal and provincial relations — "I wasn't too thrilled, to be honest, talk about dry stuff!" — but the Trans-Canada Highway fit the bill and nobody had covered it academically, so he launched into four years of obsessive digging away in libraries and at the archives. There was no Google for him back in 1993. He discovered that while Canadians have long held to the sentimental premise of the Trans-Canada being an iconic, unifying symbol of the country, politicians really just couldn't give a damn. Yes, they wanted it built, but not if they had to pay for it.

It took the Second World War for roads to be built that could avoid the United States when travelling between east and west. This had never been an issue because Canadians and Americans crossed the border freely with barely any paperwork, just a wave and a smile, but the war finally raised questions about that. The last two links within Canada were in the B.C. mountains between Revelstoke and Golden, and deep in the Northern Ontario woods between Geraldton and Hearst. Make-work crews made slow progress on the B.C. road throughout the 1930s, but once fighting began, the "Big Bend" was quickly completed in 1940. It was a three-season loop that went north to what's now the Mica Dam before dropping back south, and it took more than 300 twisting kilometres on the dusty dirt road to travel the 95 direct kilometres over the mountains. In Ontario, the gravel road through the forest was completed in 1943 to truck supplies between east and west without needing American co-operation. Those roads were built because they were practical, not patriotic, and the Trans-Canada Highway was no different.

After the war, there was a great deal of misty-eyed public enthusiasm for a national highway. The Liberal government even convened a conference of the nine provinces in late 1948 — no Newfoundland yet — to gauge interest, figure out specifications, and discuss "a great many problems to be studied in connection with a project of this importance and magnitude." Eight of those provinces said, "Sure, we can talk." Each of them had their own agenda. Quebec, however, just wasn't interested. Premier Maurice Duplessis declined Ottawa's invitation, citing "in particular, the constitutional problem which we consider of paramount importance." He was still smarting from being forced by Ottawa to agree to compulsory conscription during the war, when the rest of the country had supported it but Quebeckers voted more than 70 percent against the measure. It didn't matter that only a few thousand young conscripts were sent overseas, or that the wartime prime minister, Mackenzie King, had resigned and been replaced by Louis St. Laurent. "Duplessis just saw the national highway as an intrusion into provincial rights," said Dave, turning over the burgers on the grill.

Federal responsibility for the project was given to Robert Winters, the minister of reconstruction and an engineer by trade, though he and his office knew little about highways. Then, a couple of months later, Newfoundland became Canada's 10th province and added almost 1,000 kilometres to the highway. This was a problem for Nova Scotia, which had always considered Halifax to be the eastern terminus and would now be expected to send the road up through Cape Breton. New Brunswick wanted the highway to detour down to Saint John. Alberta wanted the Feds to pay at least two-thirds of the cost, while British Columbia wanted them to pay everything, and to end the restriction on commercial vehicles driving through national parks. Ontario — well, Premier Leslie Frost said Ontario would join if the other provinces agreed but was generally reluctant because the direct route would completely avoid the Greater Toronto Area. "They were saying, you're asking us to invest huge amounts of money into a highway that will probably see as much traffic in a year as you would see on a long weekend on the Queen Elizabeth Way," said Dave, putting the burgers on the buns and onto plates. "I've always had this image of somebody in the background saying, 'Can we teach you a little about highway economics here?'"

It was a mess and a stalemate, and when the Trans-Canada Highway Act itself was tabled in December 1949, it just wasn't going anywhere. St. Laurent wasn't all that bothered — he probably cared even less than Mackenzie King, because he could at least show the voters he was trying but claim he was being stymied by the squabbling provinces. He was insistent the highway wouldn't go ahead unless all 10 provinces were on board, because there was no way he wanted to rile Quebec — poke the bear, as it were. But then, in the six weeks after Christmas, 100,000 Canadians registered as newly unemployed, bringing the country's out-of-work total to 376,000. When the Cabinet met in the prime minister's absence that April, it was told that unemployment could more than double. Something needed to be done to put people to work. There was even the possibility that impoverished Newfoundland might hold another referendum and back away from Canada. The Cabinet considered the options, and when it recommended urging St. Laurent to move ahead with whatever provinces would agree, it shot the bullet that created David Monaghan's smoking gun.

St. Laurent met with the Cabinet on April 19, 1950, and abandoned his insistence for unanimity among all the provinces. The Trans-Canada Highway Act was signed into existence on April 25, less than a week later. Only six provinces agreed to it — Quebec, Nova Scotia, New Brunswick, and Newfoundland refused — but Ottawa went ahead, anyway. The Feds committed $150 million to the project, which is about $2 billion in today's dollars, and set a target of 1956 for completion. Everyone went home and then everything ground to a halt.

"Another burger?" asked Dave.

THE DRIVE ACROSS CANADA

David Monaghan, former curator of the House of Commons, and author of *Canada's "New Main Street."*

☐

Sleepy Ottawa is rarely described as an exciting city. I worked as a reporter at the *Ottawa Citizen* for five years in the early 1990s, and I recall my first out-of-region assignment. An unfortunate British tourist was killed in a senseless drive-by shooting, and I was sent to Rochester, New York, which was about the same physical size as Ottawa, to compare the experiences of the two cities. "We just had our first-ever drive-by shooting," I said to a Rochester police detective. "How many have you had?"

"Two," said the detective.

"Really?" I was disappointed. "I thought you'd have more than that."

"Oh, I mean two this week," said the detective, "and we're not even at the weekend yet."

Where other world capitals hammer out international policy, Ottawa's reputation is for conciliation — finding similarities among the differences. That's one reason why Canada is a member of so many exclusive governmental organizations: the Community of Democracies, the G7, the Five Eyes, and the like. We succeed because we rarely advocate for military force, and because we're so used to trying to solve the bickering among our own provinces. Ottawa does it slowly and steadily, wearing down resistance with deliberate discussion and a lack of fanfare.

"Present-day Ottawa is a sober, cautious, civil-service town of good taste, good manners, and a greyish atmosphere even when the sun shines," wrote Edward McCourt after his visit in 1963. "A Londoner carries an umbrella as a substitute swagger stick, a Parisian as a weapon with which to play Cyrano de Bergerac, and an Ottawan to keep off the rain."

☐

The main stumbling blocks for the Trans-Canada Highway were its route and its physical specifications. It was to take the shortest practical route across the country, and it was to have a right-of-way of at least 100 feet, which is about 33 metres. The road itself needed ten-foot shoulders on each side of at least twenty-two feet of roadway, paved with three inches of asphalt on top of at least nine inches of stone base. Curves could turn at a maximum of six degrees, and hills could have no more than a six-degree gradient. It was expensive at the time, even with the federal government paying half.

"Robert Winters was a remarkable man," said Dave, now grilling the second round of lunchtime burgers for Peter and me. "He was so persistent and he did believe in the project. From virtually nothing, he made it possible for the government to assemble a group of very dedicated individuals to work on the road. He was obviously a very good politician, but he was also an engineer, and engineers have a way of seeing things. They just do."

Winters helped create the Trans-Canada Highway Division, which established offices in each of the provinces that signed the act. He persuaded New Brunswick to participate that same year, despite refusing to allow the highway to branch down to the port at Saint John. Newfoundland came on after taking some extra time to think about it. Nova Scotia agreed in 1952, despite Halifax being bypassed, because it was promised the Canso Causeway. Quebec was a lost cause. Premier Duplessis told Winters that he felt the Trans-Canada was "simply the first step in an effort by the Federal Government to achieve control of all forms of transportation in Canada," so Winters just left the province alone to stew in its nationalist aspirations.

Even so, progress was slow. The Trans-Canada Highway Division took a long time to find its feet and was restructured twice. Steel and concrete was diverted to the Korean War. Mostly, however, the provinces had to build other highways first, to carry their constantly increasing traffic, and their budgets were tapped out every year. The original agreement was to expire at the end of 1956, and it was clear that no province would finish the job by then. In 1955, less than half the highway was built to the defined standard, and more than 500 kilometres just didn't exist. Sixty percent of the total budget was already spent. Something needed to be done.

Winters convened another conference at the end of 1955, and all the provinces attended, even Quebec, as an observer. He listened to the complaints that they needed more money and more time, and then offered an extra $100 million to boost the budget to $250 million. He extended the agreement to 1960 and agreed that Ottawa would pay 90 percent of the costs of up to 10 percent of the construction, which covered expensive road-building challenges in British Columbia's mountains and Ontario's swamp. Quebec still walked away without signing — it wouldn't agree to the national highway until 1960, once Duplessis was replaced by Jean Lesage and his more practical Liberal government — but with more money, most of the provinces started building with renewed vigour.

They also had the benefit of American engineering experience, because the U.S. government began building its own interstate system in 1956. Perhaps President Dwight Eisenhower had noticed the Canadian example, because his federal government paid 90 percent of the costs right from the start, and just told the individual states where the 70,000 kilometres of highways would be. It spent US$119 billion on what's been called the greatest public works project in history.

In 1957, Saskatchewan was the first to finish its allocation of the Trans-Canada Highway. Premier Tommy Douglas declared the province's 650 flat and simple kilometres open in August that year, though paving continued until the end of October and was completed just hours before the winter's first blizzard. Most of the other provinces finished most of the work over the next several years, but everything was well in hand by the time the CBC journalists drove across in 1960.

"It was a remarkable achievement when everything is considered," said Dave Monaghan as we finished lunch, "but things changed so quickly with highway design and automobile use, and it was too little too late. It was effectively a paved rural route, but it was not what we think of as a highway now. When it was completed, much of it was already substandard for the requirements of traffic in the 1960s. There wasn't a lot of foresight. It was always defined as a tourist road. At one point, there was a request by, I believe, Manitoba for the federal government to fund the building of passing lanes, and the federal government refused because it was to be a tourist highway, and passing lanes were for commercial traffic."

Online reports often state the Trans-Canada Highway was finally completed in 1971, but there's no substantiation of this. Neither the federal nor any of the provincial ministries of transportation could confirm a date to me. Wikipedia states, without attribution, that "construction on other legs continued until 1971 when the last gap on Highway 16 was completed in the Upper Fraser Valley east of Prince George, at which point the highway network was considered complete." In general, though, its traditional route was complete in 1967 when the Louis-Hippolyte-La Fontaine Bridge-Tunnel was opened in Montreal. Others might say it was in 1997 when the Confederation Bridge was opened to connect Prince Edward Island with the mainland. Some say it will never be finished.

These days, the tourist road of the Trans-Canada is being replaced by the safer twinned highway. As Peter and I found in New Brunswick and Quebec, tourists are often better served on the smaller roads that are now bypassed by the fast four-lane. Which begged the question of Dave: Had he ever driven the Trans-Canada Highway for himself? After all, he retired in 2014, after spending more than a decade as curator of the House of Commons, and now he and Frances have time on their hands for travel.

"No, I'm not much of a driver," he said. "I don't enjoy driving long distances, and the Trans-Canada Highway is a very long distance, indeed. But it sparked an interest and let me put it this way — there are plans to do it."

7

Southern Ontario

The Trans-Canada on Highway 7 west of Ottawa is a pleasant, pastoral drive that alternates between two lanes and three lanes, through the rocks of the Canadian Shield and past its sheltered forest lakes, down to the rich farmland of Southern Ontario. It's the most direct route from the capital to my home in Cobourg and I very rarely use it, though I visit Ottawa often. I'm usually in too much of a hurry and set the cruise control on the twinned highways of the 401 and 416 instead, where there's always a passing lane to get by the multitude of heavy trucks.

It wasn't that long ago that Highway 7 was still the main road between Ottawa and Toronto. It took until 1999 for the four-lane link to be completed down to the 401, and before that, drivers had no choice but to hurry through on one of several pleasant, pastoral drives. At least some stretches of Highway 7 had an overtaking lane, when the lineups behind slower vehicles became just too long and aggravating, but there was nothing to prevent head-on collisions, just like on the older roads that had long since been replaced.

These days, the highway's once-thriving motels and gas stations are mostly abandoned, though a few still exist. And then there's Howard Gibbs's gas station near Arden, which is neither abandoned nor functioning. Howard lives in a trailer behind the building, and people still stop by regularly to ask if he's the guy from the documentary. "Yeah, I guess that's me," he tells them, as he said when I introduced myself.

The Lost Highway is shown on TVO, Ontario's public TV station, once or twice a year, though it's at least a decade old now. It tells the story of Arden and some of the people who live there beside that stretch of the Trans-Canada Highway, halfway between Ottawa and Peterborough, which means it's not close to anywhere. Howard is the star of the show. "It's a road flanked by failed businesses and abandoned properties where people gave it their all and then gave it up for good," explains the show's downer website. "But what happened? And why did it happen here? And who, despite the hardship, has remained?"

Howard Gibbs has remained, that's who. He's 77 years old, and I asked him when the gas station was built. I didn't realise what this would unleash.

"Dad started it in 1930, and I closed it after 81 years," he said. "In 1952, Dad sold 1,600 gallons of Mobil oil alone, and he sold eight other kinds of oil, so he went down to Sharbot Lake and he said to Jack Simonett, he had the General Motors dealership at that time, and he said, 'I want that sedan

Howard Gibbs lives at his gas station near Arden but hasn't pumped any gas in years.

livery 1952 to tow cars here on the Number 7 Highway,' and he fixed up all the broken bones, and Dad did all that stuff you see before the ambulances and all that stuff, so, anyways, Jack said, 'Well, it's $2,100 but how much money you got?' And Dad said, '$1,500.' Well, he said, 'Give me the $1,500 and on your honour, come back and give me $600 this fall,' but he was a lonely man. He gave one girlfriend $400,000 back in the late '60s, early '70s. His wife sued because she was liberal and he was conservative, he married a schoolteacher, but anyways, she found out about it after he died and she sued but she couldn't get the money back because she was a VON nurse, I used to wait on her at the gas pumps, nice-looking woman, she was in her forties, she used to go this side of Kaladar and roust up some of them because they kept their kids in bed and didn't get them up to come out and go to school."

So, 1930 then.

"I think Howard lives in the past as much as in the present, I think maybe more than anyone I've ever known," explained Neil Graham, one of the two filmmakers who created *The Lost Highway*, when I called him later. "I'm not sure he can delineate between what was and what is, but he does not seem of this era, in his demeanour, in his language, in his countenance. He just does not seem of this world."

In the documentary, Howard hopes to transfer the gas station business to his daughter, Melanie, a single mom who's moved back home with her kids, but the government orders him to replace the corroded gas tanks and he can't afford to do so. He stops selling gas, and the station becomes even more rundown. It's an analogy for the town itself, where another couple is struggling to establish a bed and breakfast and the only operating store is a shop that sells batiks to tourists.

When the documentary was released, the people in the town hated it. And little wonder. "Arden is a really depressing place and there's just nothing there, and it just seems like a place that will never be resurrected or have any sign of life, at least to me," said Neil. "But it is home for people. If it's your home, I guess you view it differently."

Seemingly alone among the townspeople, Howard loved the documentary and his portrayal as an eccentric business owner who laments the slow decay of his bypassed community. "What you had was independence, and you saw lots of people and everything," he says on camera. "And where I loved people all my life and was born into business, it cuts your heart, half your heart, right out of you. It's just like a death in the family."

Howard's ex-wife lives in a nearby town, and her name is Hope, but the viewer never meets her. At one point in the show, Howard disappears for several days and his daughter reports him missing, only for him to turn up and say he spent the time with a newfound lady friend who, again, is never seen.

"I think Howard lives on hope," said Neil. "I think we all do, to a greater or lesser degree. We hope that things are going to work out in our way and I think Howard is no different. I just think that perhaps the thread that tethers his hope to reality is maybe just a little thinner than others."

Howard told me he was in a new relationship with a woman from Las Vegas, who might move into the trailer the following week. "There's another trailer in behind but that's getting old, so I got this one and I got the water, I turned on the pump. Dad dug a well in 1949 and they used the township pump one time and a snake dropped in the well when Dad uncovered it and Mother said we can't drink the water for so long you couldn't pump it dry, so I hired a septic tank pumper before Mother died in 2004 and he pumped it dry and it filled right back up again, so it's about 40 gallons, 50 gallons, so I've got no problems with water."

I asked if he would ever sell the place.

"Well, a guy come in last year and said, 'I want to buy this place,' he was from Cloyne, up above Kaladar on 41, and I said well not right now, I don't think I want to sell and this and that and the next thing, right now I've got to have some place to live when she comes up for this summer, so for the foreseeable future, we'll figure all that stuff out. I've got a woman who really loves me and all the rest of the stuff and she'll do anything for me."

I shook his hand, waved goodbye, and fired up the Lexus quickly, chirping the tires a little on the station forecourt. Even so, I was glad to have met Howard and shared a few of his memories. It's people like Howard who add life to a community, even when the rest of the world gives up on it and waits for it to die.

The Trans-Canada at Arden may be a lost highway, but it's still smooth and well maintained — not like the roads in 1912 when Thomas Wilby and Jack Haney left Ottawa for Toronto. The only route was to drive south to Kingston and then follow the shoreline of Lake Ontario to the Big Smoke. The better roads and sturdier bridges carried tolls, sometimes as much as 25 cents, and as Wilby lamented, "it would have been only fair had the authorities in their turn paid us whenever we had to travel a bad stretch of highway. But they never did. Instead, on one occasion, the absence of a bridge caused us to wallow through yards of mud and water and to almost break the car in deep ruts, from which we finally escaped with the aid of mud-hooks — a diabolical contrivance attached to the rear wheels whereby the machine jerked itself violently to safety." Even so, Wilby seems to have enjoyed himself, admiring the Thousand Islands and even mentioning the chauffeur humming a tune from his youth.

Of course, in Jack Haney's diary, the account of "the chauffeur" is a little different. He calls Wilby the Captain and underlines the word for sarcastic emphasis:

> Left Ottawa 7:30 am. I was ready at 6:30 but the Captain of the schooner slept in so we could not get away. It rained all day and has just finished a heavy thunder storm. Roads are rotten, full of deep holes. Had to ford two creeks today, bridges out. Came near getting stuck in one. Had to put mud hooks on, they done the business.
>
> Had a warm argument with the Captain to-day. He says it makes him sick to run over a chicken, also he is afraid to go more than 25 M.P.H. — Rather a soft outfit for the Captain of a transcontinental automobile trip. One poor devil does all the work "that's me." I am hooked up with about the worst companion that possibly could be. The work is going to be hard after leaving Toronto, and not having a MAN with me, I don't know how I'll make out.

THE DRIVE ACROSS CANADA

At Toronto, Haney took an evening to visit his girlfriend, Glen, in St. Catharines and then spent a couple of days working on the car, fixing the transmission, clutch, and shock absorbers. Maybe Glen settled him down, or maybe it was just the satisfaction of repairing the car, with proper tools in an organized workshop. In any case, the break did him good. It did Wilby good too. "Toronto proved an ideal resting-place in preparation for the wilderness which awaited me to the north of the Muskoka Lakes," he wrote. "Over the post-prandial coffee and cigars the hours slipped pleasantly by in congenial chat with fellow motorists, while the daytime had its equally congenial tasks in calls upon the Mayor and the government officials."

It's just as well they were rested, because two days later, on a sandy hill north of Gravenhurst, the Reo got stuck as it had never been before. When a team of horses finally pulled it from the axle-deep ruts, the driveshaft twisted and a new one had to be ordered, to be delivered the following evening by train. The hapless pair were stuck with each other at Scotia Junction, "a

The Reo is hauled out of the sand by a team of horses near Scotia Junction.

geographical expression set down promiscuously and irrelevantly in a swamp in the heart of Ontario," remembered Wilby unkindly. "Scotia Junction was the end of the world."

Even so, that was far from the end of it. Haney fitted the new driveshaft, and the car carried on about another 40 kilometres north before getting stuck on another hill: the grade was estimated at 40 percent with a slippery and rutted surface, so it was hardly a surprise. They took another way around, got stuck on some steep "corduroy stairs" — where logs were buried in the soft road for a firmer surface — and finally pulled themselves out with a homemade winch contraption. Wilby wrote:

> For an hour or more we wrenched away like draft horses at the block and tackle. The car performed spectacularly. It split the welkin with its roar, jerking forward with violent wrenches and jerking as suddenly backwards, in order to catapult one of us into the radiator. We multiplied human energy with a new-fangled windlass arrangement born of chauffeur genius and deftly constructed by axe and fallen birch stumps. The two tons of steel and equipment began to move, but the boughs were slim and the stubbing post took it into its head to fly hurriedly from its socket.

And when they were eventually free, there was still more. The new driveshaft was damaged and could only operate in low gear. Then they had to build a bridge. And worst of all, when they finally made it to Trout Creek, "the dingy wooden inn, thick with the tobacco smoke of sleepy lumber-men and an argumentative array of boarders, could produce no more epicurean mess of pottage than the staple of fried eggs and fried potatoes." Once again, Haney was more concise in his own recollection: "Had a good supper but have not bed yet, hope to get one soon. Wilby is pretty sore about the delay, is almost ready to give it up. The trip is a farce, anyway."

As an aside, once the trip was over, Wilby wrote a few thousand words for the Reo car company that were presumably part of the deal for its sponsorship. This pamphlet paints a much brighter picture of the whole venture, and even mentions Jack Haney, though only by his surname. At Scotia Junction, he describes how "the plucky Reo had a battle royal with the hills and muskeg and twists and turns of those narrow ghost roads."

On the corduroy hill itself, he wrote:

> Minute after minute passed, the wheels now spinning, now being locked in the deep ridges of those devilish hills, the engines roaring and moaning in protest, inch by inch she went up as the sun dropped lower and lower to the horizon line, and then as if she had given up all her mechanical courage, she would drop back again. But finally won out, and had her front paws on the topmost pitch where mud and stones presented the most fiendish surface possible.... This was the day we understood the true value of Dunlop Traction Tread Tires.

They reached North Bay the next day. There was no onward road to be found, and the Reo was loaded onto a train for Sudbury. This brought an end to driving under its own power for the first time, but not for the last.

☐

Peter and I also stopped for a few days at my home in Cobourg, a half-hour south of Highway 7 at Peterborough, and the break also did us some good. We washed our laundry, enjoyed some quality family time, and got to sleep in separate rooms without having to listen to each other snore at night. The balance of our friendship resettled and we were reinvigorated to get back on the road the following Monday morning. We drove up to Peterborough, rejoined the Trans-Canada exactly where we'd left it, and were back on our way west.

First, though, we had to head north in order to skirt around the Great Lakes. This was a challenging road to build, but nothing the engineers couldn't handle with lessons learned through trial and error. In 1957, part of the highway under construction on soft ground south of Parry Sound slipped into the Moon River; a Bailey bridge over the river helped traffic get through until engineers could figure out how to build a permanent bridge. For us, though, it's now an easy day's drive to Sudbury. The leisurely Trans-Canada is being widened into a four-lane twinned highway north of Barrie where the southbound lanes lead into the direct commuter route that rushes people to Toronto. We set the radar cruise control again, and after a while, I noticed a low, clear mesh fence that ran alongside the road — so low you could step over it with ease. What on earth was the point of that? When we arrived at Sudbury, I went looking for an answer on Google.

"Roadkill Study Shows More Reptiles Killed by Fence Designed to Help," reported the CBC in 2015. It described how low-height fencing had been installed beside the highway to prevent turtles and snakes from crossing the road and being hit by traffic, but frequent breaks in the fence had actually steered the reptiles to cross at dangerous spots. More worrisome was that, once through the fence, the reptiles often couldn't find a way back and became trapped on the road. Collisions with moose and deer make headlines because they can kill drivers, but turtles and snakes do little damage: they're just roadkill for carrion birds.

That was eight years earlier, so I phoned Kari Gunson, a "road ecologist" involved with the project, for an update. She said the original installers weren't properly trained to put in the highway fence, but now, much of the fencing has been replaced and fixed to the more obvious large-animal fencing; it's a very strong, tight mesh that's made in China and costs almost $100 per metre. I didn't realize, but we'd been driving beside reptile fencing for much of the route whenever it passed by wetlands; you just don't see it, down in the ditch, and hopefully you don't see the reptiles either, crossing in specially designed drains and culverts beneath the road.

"They prefer to nest on roadsides — they're ideal conditions for them," said Kari. "It's open, it's sunny, it's well drained. It's become their preferred site. Nine out of 10 times, they're usually now nesting in man-made environments — laneways, driveways, road shoulders, agricultural fields." Such places are great until a car comes along, and then suddenly they're not. People like Kari get involved to create artificial but safe nesting homes for the turtles to encourage them to stay near the protected culverts and off the highway.

I had no idea. I knew about the big stuff. There's a very obvious and very large wildlife bridge over the Trans-Canada just south of Sudbury that was built in 2009, covered with topsoil and landscaped. There are pictures on its walls for the motorists driving beneath to see moose, fox, and bears, and another kilometre up the highway, hidden from the road, there's an underpass that's equally as large. The Ministry of Transport has all the stats and can show that thousands of deer and hundreds of moose and bears have used the crossings, though the bridge is more popular. Apparently, almost all the animals that approach the bridge will use it to cross the road, while only half of those that approach the underpass will enter the tunnel.

Turtles and snakes and other small reptiles don't usually register, though they should. We should take more notice of them, said Kari. There's the cuteness, for one thing: "Kids absolutely freak out when they hold a baby turtle. It's that feeling of, I don't know — the world is a good place?" But far more important is that these creatures are supposed to be there and our highways are destroying their homes. "They do clean our wetlands and maintain a healthy wetland ecosystem," she said. "They eat all the rotten, decaying organic matter. They spread seeds. I mean, we only have 3 percent of our wetlands left in Southern Ontario, and we need to maintain them as best we can. The beavers build our wetlands and the turtles maintain it."

I could imagine Kari standing onstage beside Grey Owl, speaking passionately about the Blanding's turtles and the snapping turtles and the massasauga rattlers, except that she's just a regular woman in jeans and a T-shirt, talking to me on a cellphone from her home in Peterborough. When I ended the call, I knew Grey Owl was the master showman in his buckskins and feathered headdress, and he'd been on to something.

□

On the other side of Algonquin Provincial Park, 500 kilometres away, the other route of the Trans-Canada Highway leaves the capital to follow the

Ottawa River northwest toward Sudbury. It was a controversial decision in 1950 to designate the longer southern route past Peterborough as the national highway, and residents of Mattawa and North Bay and other towns along the snubbed road were furious. The mayor of Renfrew said there would be "a strong, vigorous protest." The mayor of Pembroke said, "We will protest the decision quickly and as strongly as possible." And the mayor of Arnprior said the road down to Peterborough was already highly congested: "It's nonsense to make it more so. It looks to me like a political move."

Of course it was a political move! *Duh!* It was precisely because the roads around Peterborough were congested that the Government of Ontario wanted the better highway to travel there, and Robert Winters in Ottawa rolled over quickly on that concession. Those mayors of the northern towns were envisioning a highway that would speed traffic from the Rockies and the Prairies to the Atlantic Ocean, but traffic is a product of population, and much of Canada's population lives in Southern Ontario, far from the proposed route.

Even so, the provincial government made some improvements to the northern highway and put in some signs to keep the residents happy. It was even marked as Trans-Canada on the official Ontario highway map. When Edward McCourt drove through in 1963, he wrote that "of the two routes, the alternate up the Ottawa Valley is to be preferred" because it's shorter and the scenery is more exciting; it also helps that the Ottawa River alongside was used by the voyageurs as one of the great water routes to the West. (He panned the Highway 7 route, calling it "excruciatingly dull. Peterborough provides the first break of interest after a run of 165 miles through heavily forested country." Presumably, he and his wife, Margaret, didn't stop halfway along at Arden, which at the time had a hotel, a hardware store, three general stores, and Howard's dad's gas station.) The northern roadworks and signs were just a quick and easy fix by the province, though. Everyone thought the route was now the Trans-Canada, but it wasn't and wouldn't become so for another decade.

Even the local MP was unaware of the road's status. As the *Ottawa Citizen* reported in 1965:

> J.J. Greene (Liberal — Renfrew North) renewed his complaint in the Commons last night about the condition of Highway 17 north of Ottawa. He described the highway as "a torturous trail." Speaking in an adjournment debate, Mr. Greene said the highway carries the green maple leaf, indicating the Trans-Canada Highway, and if no improvements are made the people of the Ottawa Valley will have no alternative but to pull the signs down. He said the federal government has some responsibility to see that Trans-Canada highways are up to standard.
>
> G. Roy McWilliam, parliamentary secretary to Works Minister Cardin, replied that the highway was a provincial responsibility since it was not officially part of the Trans-Canada Highway. He said the maple-leaf signs indicate it is "a provincial northern route connecting with the Trans-Canada highway."

Potato, *potahto* — the public didn't care by 1965 as long as they could drive where they needed to go in comfort. Increased traffic was clearly taking a toll. Alex Macfarlane had no problems on this road two decades earlier, and the silent movie Ed Flickenger shot for the Ford Motor Company in 1925 even used a title card to praise the dusty single-lane track north of the Petawawa Military Camp as "a fine highway through an elemental bit of country." (Again, Edward McCourt might beg to differ: "I thought I had envisioned just about everything that could happen to us on the Trans-Canada Highway," he wrote, "but had overlooked the possibility of being in a collision with a tank.")

Five years before Flickenger, in 1920, the situation for Percy and Bernadette Gomery was very different. I mentioned the Gomerys back in New Brunswick, but we've not met them yet. He was a bank manager and president of the Vancouver Automobile Club; she was his long-suffering wife and is referred to only as "the Skipper" in the book, *A Motor Scamper 'Cross Canada*, that he wrote about crossing the continent that year. He never really explains why they did it in their new Maxwell touring car, except that it was a challenge and the venture was sponsored by the Canada Motor Association to promote the building of roads across the country. Gomery wasn't thinking about the Todd Medal, because he left from Montreal and had no qualms about driving in the United States when necessary. He wrote weekly newspaper accounts during the journey that extolled the pleasure of driving, though his book is a more honest account of the many challenges. Like Wilby, there were no road maps to find their way, but for Gomery, that only meant there was nothing that stated definitely that a road did *not* exist:

> I had written many inquiries in advance as to possible routes and roads — if any — through parts of the country not covered by guide books. The more replies we got the worse that Upper Ottawa road sounded.… One authority at North Bay said it could be done. Another said it couldn't. The Ottawa Board of Trade believed it "might be feasible in dry weather," and Pembroke came along with a detailed description, section by section, of the road — the outcast among roads — except the sections they did

Percy Gomery with his Maxwell touring car before venturing into the Ontario woods.

not know about! None of my advisors, however, seemed to know of anybody who had ever driven a car through it.

Reading his book today, chuckling in the comfort of armchair travel, the journey seems barely fathomable. Percy and the Skipper drove fairly easily to Petawawa "and, as though to tantalize us to the stinging-point, the roads through the military encampment were of a faultless tar macadam. At the boundary, however, we just pitched off and were confronted with a wilderness of sandy plains laid out in a network of trails neatly arranged, like tangled string."

They made some wrong turns but eventually found their way through to stay in a rough woodsmen's hostel, kept awake that night by the sounds beneath their loft floor of French songs and fights, and by revellers trying to get into their room. And then, driving the next day: "Things went reasonably well for a few miles, our main difficulty being to follow the road at all. And, when I say that there is no other road for a hundred miles to the south and unspeakable miles to the north, you will know what I mean. Repeatedly during those days I had to get out and skirmish around to find traces of a road at all, and, just as often, the car slipped away unconcernedly until it came to a halt in a marsh or against a stubborn concealed log."

They pressed on. At one point, they drove out of the bush and found themselves at the riverside village of Stonecliffe where the hotel manager said the Gomerys' Maxwell was the first car to ever drive there. It was also the first car the man's five-year-old son had ever seen. And then, after a surprisingly good lunch, they were back on the road — or lack of it:

> As the world is said to grow more giddy and dangerous with the declining sun, that execrable road did the same. For miles together it was just a succession of hidden mines into which the car plunged every few yards. Rank growth of years of grass hid both the pits and the huge rocks that threatened to tear the in'ards out of the engine if it was moving more than about two miles an hour. As it was,

the car was buffeted about brutally and so frequently was something being bent or smashed that it ceased to be a matter of comment. Then would come an awful hill, a sort of precipice cut into broad steps on which were strewn boulders about the size of perambulators. Now and then we would gain a height from which we could look a mile or two ahead over a peopleless wilderness of foliage, with just the suggestion of a different shade of green showing where once a road clearing had been made.

"Is that where we've got to go?" the Skipper would groan....

After dodging fallen trees, raising others and repairing bridges, I miscalculated the height of a suspended trunk and the car top was torn off. The only thing in our favour was the weather and, about five o'clock, it commenced to rain. We cast longing eyes at a rather homey boarding house at Deux Rivières station (the first hamlet in twenty-five miles), but decided to push on for Mattawa.

Immediately away from the houses, we passed into the woods again, there being no habitations or buildings whatever for fifteen miles. However, several miles along, the wheels dug their way into hopeless mire and insisted on calling it a day. I think a shovel would have saved us that night, but it was missing from our kit.

Sadly, we fished out the very necessaries, including the typewriter, and left our desolated little home with its broken running board, broken spring, broken lamps, flattened gas-tank, bent windshield and smashed top to the mercy of the rain and started back for Deux Rivières. Our arms were full of parcels; it was wet and hot; the mosquitoes were eating us alive and we were desperately tired. Several times the Skipper became hysterical. I comforted her as well as I could; in fact I recall telling her how these hardships could only make us better pals.

The Gomerys found their way back to the boarding house at Deux-Rivières where Percy remembered he had to file his weekly newspaper account. This was after not getting any sleep at the woodsmen's hostel, don't forget. So he pulled out his typewriter:

> Wearily I arranged the carbons, metaphorically put on my jester's costume, and proceeded to inform the motoring public of the cities of Canada and New York what a blithesome lark it is to wheel across the continent on a new road.
>
> When your luck starts to skid it generally slips on to the day's end. At half-past one, when I had scratched my hands on a mountain of cinders on the way up to the railway station post box and torn my trousers on a barb-wire fence on the way back, I looked up at the clouds and managed to see just one or two stars between. I claim a smile for noticing that there were still one or two stars.

Percy Gomery's article was published that Saturday in Montreal's *Gazette* and other newspapers, but he didn't sugarcoat the experience of the drive too much. Its headline read: "Some Roads So Good They're Very Good, but Some So Bad They're Horrid," and he cajoled the Ontario government for its roads being inferior to Quebec's. At the end of it all, he explains: "As I write this, late at night at the settlement of Deux Rivieres, my car, mired to the gas tank and containing everything we own save toothbrush and night gear, lies deserted in the forest three miles away, and within a paltry seven miles of the end of the terrible north Ottawa road."

It's easy to feel sorry for the guy, a self-described plump little husband, and especially when you've read his book and know that worse was to come the very next day.

☐

I'm inclined to agree with Edward McCourt that the northern route following the Ottawa River is the better way, if you have the opportunity to take it. I've driven it a number of times on adventurous weekends as a route to North Bay or around Algonquin Park, and it's both scenic and comparatively slow. The safely twinned, four-lane highway ends with little fanfare somewhere west of Arnprior, less than an hour from Ottawa, and the first traffic light — the first since Nova Scotia — is just outside Renfrew, the next town along. The woodsmen's hostel is still in the Quebec village of Rapides-des-Joachims on an island in the Ottawa River, and it's now being renovated by its new owner, Said Abassi, to be a fishing lodge. Said told me he used to visit from his home in Newmarket, Ontario, and one day the previous owner wanted to sell. "He said, 'I'm sick and tired of here,' and bang, bang, bang, after three or four days, he was gone and I owned the place. Now I go fishing every day."

The road hugs the Ottawa River and the Quebec border as a well-paved pair of lanes all the way past Gomery's landmarks of Petawawa, Stonecliffe, and Deux-Rivières before turning away from the river at a roundabout in downtown Mattawa. Then it's an easy half-hour on to North Bay or two hours all the way through to Sudbury where the Trans-Canada becomes a twinned highway again for a while.

It wasn't so simple for the Gomerys in 1920, of course, when the Mattawa road really didn't exist because travellers used the railway or the river. Even Percy admits in his book that it was just a trail. Still, the two of them returned to their car the next morning with a small group of men and horses and dug the Maxwell out of the mud, then pressed on alone on the "eternal grass-grown trail winding now over flowery hills or firm sod, now into the dark terror of wooded swamp." Somehow, they made it across a crumbling bridge until finally, after six kilometres, they sank into mud that was as deep as it was black. Immediately, bugs swarmed them. "The thing was hopeless; we seemed to be only at the beginning of the swamp anyway," he wrote. "Taking the Skipper to some higher, airier land ahead I left her, I hoped comfortably, with a rug, a book, mosquito netting, the revolver and such oddities, while I started for help. I told her there was no danger, but I omitted to tell her that the country we were in was famous for big game." He means bears.

Just pause for a moment and reflect on Percy Gomery's predicament. He'd driven a heavy, rear-wheel drive, vintage car far off the road, through the forest and into a swamp, and expected to continue on through. These days, you'd probably not take a Jeep Wrangler mudding like that unless you knew the route and had your electric winch ready. He had no map, narrow balloon tires, a shredded roof, and an exhausted, terrified wife. He was a banker by trade and could only hope that all would turn out for the best. After all, he left her with a book and a rug and oh yes, a gun. You've got to wonder at the thickness of the thread that tethered his hope to reality.

Out-of-shape Percy ran eight kilometres ahead to a log farmhouse where he found two small boys who would bring a pair of cart horses to haul the car from the mud, and then he ran eight kilometres back, where the Skipper had returned to the perceived safety of the mosquito-infested car. She'd heard rustling in the bush behind and reasoned the noise of the car engine might scare away aggressive carnivores. When the boys turned up, their Clydesdales strained for an hour without success to move the mired, lifeless car, until Percy finally thought to start the engine and try to drive it out with the horses pulling. They'd not done this because they'd assumed the horses would be terrified by the noise, which they weren't, not in the least. The ripped and dented Maxwell touring car made it clear, and they drove the eight kilometres to the farm, with the boys and horses following just in case.

The Gomerys weren't quite through yet, for there was rain and thick mud on the road to North Bay, but the highway on to Sudbury that didn't exist just eight years earlier for Wilby and Haney was now built, and "hard as a table, though narrow as a ribbon. The temptation to speed was irresistible." Alex Macfarlane would attest to that 26 years later.

□

Macfarlane turned north at North Bay to take the Ferguson Highway through Kapuskasing and into the forest far above Lake Superior. This is Highway 11, a continuation of Yonge Street, once considered the longest street in the world, and this 1,000-kilometre stretch between North Bay and Nipigon is now also designated as being the Trans-Canada Highway. You wouldn't think it from looking at a map, but it's actually 30 kilometres shorter than the more wiggling, traditional Trans-Canada route that stays close to Superior's north shore.

The rest of us have all now reached Sudbury, famous for its lunar landscape. Since nickel was discovered here in the 1880s, and then copper and platinum, miners smelted the iron ore to extract the metals, which both deforested the area of firewood and polluted it from the sulphur released in the process. Thomas Wilby and Percy Gomery don't seem to have noticed any environmental damage, but by the time Edward McCourt came through in 1963, he described the next-door community of Copper Cliff as "an impressive spectacle in an awful kind of way. The copper-smelter and slag heaps are an immensity in keeping with the enterprise of which they are the culmination." To deal with this, the Inco mining company later built a chimney 381 metres high at Copper Cliff to dissipate the sulphur dioxide emissions higher into the air and so over a wider, more diluted area. When it was finished in 1972, the Inco Superstack was the tallest free-standing structure in Canada (until the CN Tower was built in 1975), and the tallest chimney in the world (until a chimney in Kazakhstan pipped it by 40 metres). It still holds second place for both those titles.

The Superstack stands sentinel but was turned off in 2020, and its new Brazilian owners say it will be demolished when they find the money to knock it down. They've discovered a more effective way to clean the gas that comes off the smelters and to reduce the emissions, for which we should all be grateful, though it's too bad the chimney can't be kept as some kind of landmark. It helped put Sudbury on the map, after all.

The maps that existed back in 1912 showed a road heading west, but it only went to the small port of Cutler in the channel above Manitoulin Island at the north end of Lake Huron. Wilby and Haney drove there and loaded the Reo onto a tug that took it the 30 kilometres west to Blind River, then drove from there through to Sault Ste. Marie.

The road from Cutler was being built when the Gomerys arrived in 1920. They were advised to put their car onto the ferry just as Wilby had done, but instead they drove blithely through the roadworks, cheered on every three kilometres by road gangs. At least, Percy says they were cheered on. He fitted tire chains to each of the Maxwell's four wheels and chewed his way forward, tearing "holes a foot deep in mud or grass, but always we got through." Well, except for the first day of this, when they found themselves stuck, the night grew dark, and they limped their way back to the nearest road crew. That was where "the forty men, it seemed, slept together in a tent about large enough for them if their legs did not mind staying out; the cook, his wife and baby slept in the tiny kitchen; the superintendent slept in his office. Puzzle: where will the visitors go? I knew the answer, but the superintendent did not at first seem to get it. I thought he was a bit obtuse." In fact, it was Bernadette who persuaded the superintendent to give up his office and sleep with his men, so she and Percy could have his bed for the night. These were different times. Very different times.

There's no port at Cutler anymore. It's an Indigenous community where the clerk at the local cannabis store told us of the wreck of a vintage car in a creek just up the road, and Peter and I went to search for it. I hoped it might be a car that Percy Gomery saw wrecked, mentioned as the only vehicle he'd heard of that travelled the trail through from Blind River before him — "the story was that five men accompanying this prehistoric pathfinder literally carried the juggernaut no small part of the distance" — but we couldn't find it. That's okay. The clerk also told us that shape-shifters routinely travel across the country, and from planet to planet, in the blink of an eye. He was absolutely convinced of this, sitting behind the counter at the cannabis store. Who am I to say otherwise?

◻

We'll bid goodbye now, for a while, to Wilby and Haney, who put the Reo on a lake steamer and sailed the length of Superior to Port Arthur. Their only other option was to drive across the border into Michigan and then follow the American roads south of the lake to Duluth and up to Manitoba. That's what the Gomerys did, so we'll say goodbye to them, too, for a while. Don't think badly of them. There literally was no road through Canada for the next 1,300 kilometres. Besides, the American road was no picnic: "The landscape was depressing, population thinned out until we crossed a sort of desert twenty miles across with only one house to be seen," wrote Gomery of the route across Michigan's Upper Peninsula. "There were not even any fences; the only construction of man being a sign, DIXIE HIGHWAY."

More to the point, Bernadette needed a break. They'd planned to take the lake steamer but were told how pleasant the road was and chose that instead, only to discover it really wasn't. "My partner tearfully admitted that she had been more or less on the edge of a breakdown almost since we left Ottawa," wrote Gomery, as if he'd only just noticed. "She had tried and tried to force herself to believe that the painful experiences would soon be past, but it was no longer any use." They resolved that she would travel home to Vancouver on the train after a night's sleep. Percy persuaded a local couple in a pleasant home to offer them a bed, which was so comfortable that Bernadette slept for 16 hours straight. In the morning, she "was smiling and ready for the road once more." She was built from strong stuff, the Skipper.

8

Northern Ontario

We're now in Sault Ste. Marie, close to one of the Trans-Canada Highway's greatest challenges at "the Gap" — more than 100 kilometres of impenetrable rock and swamp on the east shore of Lake Superior. When the railway came through in the 1880s, it stayed inland where the going was a little easier, and that's the route chosen by our two pathfinders in the mid-1920s.

Ed Flickenger fixed the steel wheels to the Model T and set off with the local Ford representative behind a similarly shod roadster that led the way as a pilot car. The two funky Fords rode the rails over high trestle bridges and through the Agawa Canyon. It was smooth and easy driving — probably the smoothest and easiest of the journey, pulling off onto a siding every now and again to let a train pass. The Model T was registered as a train with the railway company, and a title card in the silent movie shows the arrivals board at White River where the "Ford Special" is on time to arrive at 12:10 p.m. The car took a few days to run through to Nipigon, likely following the pilot the whole way, before leaving the rails to drive the last few hours on to Fort William.

And then there was Jimmy Oates on Toby, his motorcycle. Remember him? When he turned up at Sault Ste. Marie from Toronto in 1928, he'd forgotten to ask the Algoma Central Railway for permission to ride on the tracks. He'd asked Canadian Pacific, but nobody in the Soo knew who he was. It took three days before the permission came through, and presumably he used the time to heal up from his lack of sunscreen. "Sun and wind very tiring to my face," he wrote, "which looks more like a cherry and is so sore that the slightest rain spells agony."

When Oates finally set out, the ride was very different from the Model T that glided along the tracks because he had to ride the bike on the wooden ties, where the motorcycle wheels fitted between the rails and the sidecar wheel sometimes did, too, though more usually hung out on the right side. He bumped like that for 150 kilometres before coming to the high trestle bridge above the Montreal River. The track's cross-members were spaced so widely apart that the bike's 26-inch wheels would fall right through.

Was he screwed? Was he hell! This was Jimmy Oates the one-eyed Manxman, who didn't know how to give up. He went back to the nearest telephone pole and shimmied up with his climbing spikes to clip his field telephone to the wire. He ordered a couple of long planks of wood that were delivered on the next train, and then, when he knew the way was clear for the rest of the day, he laid the boards lengthwise between the rails, leap-frogging them into place as he progressed forward over the long bridge, the sidecar wheel balanced on the right-side steel track, 80 metres above the river with no fence or railing. The Fox newsreel company found out about this and contacted him two days later. It asked if he'd repeat the crossing for the cameras — now that was a brave producer! Amazingly, Oates agreed to do so, travelling back on a flatcar and repeating just the last few metres of the bridge.

Of course, the bumpy ride took its toll on the bike. The clutch had to be recorked many times, and the exhaust pipes were so bashed in that Oates sawed them off, leaving only short downward pipes that must have been deafening. The sidecar axle broke, and he rode 20 kilometres with its chassis skidding on the rail until he reached a forest fire air base whose people airlifted him back in a seaplane to Sault Ste. Marie to make some stronger axles. At one point, the sidecar broke off completely, and once, he somehow flipped the wheels over the rail and almost rode Toby into Lake Superior,

ACROSS CANADA
FROM
ATLANTIC TO PACIFIC
5000 MILES — 21 DAYS
1928

Jimmy Oates found it rough going riding on the bumpy ties of the railway.

wedging it into a hornets' nest instead. Each time, however, he fixed the bike and fixed himself and carried on westward. The ride had its lows but also had its highs.

"Accepted invitation to go to Sand Lake," he wrote, "misnamed, should be Lake of Flies but possessing compensation inasmuch as it possesses a girls' camp. I stayed a few days enjoying camp life in a wonderful manner and I was only sorry to leave." But in the same journal, he also wrote: "Bad road bed and bridges bump teeth out, arms ache and eyes watching ties.... Everyone just splendid, taking meal in Fire Depot's shack.... Received letters, feeling fed up with the whole trip, have gone through hell and yet I seem to have done nothing and no person seems to be interested."

People were interested, however. The papers were following him, and so was the Fox newsreel company. Later, in Winnipeg, Oates went to the cinema and watched the report from the Montreal River bridge. "Scenery beautiful and altogether a good picture," he wrote. "Rode into the camera and faded out in the distance after having stopped to light cigarette and then rode on. Not a movie star by a long shot." Except, he sort of was.

☐

One person who knew the value of publicity in the 1950s was Al Turcott, a businessman in Wawa, 230 kilometres up the lake from Sault Ste. Marie. The mining town was only reachable by lake steamer, seaplane, or railway, and Turcott knew the importance of a road connection. He owned the dry goods and clothing store, and he also knew the value of tourism.

For years, politicians had promised a highway that would link Wawa to the Soo, and the make-work projects of the 1920s created a road that stretched north for 110 kilometres from Sault Ste. Marie to the Montreal River. Men with picks and shovels laboured a metre at a time for 15 cents a day. The project petered out during the lean years of the 1930s, but then conscientious objectors during the Second World War were put to work pushing the road farther north, finally ending 80 kilometres along the lake's shoreline from Wawa. The Precambrian rock in that last stretch of wilderness was just too hard, and the muskeg swamp just too much of a challenge to finish the job.

In 1951, the Ontario government had committed to the Trans-Canada Highway, but Turcott saw nothing was happening to complete a road through the Gap, as it was called. He was concerned the road planners might seek an easier route to bypass his town, perhaps staying close to the railway through Chapleau, 130 kilometres inland. So he dreamed up "Operation Michipicoten," named for the river close to Wawa, in which four local men trekked the distance through the bush, following the remnants of an old survey line, to prove it could be done. Conveniently, the trek was made in October, just a month before the provincial election. It seemed an exciting and gruelling trek through Lake Superior Provincial Park, followed in the local papers; one of the trekkers was the Wawa bureau chief for the *Sault Daily Star*. It was supposed to take 10 days but required more than two weeks. The original leader fell sick and then the replacement leader injured his foot and was ferried out by rescue boat three days later. At one point, the group was lost for several days when they didn't report in by radio: "Wawa Men Bound to Soo Unheard from Since Monday; Start Search" led the *Sault Star* on the Saturday.

But they made it. The four men walked out of the bush at the Montreal River 16 days after beginning the trek. "Says Road to Wawa Feasible," proclaimed the *Star* above its bureau chief's story. The journey was made during the same time that young Princess Elizabeth was visiting Canada, and a photo shows the group standing with the three prospective local MPs; trekker Ed Nyman holds a sign proclaiming PRINCESS ELIZABETH LINK, which was the proposed name for the road to be built. Next to him is Harry

The four local men who made their way through the bush from Wawa for Operation Michipicoten in 1951 — seen with an unknown interviewer, from left to right, Derek Baker of the *Sault Daily Star*, Ed Nyman, George Kimball, and Paul Villeneuve — described the trek as a daring adventure. It really wasn't.

Lyons, the hopeful Progressive Conservative candidate, who declared in a story beneath that "I will resign my seat if substantial progress has not been made on a Lake Superior road through Wawa in 18 months." Lyons was elected in a Conservative landslide. The chant went up in town for "A road to the Soo in '52!"

And nothing happened. The money wasn't there for the 175 kilometres to build a road through the Gap both south and north from Wawa — it was being spent on roads in Southern Ontario. Lyons didn't resign. It wasn't until 1955, when the federal government agreed to fund 90 percent of the cost, that construction began. The chant changed to "Out of the sticks in '56!" The road pushed through the rock next to the shoreline, then took an inland course for the second half of its stretch through the provincial park.

The CBC journalists were given special permission to drive on the road in 1960 while it was still being built, and they followed a four-wheel-drive government vehicle prepared to pull them out of any problems. Percy Gomery would have been right at home. "About 10 or 15 miles from the community of Wawa, we saw why the Highways people were so cautious," said Doug Brophy. "The pavement ended and walking the road — and I use the term loosely — were a couple of giant power shovels, the largest trucks I've ever seen, and a stretch of ground that had less resemblance to a highway than anything I've ever seen before.... In our little convoy, we had to pick our way around the boulders, some larger than a kitchen chair, and through sand and earth that must have been a foot deep in some stretches. I'm glad you were at the wheel there, Ron."

"Well, I was sorry for a little while, Doug," said Ron Hunka, "but I'm sure the engineers for this particular stretch of the Trans-Canada Highway will forgive me for saying that this is by far the roughest day that we've yet been through on this Trans-Canada tour. It's been a testing ground for Chevrolet's Positraction rear axle...." You know the rest. Suffice to say they made it through to Wawa, and then continued on through more construction to the asphalt at White River.

The road was officially opened on September 17, 1960, and a nine-metre tall statue of a Canada goose was unveiled that day to mark the occasion. It was commissioned by Turcott and made from plaster, chicken wire, and steel. It weighed an astronomical 68 tonnes. Residents called it "Turcott's Folly," but when it began falling apart it was moved away from the road and replaced with a sturdier, much lighter, and slightly larger steel goose that's still pointing the way outside the town's visitor centre next to the highway. The original goose is now restored and sits above the general store downtown. There's even a third, smaller goose above the Wawa Motor Inn.

Turcott opened the first motel in Wawa and died in 1974. He's remembered fondly by Ed Nyman, the trekker holding that sign in the newspaper photograph. I visited Ed in 2012 at the seniors' centre drop-in, and again at his home in 2023.

"Why did you make that walk, anyway?" I asked him.

"I was only 17 or so, and Mr. Turcott talked me into it," said Ed. "He was a great bullshitter. We had a radio and supplies were dropped in by a plane, but it really wasn't difficult. We could have done it much more quickly, but Turcott wanted the publicity so we took our time and went slowly."

"Do you think the town was better for having the road?"

"We used to more or less trust anybody," he said. "Nobody had locks on their doors. These days, everybody has locks."

Ed reminded me of Lloyd Adams, who surveyed the road across Newfoundland so it would only take 45 minutes to get to Walmart. I guess that's progress.

□

There's another route, of course. Back in the earlier days, it was considered the only route through the trees and relatively flat swamp of the Northern Ontario forest at the end of the Ferguson Highway. That's the road that was taken by Alex Macfarlane after the Second World War, but in 1930, 10 years before the road was built from Nipigon to Geraldton, and 13 years before the final gap was filled in between Geraldton and Hearst, a newspaper journalist from Edmonton named Healy Needham thought the virgin land should be navigable. He set off in September from Halifax at the wheel of his new McLaughlin-Buick straight-eight roadster and was, apparently, "brimming over with confidence," according to the *Ottawa Citizen*. Needham said he was determined to win the gold medal for being the first to cross the country. He told reporters in Ottawa he'd spent two and a half years in the bush preparing for the journey — which was a year longer than he told reporters in Halifax the week before — and had already blazed a trail that should get him to Winnipeg by Christmas. The colder weather would give the car a better footing on the soft ground, he reasoned. Nobody, of course, checked out any of this. The newspapermen just scribbled his comments in their notebooks and went along with it.

"This is not a stunt," Needham told the *Citizen*. "It is an earnest endeavour to convince the Canadian public that a trans-Canada highway can become a reality. I am positive that I will succeed."

Right. Anyway, Needham had no problem making his way up to Hearst where the gravel road ended. Before launching into the 400 kilometres of bush, he persuaded Gus McManus, a prospector and the town's pioneer mayor, to come along with him as mechanic in the passenger seat. The car had its fenders and running boards removed to clear deeper mud, and was

Healy Needham had his McLaughlin-Buick roadster customized with strengthened wheel hubs and a winch.

fitted with a winch to pull itself clear in swamp. No one can deny the off-roading was tough. It took them three weeks to push 15 kilometres into the bush. Needham blamed the slow progress on the unusually mild, wet weather. Vancouver's *Daily Province* reported:

> The shortest forward move of the Nova-Columbia, as the car is christened, involves terrific labours. The trail is marked with poplar sticks half a mile ahead; marked so that the car will avoid some holes and straddle others. Burnt stumps, if sufficiently rotted, are knocked over and used to fill pot holes. The trail finally being marked, Needham climbs to the driver's seat. He sends the car careening over hummocks and low spots. The car plunges, dives and twists. At times all four wheels are in the air. Vegetation claws at the wheels and progress is slow. But Needham "gives her the gun." He accelerates, and the car picks up speed again. The rear end sinks through brush into a hole. The car stalls. It is jacked up and poles placed beneath the wheels. Time after time the same thing happens. Meanwhile, black flies, the scourge of the north, are making life miserable for the pioneers.

Soon after this, the weather cooled and the pace picked up, and by early December, Needham had made his way through more than 150 kilometres of bush and muskeg. Most would have considered the winter drive a non-starter. "My woods experience tells me that it is practically impossible to move an automobile under its own power and on wheels through that country at that time of year," wrote local historian L.M. "Buzz" Lein in 1982.

> Swamps do not freeze up under a couple of feet of snow, and in January with temperatures that could go as low as -50F, a 1930 automobile with the type of oil and grease available then would have a rough time. I do not recall that we had anti-freeze then, but we sure did not have

anti-freezing grease. We used to have to drain our winter-used engines in 1937 of radiator coolant and engine oil if the engine was going to be shut down — or if it suddenly stopped and could not be restarted, then the engine oil had to be drained to be reheated over a fire before it could be put back in the engine and the engine restarted if the shut-down trouble was found.

Still, Needham made it close to the railway town of Nakina where residents helped clear a trail to reach them and he was given a hero's welcome. He moved on fairly quickly after that, hoping to drive across frozen Lake Nipigon, but cracked a rib and then developed pleurisy under the strain of trying to free the heavy car from frozen slush. In January, he was hurried to a Montreal hospital for X-rays and tests, near his family home, leaving the car with Gus McManus.

Then, the following month, the minister in Nakina, which is close to current-day Geraldton, wrote a letter to the newspaper. "Needham Drove on Railroad Tracks," shouted the *Sault Daily Star* on February 7. "Rev. J.A.C. Kell, Nakina, Claims That 142 Mile Trip Was Fraud."

"I have had lots of fun lately exposing the latest fraud which has appeared in our midst," wrote Jack Kell.

> You have perhaps heard about a Mr. Needham and his car, the "Nova-Columbia," in which he intends to ride across Canada. The distance between Hearst and Nakina, 142 miles, is the bugbear of all who covet the honour of being the first to cross Canada in a motor car, not using the railway track on which to drive. Mr. Needham claims to have travelled the distance by tote road, river, creek and bush. Everyone here knows that he came most of the way on the railway tracks, at night time between trains. One of our local men told me he saw him at Savoff, 8 miles from here, two days and a half before he actually arrived here. The country between here and Savoff is very marshy, low lying,

and everyone knows that he could not have done it unless he came right along the railway track. Another man heard him pass his shack which is located close to the track a few miles east of here. Others saw him coming into the town about 1 am Wednesday morning, Dec. 10th, and I myself saw the tracks of the car where he turned off the rails. In the face of all this he is claiming to have, after encountered tremendous difficulties and hardships, been the first to motor through the bush. I went to him and told him I was going to expose him if after investigation I found he was not genuine. So I have sent a report to the concern that is sponsoring him and a copy of it to the *Mail and Empire*. Perhaps they will hush up the whole business, but I will not let that fellow have the honour of being the first man to motor across Canada (without using the railway track) if I can help it.

Needham never commented on the accusations. I can find no mention in Toronto's *Mail and Empire*. He stayed in Montreal and didn't return to his Nova-Columbia car. Gus McManus, however, wasn't finished. He put skis on the front wheels, sawed down the convertible roof to make escape easier if the car should go through the ice, and pressed on over the length of frozen Lake Nipigon. There's a grainy photo where the snowbound roadster looks like something out of *Mad Max*. He reached Fort William in mid-April but knew he was only halfway to Winnipeg and couldn't carry on in the warmer weather. He told reporters the car would lay up in Fort William for the balance of the summer before resuming the attempt. Funnily enough, there are no more reports after that. The car disappeared, probably into a puddle of rust, and the journey was never continued. Can't say I blame him.

There was another attempt that summer on the same route by a different team, however: "an independent, non-political project promoted solely in the interest of the Trans-Canada Highway." This time, E. Wharton Shaw, with his daughter Phyllis and a young mechanic named Harold Puxon, all of Hamilton, drove from Halifax, Nova Scotia, to Hearst, where they met with

Shaw's friend and fellow investor, V. E. Steers. The four of them then set off into the bush with a tractor that towed a truck and trailer. "Those seeking adventure are given the opportunity of joining the expedition," wrote the *Hamilton Spectator* beforehand. "Where possible, the railway right of way will be used — namely, the cleared area at the side of the tracks." The expedition lasted until mid-July when it ran out of money and was abandoned after taking six weeks to make it 80 kilometres off the road.

Whatever the truth of the matter, you've got to admire the sheer chutzpah of all these people. Both Ed Flickenger and Jimmy Oates had already made the drive by rails, so there was nothing special to be gained by doing it again, and Healy Needham did admit he wanted to win the gold medal. As far as promoting the cause for a Trans-Canada Highway, what does it really matter how it was done, as long as the journey stayed north of the border? There are only a few photos of Needham and his massively overloaded Nova-Columbia, and when I look at them, I can imagine Grey Owl sitting in the passenger seat, smiling broadly in his appropriated native finery and high-fiving the driver.

Wanting to know more about Healy Needham, I spent many hours down online rabbit holes looking for something, anything, that would help me close his circle. I found a few newspaper articles from April 1931, three months after his hospitalization, when Needham had apparently gone to Nova Scotia to organize a drive around the world. "Mr. Needham, who is at present staying at the Halifax Hotel, is busy sorting applications from all over the continent from adventurers who have expressed a desire to participate in his next trail-blazing tour," reported the *Halifax Mail*. It then quoted him directly: "Everything we shall use on the car, including clothes, equipment and appointments, will be of Canadian manufacture as well as the car itself. The body of the car will be made of Canadian nickel and it will be the first of its kind and will fully demonstrate another way in which the great Canadian metal may be used." The car would be upholstered in red leather and built in a torpedo-shape, said Needham, with its name, "Miss Canada," painted on the sides in scarlet. He added that he had received many offers from wealthy Americans to accompany him but was holding out for a Canadian, preferably from Nova Scotia. He planned to set out on

May 15 to drive across Canada "as a tune-up" and then on to Japan and Australia. From there, "we shall load the car on the boat at Freemantle for either Calcutta or Capetown. It will be Calcutta if I decide to make the trip a time-record affair, and to the Cape if it is to be a trail blazing attempt." There are no photos of Miss Canada to be found, if she ever existed. And don't forget, this was in April, just as Gus McManus was finally getting the chopped-down Nova-Columbia over the melting ice to Fort William.

There's only one other mention of the man after that, in a stand-alone article published on page 19 of the *Montreal Daily Star* on June 16, 1931:

> Around the world by automobile and steamship in a race against time, and in an effort to beat the present record of 153 days now held by R.G. Stokes, an Australian, is to be made in August by Healy F. Needham, a Canadian motorist.... It was Needham who took the first car through the Rocky Mountains and who essayed the trans-Canada motor trip which ended in disaster at Mud River, Lake Nipigon, when the car overturned, broke his ribs and he had an attack of pleurisy, after having blazed a trail for 300 miles through the bush. Needham records this as a mere incident and a good preparation for his trip around the world in a Canadian-made car with a chromium-plated monometal body and engine block of chrome nickel. For four years he's been waiting till the steamship schedules fitted in with the motor end of the trip.

There's nothing else. Part of me is glad I don't know what happened. I hope the rest of his life was everything he dreamed it would be.

Fifteen years later, Alex Macfarlane made excellent progress, of course. He and Ken MacGillivray drove through on the new gravel road where "our only competition was from Deer and the occasional Moose and Red Fox, [and] we made better time over it that I would like to admit." Certainly, they did. It was 16 hours and 1,144 kilometres from North Bay to Port Arthur, their longest day yet, which included a couple of flat tires, and then they were back on the road the next morning: "The somewhat mountainous nature of the country necessitates a multitude of curves, and curves don't add to the pleasure or safety of driving." They also ran into 10 centimetres of May snow that continued to beyond the provincial border, though Macfarlane doesn't say if that actually slowed them down at all. Probably not much.

□

I've driven the Lake Superior highway a number of times, and it has a well-earned reputation as a tourist road. It's not a continuous coastal vista by any means, like California's famous Highway 1 or Quebec's Gaspé Peninsula, but it peeks out at the lake from behind the rocks enough times to make a visitor gasp at its beauty. The sunsets over the water at Batchawana Bay are unsurpassed anywhere in the world. Peter and I drove north easily on the two-lane highway from Sault Ste. Marie and paused at a cairn near the Montreal River that declared itself the halfway point of the Trans-Canada, though that position changes constantly as the road's bypasses are built and its curves are straightened.

We stayed the night at one of Wawa's many motels, then paused an hour up the highway for breakfast at White River. There, I sought out Walter Spadoni, who I'd met in 2012, but was told he's since died: he would have been more than 100 years old. In 1935, he had his five minutes of fame on the way to school when he saw the thermometer of Rumsey's General Store, which read minus 72 Fahrenheit. That was minus 58 Celsius, and the coldest temperature ever recorded in Canada at the time. It's why there's a giant frosty thermometer billboard on the edge of town. Many people question the true temperature that morning, saying the thermometer was broken, but I'm sure it was still damn cold. Anyway, these days the town doesn't need it for publicity. It markets itself as the train station where a Canadian soldier, on his way from Winnipeg to England to fight in the First World War, bought an orphaned bear cub he named Winnie, which was taken in by the London Zoo and became the inspiration for Winnie-the-Pooh.

Those woods north of Lake Superior are full of black bears. They're one of the reasons the area was so well suited for prisoner-of-war camps during the Second World War. The German prisoners really couldn't escape to anywhere because there were no roads through the hundreds of kilometres of dense bush, though there were bears, and bugs. There was no need to build more than a rudimentary fence around the camps — where could an escapee go? The railway line was the only way out, and it was well guarded.

Canada detained more than 30,000 German soldiers, merchant seamen, and civilian internees during the war at a couple of dozen permanent camps and hundreds of smaller work camps. Nowadays, there's barely any evidence of the Lake Superior camps. Peter and I stopped at Neys Provincial Park where the woods still have a few chunks of stone foundations, and there's a mysterious star shape of rocks on the ground that may have marked the flagpole of Camp 100, home to more than 500 prisoners. This was where the "Black" Germans were held — the most vehement believers in the Nazi cause, compared to the less committed "Grey" and "White" Germans who were kept at nearby Camps Red Rocks and Angler. Nobody ever escaped Neys. Some tried, but if they made it into the bush, they'd inevitably return after a few days of summer mosquitoes and blackflies, or frozen winter snow. One prisoner fashioned skates from an old bedstead and set off over the Superior ice for America but turned back long before completing the 170-kilometre crossing. Why would anyone want to leave, anyway? At Neys, they had a soccer field and an ice rink for hockey, and if they signed a pledge to not try to escape, they could go down to the sandy beach and take a swim in the cool water.

After the war ended, the prisoners returned home to Germany and the camps were closed, but some of the detainees returned to Canada, impressed by the humanity of the Canadian guards and the promise of the country. I called around and people kept mentioning Paul Mengelberg at Camp Angler, who died in 2013. His daughter, Doris, in Kenora was proud to tell me about her dad.

"He was no Nazi, though he was caught up in the war effort and served in a U-boat before he was captured," she said. "He had no idea what Canada was like when they brought him over here, but any opportunity that came along, he embraced it and made the most of it." After repatriation to Germany, he married and brought his wife, Agnes, back to Canada where they settled at Longlac and he began work as a heavy equipment mechanic. He also served as a scoutmaster for three decades, teaching bushcraft and leadership to the Scouts in his care. "He loved the life here," said Doris. "He loved the freedom and the outdoors. He loved Canada."

◻

Farther up the highway, beyond Nipigon and close to Thunder Bay, the Terry Fox Monument marks the point where Terry was forced to abandon his Marathon of Hope across the country. He'd left from St. John's in April 1980 and spent more than four months running a marathon every day as he made his way west to the Pacific, hop-skipping on the artificial leg that replaced the leg lost to osteogenic sarcoma when he was 18 years old. He ran more than 5,000 kilometres before the cancer returned and he was forced to go home to Vancouver for treatment, where he died the following year, age 22. Since then, the Terry Fox Foundation says its annual Terry Fox Run has raised more than $850 million for cancer research.

The three-metre-tall bronze statue is about four kilometres west of the point where Terry actually ended his run. It's in a dedicated park and looks out from a high hill over Lake Superior and toward Thunder Bay, 10 minutes to the west. Peter and I didn't speak as we studied the statue, but we were both thinking how simple it had been for us to back our wheels into the Atlantic and drive to this point, while Terry dipped his foot into the water at almost the same spot and then found his way here with little more than perseverance and bloody-minded determination.

"To every Canadian, he left us his challenge," read the inscription. "A challenge each of us will meet in our own way."

◻

Of the Trans-Canada Highway's roughly 7,700 kilometres, more than a quarter are in Ontario, and when we reached Thunder Bay, we still had more than 550 kilometres before getting to the Manitoba border. There are two routes to choose from: the traditional Highway 17 that heads northwest through Dryden and Kenora, and the newer branch that drives directly west to Fort Frances, across from International Falls on the American side of the border, and then north to rejoin the route near Kenora. I took that two-sided one a few years ago with my family in an RV, and I remember it as the most monotonous drive I've ever endured before or since. Perhaps I'm being unkind and my memory is faulty; probably I went into a funk because my wife complained there was no Tim Hortons, or my kids griped that they just wanted to stop and do some fishing. But aside from Fort Frances itself, I don't remember a single community or even store alongside almost 500 kilometres of road. Nothing. Just a few lakes on the old road that heads north. And trees.

As Edward McCourt, who drove the traditional route, wrote in 1963: "Even the man who passionately believes that he shall never see a poem as lovely as a tree will be disposed to give poetry another try after he has driven the Trans-Canada Highway."

Half a century earlier, Thunder Bay was divided into the two competing towns of Port Arthur and Fort William. Thomas Wilby and Jack Haney were able to take the Reo off the lake steamer at Port Arthur, drive around town, and that was it. Wilby met with local officials and dodged trains running down the centre of Main Street; Haney fixed a spring on the seat and then loaded the Reo onto a railcar for Manitoba. Tensions between them were high. Haney stayed in the car on the steamer and wrote that he was getting sicker than ever of the Captain, and then, once in town, "had trouble with Wilby concerning the signs on car. Again says he will get another man if I do not do as he commands. Hurrah! Watch him walk to Vancouver." The next day, after finally taking a bath, he travelled alone on the train to Kenora and then on to Manitoba. I'm sure the separation did them both some good. Maybe the bath too.

Ed Flickenger had been able to leave the railway at Nipigon and drive the final 100 kilometres to Fort William on the highway under construction, then made it another 50 kilometres west before having to put the steel flanged wheels back on the Ford Model T. He travelled another 300 or so kilometres before leaving the tracks again and taking a new road to Dryden, where Perry Doolittle joined the entourage. The car went back and forth from road to tracks to road to tracks, needing two hours for every change of the wheels, until it finally made it to Manitoba and left the rails for the roads across the prairie.

Flickenger, now travelling with Doolittle for a while, found the roads far bumpier than gliding along the railway tracks, but three years later, Jimmy Oates left the jarring rail ties for the smoother pleasure of the rutted roads. He, too, finally went back onto the rails for the crossing through to Whitemouth in Manitoba, though he did so "with feelings of great regret."

☐

Peter and I pressed on from Thunder Bay along Highway 17, the traditional Trans-Canada Highway. After an hour, we crossed over to the Arctic Watershed, where rivers and streams drain into Hudson Bay instead of the Great Lakes; 10 minutes later, we gained an hour when we drove into the Central Time Zone. In fact, time seemed to stand still on the long road through the trees. There were few of the curves that Macfarlane decried, though we did see a mother moose and a pair of calves crossing the highway far ahead. A couple of closer cars had also seen them in time, fortunately for everyone, and they were safely in the trees by the time we passed.

Farther on, beyond Dryden, we were pulled over beside a lake for Peter to smoke a cigarette when a couple of cyclists rode in on a pair of recumbent tricycles. Bryan Cowie and Kelly Durst were happy for a break — they'd been pedalling since Kenora that morning and left Lethbridge 20 days before, on their way to Newfoundland. Both said they'd made the cross-country ride before, in separate years before meeting, though she'd used a regular bicycle instead of the laid-back trike. Bryan said his trike kept breaking, which slowed them down, but they were in no rush and were pedalling for the pleasure of it.

"It's a wave," said Kelly. "It's just like life, cycling. You have to ride the wave up and down, but the downs usually end up as something you appreciate more. Like, when we had the breakdown, but the next thing we knew, we had people helping us out. There's always a bright side to the dark side, and when we go back to normal life, things are just easier to deal with. I think that's why we do it."

I nodded. I was thinking of Jimmy Oates bumping along the rail ties, hoping for a few days fishing at the girls' camp.

"The hardships allow you to enjoy life more," said Bryan, and I thought of Percy Gomery digging his two-tonne Maxwell out of the mud.

"Nobody ever talks about bugs, but they're the bane of our existence when we're doing this," said Bryan.

Kelly chipped in: "We've already been bit a lot. They swarm the trikes because we can't go fast enough with the tail winds to get away from them, and it's just like a cloud of bugs around you. It's pretty funny."

And I thought of the Skipper, sitting there alone in the gummed-down Maxwell under a mosquito net, holding a book in one hand and a revolver in the other, then a few days later, after a good night's sleep at last, game for more. Some things, and some people, never change.

We left them pedalling east as we sped west toward Kenora. A new bypass splits the Trans-Canada there for a few kilometres and offers an alternative to driving downtown. Then we slowed for roadworks where the highway is finally being twinned through the far west of the province to the Manitoba border. It was a long day of relatively uneventful driving past lakes and trees, and we both felt a little tired by the time the forest thinned and we reached the Manitoba border.

Six provinces down and four to go. Almost there, surely.

LEGEND

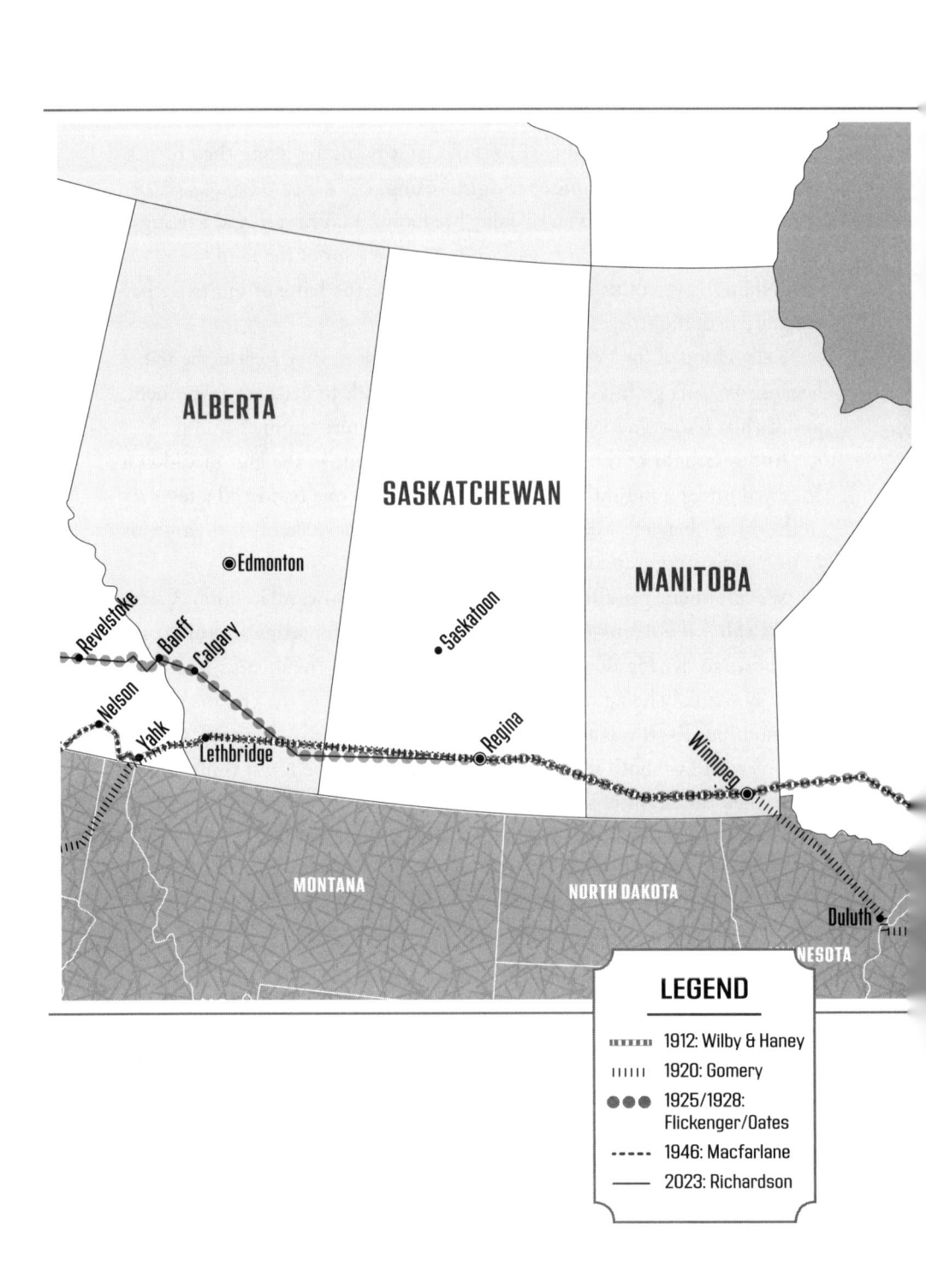

- ▪▪▪▪▪ 1912: Wilby & Haney
- ∣∣∣∣∣ 1920: Gomery
- ●●● 1925/1928: Flickenger/Oates
- ----- 1946: Macfarlane
- ——— 2023: Richardson

9

Manitoba

Winnipeg is a fine place to take a break for a while. All our pathfinders did, since it's the first big city on the road west after Toronto. The national highway bypasses to the south, but if you want to, you can follow the Trans-Canada right through the centre of everything. Take Main Street over the Red River, then across the Assiniboine River a minute later (if traffic's not too bad), turn left on Broadway, and skip over to Portage. Then follow Portage all the way west, past the stores, bars, coffee shops, laundromats, hotels, and everything else that makes a city a city, and you're on the Trans-Canada Highway all the way. Canada's New Main Street. Let the trucks use the bypass. If you're a tourist, or if you want to take some extra pleasure in life, head downtown.

Peter and I went into the city for the evening with my friend Winnipeg Willy, a biker who seems to know everyone. We ate burgers at his favourite diner in St. Boniface, then drank beers nearby at the Marion Hotel. The place was quiet — the strippers weren't onstage that evening. We went outside onto the sidewalk deck so Peter could have a cigarette, where a plaque made it very clear on which side of the railing you could and couldn't smoke. "Enter at your own risk," it warned, pointing at an open spot to the left of its wooden post. It continued in smaller type: "If you really need to smoke — don't. It will kill you. — michele smith." And underneath that, printed in a flowing, misspelled font, "If you don't give a fuck, do it hear — Doug Smith." We both liked the easygoing Marion. We felt completely comfortable and left soon after dark before any fights might begin.

I was happy to relax with a beer for the evening. We'd made it through to the next stage of the journey, the great flatland, very clearly different from anywhere else we'd driven so far. As soon as we crossed the border, the highway widened and twinned itself into pairs of lanes with a rocky and then grassy median between them. The trees ended quickly past Falcon Lake, and by the time we reached the road sign for the longitudinal centre of Canada, we were well onto the prairie. The city rose up on the plain ahead, towers in the sky that seemed closer than they really were, still far away.

Winnipeg has long been a destination for travellers, especially coming from the West where it marks the end of Big Sky Country. America has the Mississippi to separate East and West, while Canada has the Ontario/Manitoba border.

In 1916, H.W. White drove his wife and one of his three daughters to Manitoba from their home in Vancouver. It was a nostalgic visit for Harry and Lydia. They lived in Carberry before moving to the West Coast, where he was the area manager for McLaughlin Motor Cars (which became General Motors). A wealthy family, they didn't do things by halves on the journey: his open Cadillac towed a Warner camping trailer, described by the *Manitoba Free Press* as "a regular house on wheels, a complete camping outfit, containing two bedrooms with full-sized beds, springs and mattresses, a dining room and kitchen." He left Vancouver and made straight for the international border, driving on American roads and then crossing back into Canada near Cranbrook, British Columbia. There was some excitement: they had to drive for three kilometres on the railway tracks where the road bridges were washed out. At Calgary, they took a three-week break to recover from the rigours of the mountains.

I mention this journey only because, at the end of it, Harry White claimed the gold trophy offered by the Vancouver Automobile Club as the first person to drive between Winnipeg and Vancouver. He knew about the trophy because he was vice-president of the club, and it was different from the medal offered by Bert Todd in 1911 for a Winnipeg–Victoria drive that had to stay within Canada — that would be awarded to a pair of Americans in 1924. There's a photograph of the White family leaving Vancouver in the Cadillac, all formally dressed, with Harry sitting stiffly at the wheel and the two women behind in the second row; in the front passenger seat is a thin-faced man wearing a chauffeur's uniform. He's unnamed. I'm sure Jack Haney would sympathize.

◻

The original road east of Winnipeg crossed the border with Ontario at the same rocky place as it does today, then skirted up toward Whitemouth to pick up the rail line west into Selkirk, just north of Winnipeg proper. That was a contentious road that Manitoba laid down in the 1920s with the help of federal money, intended to link the West to the Ontario tourists of Lake of the Woods and Kenora. It was only 75 kilometres, but it took a decade to build.

Sometime in the mid-1920s, Ontario's minister of lands and forests — James Lyons, whose son, Harry, later took his seat in the province's legislature and pushed for the road to Wawa — made a bet of a silk hat with William "Billy" Clubb, Manitoba's public works minister, that the Ontario section of road from Kenora would reach the provincial border before the Manitoba one from Winnipeg. Ontario's highway was about 50 kilometres shy of the line. The Manitoba minister was happy to take the bet. Both men were strong advocates for a Trans-Canada Highway, and Clubb wrote an eloquent editorial in Toronto's *Mail and Empire* extolling its advantages:

> A highway joining the east to the west must be a potent factor in establishing and maintaining cordial relationship.… The aviator may fly with the swiftness of a falcon from one place to another, but, cut off from all association with his fellow, he flies in the chill isolation of the clouds.

> Travelling by rail is a very formal affair. The traveler is hurried along by a rigid officialdom whose great aim is to detrain him at a certain destination on the moment of time specified. He has but one choice — the choice of destination.
>
> The vision of a completed Trans-Canada highway presents to the mind of the motorist many pleasing and educational prospects. He may loiter at will by many a shaded dell or meandering stream; and he may deviate from this broad highway to acquaint himself with strange communities and strange peoples.
>
> Racial animosities and interprovincial differences — and these are largely due to ignorance on the part of both in regard to the other's point of view — are being dispelled by a freer intercourse, and, undoubtedly, the construction of the Trans-Canada extension east is another great step towards perfecting our national unity.

These were high hopes for the Trans-Canada, but it took until 1932 to finally link the two provinces by road, eking out the dwindling budget before the leanest years of the dirty thirties. It's still the only crossing between the two provinces, save for a couple of minor roads that drive into Ontario communities near the border and don't continue. If you want to drive across Canada, you have to take this road — there is no alternative without going into the United States. Aside from Prince Edward Island, it's the only border between provinces or even states in the two countries that has only one through-crossing. Ontario finished its length of highway first, but Lyons was no longer in the Cabinet and wasn't at the ribbon cutting, and his successor and Clubb are both bareheaded in the photo of them shaking hands across the provincial border. Hmmm. Maybe Billy Clubb sent the hat through on a bus and boat to Sault Ste. Marie.

Before then, the only connection was by train, and in 1912, Jack Haney travelled through to the Selkirk rail depot to collect the Reo. He met a guide and they drove the 30 kilometres back into the city through drenching rain where, according to Wilby, they were "covered from head to foot in mud, and in a spirit of covert mutiny.… It had taken them the greater part of the day to navigate the seas of mud which they encountered." It was almost a mutiny too. Haney refused to leave the next day, saying the weather was too bad and the car needed attention to its valves and clutch. He'd be the one digging in the mud, after all. They ended up staying a couple of days while Haney fixed the car, and Wilby took the opportunity to visit the wonderfully named Sir Rodmond Roblin, premier of Manitoba.

"We talked considerably about roads, for the gumbo variety of which the premier expressed no particular fondness," wrote Wilby. "He had gumbo on his own premises, and he confessed to having been held up by it in his motor-car before his own front door only a few evenings before. 'The worst of it was,' he said laughingly, 'my son and I were in our dress clothes, and it was a question which of us was going to crawl under that car and release us from durance vile.'"

Manitoba is famous for its clay-rich soil, and when it rains, that soil turns into thick, sticky "gumbo." When roads were simply tracks, without the benefit of gravel or tarmacadam, they were fine and hard when the surface was dry, but became almost impassable in the wet. And when Wilby and Haney came through in 1912, it was very, very wet. The going was very, very rough. "Where the city pavement ended, black gumbo commenced," wrote Wilby. "In a flash the road became inky and spongy. It was as if the prairie, conquered by the city, here cried aloud and defiantly: 'Stop where you are. The rest of the land is mine.'"

Nothing had changed 12 years later when a Quebec motorist came through on another cross-country jaunt. I've not mentioned C.K. Graham until now because his drive was adventurous only for its time. He set out for Vancouver in his Dodge with his son and nephew, and also his friend, Mark McElhinney, a dentist and one-time president of the Ottawa Automobile Association, who wrote about the drive for his club magazine. They put the car on a lake steamer from Sarnia to Duluth, then drove through Minnesota to cross into Manitoba south of Winnipeg.

"We struck the real prairie this side of Crookston and it was a revelation. The dry gumbo was like a pavement," wrote McElhinney. And then the weather turned briefly wet, blowing through as quickly as it arrived:

> It was soon over, the sun came out brightly and we struck out bravely. In less than two miles we solidly gummed up in the black, sticky muck. It was wadded full between the wheels and the body and mud-guards. We tried all sorts of ways to remove it, finally having to claw it out with our bare hands. It took nearly four hours to get back to Hallock where we stayed for the night. Gumbo has one virtue besides growing good wheat, it dries quickly so that next day we made the ninety miles through Emerson to Winnipeg in time for lunch.

However, the ground was dry in 1920 when the Gomerys crossed back into Canada and made their way up to Fort Garry, as Winnipeg's downtown was then known. They were both in good spirits, happy to return to their country on "that perfect clay road" beside the Red River and looking forward to a couple of days of pampered urban civility. In fact, Percy was in such a good mood he overtook a police car, driving almost three times the speed limit at 65 kilometres per hour. In his defence, he didn't realize it was a police car; in fact, "I called to the Skipper to have an eye open for a possible policeman while I put this fellow and his rattletrap of a car in their places. It was an easy victory, and we resumed our pleasant conversation about roast duck on the half shell."

The driver was Fort Garry's town constable, and he caught up with the Maxwell and tried to fine Percy Gomery $10 for speeding. Gomery refused to pay and insisted on speaking with a magistrate, who offered to drop the fine to $5, but Gomery still refused, despite the threat of arrest:

> "What do you expect will happen, Mr. — er — Gomery, if you are — locked up?" asked the magistrate.
> "Oh, nothing particular, your honour, except that every newspaper from Halifax to Vancouver will announce

tomorrow morning that I have been put in gaol for driving this car from Montreal. And about half a million motorists will have a long laugh at you and me and the Municipality of Fort Garry."

The irony is that Gomery was guilty as sin for speeding at 40 miles per hour in a 15-mile-per-hour zone, and yet he had total confidence that his superior station in life would exonerate him, especially when laughed over with a convivial judge of similar status. His words squirm with the more critical reading of today's perspective, especially when he mocks the francophone police officer's heavily accented English while blithely admitting that he himself could speak barely a word of French. Even so, he read the room and softened while talking to the constable; he began to flatter him, telling the judge: "He's done his duty and done it well. No motorist will ever bargain with him." Gomery talked himself out of the ticket and went on his way without paying any penalty. As I said before about Gomery, it was a very different time.

As an aside, when I drove the Trans-Canada Highway in 2012, I overtook a long line of vehicles in Cape Breton that seemed to be crawling behind a slow-moving truck. After I caught up to the truck and began to pass, with the Camaro moving much more quickly now because the dotted yellow lines had become solid as a hill approached, I realized the truck was itself following close behind a slow-moving police cruiser. I overtook the cruiser and then pulled over to face the music in a parking lot at the top of the hill before he even switched on his lights. He drew alongside, and I was polite and acquiescent, but he still charged me with "driving to left of solid double line," as well as "changing lanes unsafely." Each charge carried demerit points and a fine of more than $200. It didn't help in the least when I told him I was driving across Canada and blogging every day in *Maclean's* magazine. I think it was my out-of-province licence plate that did me in. I contacted a lawyer — no cheaper paralegals allowed in Nova Scotia — and said that while completely guilty, I felt it was grossly unfair to be penalized twice for essentially the same offence, and wanted one of the charges thrown out. It didn't matter which one. The lawyer agreed, took on my case, had an excellent lunch at my expense with his friend, the chief prosecutor, and the cheaper charge was dropped in exchange for a guilty plea to the other one. The whole sordid affair cost me about $1,000. On the positive side, I've learned my lesson and not overtaken any more police cruisers on solid-double lines.

It was in 1920, the year the Gomerys visited, that the Canadian Automobile Association met in Winnipeg, intending to listen to a presentation from the Manitoba Motor League on how best to mark and signpost the country's highways. Until then, there had been no standardized maps; drivers found their way by getting written directions, or travelling with a pilot who knew the best way through. Wilby and Haney got lost somewhere beyond Portage la Prairie, where all they could do was follow ruts through the fields that seemed to head in the right direction. The Manitoba Motor League, however, led by its director Arthur Coates "Ace" Emmett, was endeavouring to end such confusion: As historian Karen Nicholson writes in "A.C. Emmett and the Development of Good Roads in Manitoba" in the journal *Manitoba History*, volunteer crews from the automobile club were supplied with paint, brushes, and stencils to cut *R* (right) and *L* (left) turns on trees, fence posts, and whatever was handy along rural roads, the markings coordinating with Emmett's maps. It was a colour-coded system that seemed sensible, and Emmett was looking forward to explaining it to the CAA delegates. However, on his way to the meeting, he noticed the city's streetcars were all numbered, and this gave him an idea.

When he was introduced to speak, Emmett said, "Gentlemen, you will see that I made elaborate preparations to show you our highway marking system but now I find that this preparation was unnecessary and the model can therefore be neglected and my prepared address can go into the wastepaper basket. I will give you the shortest address you have ever heard, viz: Number your highways!"

Ace Emmett is credited with originating the idea of numbered highways. You can imagine all those besuited delegates slapping their foreheads as one and groaning, "*Duh!*" The first jurisdiction to do so was Wisconsin in 1925 — the state's representative had been at the Winnipeg meeting — and

Manitoba followed the next year, where the Trans-Canada, of course, would be designated as Highway 1.

☐

Winnipeg was proving an excellent city for travellers to take a break from the road. Jimmy Oates spent a week there in 1928 to rest and spruce up Toby, and even Alex Macfarlane and Ken MacGillivray indulged in a day off in 1946, while mechanics went over their Chevy to clean it, grease it, and tighten its nuts and bolts. I suspect Macfarlane had been concerned somebody else might learn of his attempt at the Todd Medal and set off at the same time, or perhaps a day earlier from Halifax, to beat them to it — this would explain why he didn't write to the medal committee to register the drive until the day he and MacGillivray actually left home for the East Coast. By Winnipeg, he would have been comfortable that nobody else was on their heels.

Back in 1925, Ed Flickenger and J.L. Scrymgeour drove the Ford Model T off the rails and into town for an informal dinner hosted by the Canadian Automobile Association. The local dealership was running a contest to guess precisely what time the car would arrive, and somebody with the closest answer won $25 when the car honked its horn outside the city hall. It didn't need to honk its horn — the mayor was in another car immediately behind, with various motoring dignitaries who had driven out to the start of the road at Whitemouth to meet them. Perry Doolittle, the president of the CAA, was also there after coming in from Dryden with the Model T on his way by train to a conference in Vancouver.

The late-September weather turned wet, however, and developed into one of the worst rainstorms of the season. Doolittle urged the Ford team to wait a few days until the gumbo could dry out. He was apparently ignored. "Dr. Doolittle held an all-afternoon session with the crew in the Royal Alexandra Hotel Wednesday," reported Regina's *Leader*, "trying to show them that they would assuredly get stuck in the 'gumbo' west of here, and would have to sleep in the mud for several days. But J.L. Scrymgeour, newspaper man of the party, who is sending out daily stories of the trip to the principal dailies of the United States and Europe, held that the trip had been too easy so far and that he was 'just aching for some exciting hardships to write about.'"

In Vancouver, the *Province* saw the news the car would drive on and editorialized that "Gumbo is Manitoba mud. Its adhesive qualities are world famous. Fish glue is clear water compared to gumbo. Properly flavoured, it would make ideal chewing gum.... Mr. Scrymgeour will find no excitement tackling gumbo. Hard, dirty work will be his portion, and in the end he and his companions will probably pick up the car and carry it westward until the roads dry up or freeze over."

There's no account I can find of the Model T's drive the next day, but in the movie itself, the weather is dry and the title card states that "leaving Winnipeg there is a fine 40 mile stretch of roadway." The dirt road is clear and not at all wet, though it turns to deep, rutted gumbo before Portage la Prairie. I'll wager a silk hat that the party took Doolittle's advice and stuck around for a couple of days so they wouldn't get stuck in the outskirts of the city.

Ed Flickenger's Ford Model T found it rough going when it ran into gumbo on prairie roads.

Peter and I headed west out of Winnipeg the next morning, neither of us speaking, the radio silent. It's about two hours to Carberry, and we knew what we'd see there: a charred circle in the long grass of the southern verge, a makeshift memorial of rough crosses, flags in the town at half-mast. When we arrived, it was exactly as the news photos and video reports had shown it to be. Peter didn't want to stop. He knew I would pull off, drive into town, talk to people, take a look. It's what I do, for better or worse, and it couldn't be ignored. It needed to not be ignored.

We'd heard the news a week before: a small bus carrying seniors from Dauphin on an outing to a casino near Carberry was hit broadside by a tractor-trailer as it crossed the Trans-Canada Highway. The bus was travelling south on the road from Dauphin, two hours away, and it went past the first stop sign and into the waiting area between the pairs of lanes, and then for some reason it drove past the yield sign into the path of the truck, which police said was driving at the speed limit and had the right of way. The bus was slammed onto the verge where it exploded in a fireball. Fifteen people died at the scene, another person died later that day, and another person died the following month. Eight people survived, including the two drivers. Most of the victims were in their eighties, and as people told reporters later, everyone in the small town of Dauphin knew somebody on that bus. It was one of the worst highway crashes in Canada's history.

I wasn't sure who to talk to, or what to ask. I'd covered many fatal collisions as a young reporter in Ottawa, and before then, for a summer at the *Leader-Post* in Regina, but those seemed different. They were spot news, focusing on the facts of the case. Now, the facts were known that many innocent people had been killed and police were investigating the cause. It would be ghoulish of me to ask questions but irresponsible to merely drive by when I wanted to know about the relationship of the Trans-Canada Highway to the community. It was the elephant in the room. Peter refused to get out of the car, and I didn't blame him. The clerk at the local motel had nothing to say; the local librarian told me the event had traumatized the whole community, which mobilized all its first responders to attend the horrific scene of the carnage. That was enough. I put the car into gear and got the hell out.

But we still had to drive past the accident site to get back onto the Trans-Canada. The burnt circle couldn't be ignored, and the heavy skid marks on the asphalt couldn't be avoided. Something terrible had happened here. I pulled over at a safe place well away from the highway and walked over to the circle. Peter stayed in the car, eyes closed.

The sun was hot, the sky was clear, long green grass waved gently in the soft wind. Somebody had mown an area where others had placed flowers, perhaps a dozen bouquets both plastic and real. A small paper Canadian flag on a stick. A dreamcatcher. Some bundles of sage grass. There were no crosses; those would come here later but were already at Dauphin where everyone was mourning.

I walked to the burnt area, silent except for sporadic traffic up on the highway. The grass was scorched completely away, leaving just a layer of blackened ash. I squatted beside it and tried to imagine how it must have been just nine days before, the explosions, the shrieks, but nothing came. The long grass all around the circle waved like ripples on a quiet lake.

A makeshift memorial beside the Trans-Canada Highway at Carberry, close to the site of the crash where 17 people were killed in 2023.

Something fluttered in the dark bed of horror. Something white. I moved closer to look and saw it was the singed pages of a charred book. An owner's manual for a bus. It was open to the last page of its first section, entitled "Replacing Restraint System Parts After a Crash." "If you have had a crash, do you need new belts?" it asked. I took a photograph of it. I'm not sure why. I went back to the car.

"You'll never believe what I just saw," I told Peter.

"I don't care," he said. "Please — can we just go?"

The investigation would continue for a long time. It's still happening as I write this, and the bus driver is still in the hospital, unable to speak with police. Whatever the cause, it's agreed something must be done to make the intersection at Carberry safer. The provincial government moved quickly to install additional flashing lights, signage, and rumble strips, and announced the following January it would follow the recommendations of a report to spend $12 million on improving the intersection — either installing a roundabout, making the median area wider, or creating a restricted crossing U-turn (RCUT). The roundabout would slow down Trans-Canada traffic considerably but might itself cause collisions from drivers who rush it, or don't expect it. The wider median, with a second stop sign, would theoretically give paused drivers more space and leeway for making the second half of the crossing. The RCUT would create lanes in the median for a few hundred metres to each side of the crossing so that north-south vehicles would first turn right, then make a protected U-turn in the median to turn left; effectively, it would prevent drivers making a dash straight across four lanes of traffic. The premier called these "medium-term options" and promised to listen to public feedback before making the decision on which to build.

Immediately after the crash, many people phoned in to radio shows and wrote on online forums that the Trans-Canada Highway is a disgrace and should be twinned and restricted just like the American interstate system. This would undoubtedly be safer, but it would also be extraordinarily expensive, and few people are prepared to pay the extra taxes it would require. Even fewer are willing to pay for tolls to cover the cost, which would probably be inadequate given the relatively light use of the highway in rural areas like Carberry. The Manitoba Ministry of Transportation and Infrastructure estimated 5,000 vehicles drive past the intersection each day, which makes it tough to justify costly upgrades when busier highways in the province also need work; the Perimeter Highway around Winnipeg — the Trans-Canada bypass — carries up to six times as much traffic. A new interchange built near Calgary in 2023, with an overpass, on- and off-ramps, and a bridge, cost $65 million and was warranted because it services more than 80,000 vehicles per day.

A restricted interchange at Carberry is inevitable, Premier Wab Kinew told a press conference, but not until traffic use is high enough to justify it — whatever that number may be. "There will be an interchange at this location in the future," said Kinew. "The engineers tell us that that's probably in the 20- to 25-year timeline, in terms of when that makes sense."

In the meantime, change can't happen quickly enough for the Carberry intersection. A month after Peter and I came through, a truck drove southbound across the Trans-Canada Highway just as the bus from Dauphin had done, and it was hit broadside by an SUV driving toward Winnipeg. The passengers in the SUV were taken to hospital with severe injuries, including two brothers travelling to the city to make funeral arrangements for their mother who had died hours before. The SUV driver was airlifted to Brandon where she remained for a month after spending five days in a coma. The driver of the southbound truck was charged with proceeding through the intersection before it was safe to do so — making a dash across four lanes of traffic — and fined $174.

A highway is many things, but as much as it must be appreciated, it must also be respected. A moment's inattention can create unimaginable tragedy. As long as drivers are responsible for their own vehicles, all highways carry this risk. There are small white crosses everywhere on the nation's roads, and many of them mark the deaths of careful drivers caught out by somebody's poor decision. When the Manitoba government released its report on improvements to the Carberry intersection, Minister of Transportation and Infrastructure Lisa Naylor told the CBC the province was reviewing its entire highway network to look for safer approaches in design. "This approach aims to create a more forgiving road system," she said, "meaning that the system accepts that people make mistakes and are vulnerable — so road systems are created to prevent tragedies."

The Trans-Canada Highway is no different. It may be a great step toward binding Canada's national unity, but it can also be unspeakably cruel. "Can we just go?" asked Peter again, and I slipped the Lexus into drive, negotiated the median, and headed west across the rolling open land to the provincial line, neither of us speaking for an hour and a half until we reached Saskatchewan.

10

Saskatchewan

People who have sped through Saskatchewan sometimes decry the province as a backward wasteland. "If you're on a road trip, just fly over the Prairies to Calgary and go from there," they advise others who have never visited. "There's nothing to see on the Prairies. You won't miss anything."

It's true the landscape can be flat and monotonous. When I drove my family across Canada in an RV, my teenage nephew moaned there was no reason to look out the window since leaving Ontario. He was used to today's constant stimulation. "When are we getting off the prairie?" he sobbed. I pointed out we hadn't yet reached Winnipeg.

However, I love to drive under the huge sky that only magnifies the vast open land beneath it. The old joke about spending three days watching your dog run away from home holds true, and when I spent a summer in Regina working for the *Leader-Post* newspaper, I fell in love with the province — at least, the province in the hot weather of summertime.

Edward McCourt also appreciated Saskatchewan where he taught English at the university in Saskatoon, but he was a realist. "Even those of us who, irrationally, love almost everything about Saskatchewan admit that the tourist won't be tempted to linger on the eastern stretch of the highway," he wrote in 1963. "Empty land. Empty sky. A stranger to the prairies feels uneasily that he is driving straight into infinity."

Neither McCourt nor Peter and I had to stray from the smooth asphalt of the Trans-Canada Highway as we sped west. It's 240 straight kilometres from the provincial line to downtown Regina, and you can say confidently that the distance will take two hours and 15 minutes to cover because there's no reason to slow down unless you need gas or coffee. The twinned highway is wide, flat, and seems featureless, though in truth, it gets even flatter on the other side of Regina. The broad wheat fields here ripple and chop like a lake beneath a light wind. There are hills on the prairie, and river valleys, but the paucity of trees smooths them down to the eye and expands the perception of their reach.

But, as with everything about Canada, there's always something unexpected if you take the time to look for it. Before the highway came through, in fact even before Wilby and Haney drove over these fields, this supposedly empty area of Canada was one of the most socially aristocratic regions of the continent. It was home to at least nine French counts, escapees from the heavy taxes and anti-monarchist sentiment of their home country, who saw a land of endless potential on the unfenced prairie.

The first of them settled in the mid-1880s and sent word back to France that this was a land of rich opportunity. They brought European funds and investment to the region, as well as servants, craftsmen, and skilled labour, though they didn't bring business acumen or farming expertise; their various ventures ended mostly in failure. In fairness, farming on the prairie was still finding its way in those years, and if it wasn't wheat, it was probably experimental. The pasture soil was too alkaline for the Gruyère cheese the Comte de Seyssel attempted to produce, and the end result was inedible. The chicory grown by Baron de Brabant was mixed incorrectly with coffee and made it undrinkable. Sheep and pigs could never be raised by the Comte de Jumilhac in sufficient numbers to be profitable. The Comte de Roffignac's sugar beets grew very well and would have supplied a local sugar refinery, but their production also created alcohol, and the government refused to issue a permit; the bureaucrats were concerned the alcohol would create unrest among the Indigenous population. The counts gradually accepted defeat, and the last of the nobility left around the turn of the century.

But in the meantime, what a pair of decades it was! As the archaeologist Kristian Sullivan writes in "The French Counts of St. Hubert: Local History as Social Commentary," they built homes lavishly decorated by artisans brought over from France. They ate imported foods and drank imported wines. They used coaches with coachmen and footmen, and the women wore Parisian gowns, silk parasols, and elaborate hats. "Meals were often feasts: one culinary delight presented by a count included pig stuffed with whole goose, enclosing a whole fowl filled with epicurean dressing, with a side dish of oysters." One year, they took over the hotel in Whitewood and threw a party that's still remembered at the local museum. "It was astonishing, the number of white shirt fronts that were mustered, not to mention white kid gloves," wrote Mrs. R.S. Parks. "Many pretty dresses of the style of the late eighties were in evidence, souvenirs perhaps of better days across the sea. The vivacious Frenchwomen of gentle birth and breeding in fashionable décolleté gowns and jeweled neck and arms lent a distinction in spite of the incongruity of the crude setting."

At the same time, a further 30 kilometres south, an English army captain established an agricultural college named Cannington Manor where the sons of wealthy British families came to learn about farming in Canada's West. The captain didn't know much about farming, however, and his main ambition was to charge tuition to those wealthy families while their sons played tennis, cricket, and rugby, as well as billiards in the 26-room house. They especially enjoyed fox hunting and chukkas of polo, and, of course, hanging out with the French counts. The community died out around the same time as the counts moved, mostly because it was bypassed by the new CPR branch line. All this in an empty land that motorists now speed through on their way to somewhere else.

□

Thomas Wilby would have liked to speed through in 1912. "The beauty of the average prairie town is not so conspicuous as to induce one to linger

THE DRIVE ACROSS CANADA

for its contemplation," he wrote, but even so, the going was slow. They had no maps and it was essential to travel with a local resident who knew the area, for there were no roads to speak of, just a track through the fields that "would stop dead or fade away and defy sight or scent to pick it up again, and it was soon evident that its nefarious intent was to lose us in the bushland wilderness and there leave us to the coyotes." At Moosomin — "a town hardly big enough to hold its own name" — the pilot agreed to guide them the 250 kilometres to Indian Head but got lost along the way as the mud obscured all landmarks. It eventually took two days to reach Regina.

I shiver to think of the conversation in the Reo as the pair trekked west with the confused pilot. Wilby's book at this point is full of slurs against Indigenous Canadians and comments on, shall we say, the lack of aesthetic appreciation displayed by early settlers, but these are characteristic of so many outside observations from this period. Haney was probably slumped over the wheel when he wasn't battling the car through a swamp. He'd been sent a telegram in Brandon from the Reo head office confirming that "Wilby is <u>Captain</u>. Come damn near bidding the Red 'a trip to Hell' and I would get another job, but have concluded to stick it out till I get across or fired."

By "the Red," he means the All Red Route, which was the colour of the British Empire on all world maps, and the point of this journey was to not stray out of the red and into the yellow or green of the United States. Wilby's sycophantic pamphlet for his sponsor was entitled *'Cross Canada with the "All-Red" Route Reo*. It must have irked the author no end that the opening page held a portrait photo of F.V. Haney, with no picture of Wilby himself.

In Regina, the pair were joined by Earl Wise, a young man the same age as Haney, who worked for the local Reo dealer and came along to assist with the car. He probably helped a lot with its passengers, too, as a middleman and buffer between the driver and the Captain. Wise was from Michigan, but his parents were English, so perhaps that made him more acceptable to Wilby. He sat in the back with his legs hanging out of the car, but he moved around and occasionally he'd even ride on the hood itself. "Sometimes he went on duty as second engineer," wrote Wilby, "and while the car was devouring distance, he displayed extraordinary acrobatic nimbleness by climbing out to the front mudguards to take long hungry looks at the carburettor, or the radiator cap or the valves. Apparently satisfied, he swung back to civilisation again, unemotional as a Dervish, and, solemn as a judge, cuffed the chauffeur *en passant*, rolled a cigarette at an angle of forty-five degrees to the horizon line, and sank into the placidity of a sack of potatoes." Wise was an affable, easygoing guy who stayed with them for the rest of the journey, and he turned out to be essential to reaching the end. True to form, he's never named in Wilby's book.

The going was still rough across the prairie. Part of the problem was that, as in Quebec, farmers had the choice of either paying a tax for the province to maintain the roads or avoiding the tax by looking after the roads beside their properties themselves. You can guess the most popular choice among the hard-working, penny-wise residents. A British motorist, Donald Gooch, lamented this while driving across the prairie with his dog in 1913, seeking out potential Canadian dealers for Austin cars. "Through the use of either a scoop-shovel or a spade and stone-boat, the farmer succeeds in piling up a zig-zagging ridge of loose 'gumbo' soil and then abandons it to work itself down," he told a newspaper reporter at the time. "The result of even a light rain upon this may be better imagined than told. True, he has nominally conformed to all road requirements exacted of him, but when he wants to travel, either via motor or buckboard, he calmly shifts his course to the remaining 'undisturbed' portions of the grassy veldt with its few more worries than the treacherous gopher hole."

Seven years later, Percy Gomery commented that "this wonderfully rich and growing province ... would be pleasant driving to the Red Route motorist, were it not for the neglected state of seventy-five per cent of its roads, resulting in broken springs and over-worked patience." He wrote an article for the local paper that lambasted Saskatchewan for the poor condition of its roads — thick, sticky gumbo after any fall of rain, poorly signed, and following the right-angled criss-cross of township lines, rather than direct routes between towns. Settlers were permitted to return any roads next to their newly established property to farming use, as long as they replaced them with equivalent roads nearby, and many neglected to follow that through.

The gumbo wasn't getting any less sticky for Ed Flickenger's Model T in Saskatchewan.

Mostly, Gomery voiced the usual criticism that Canada needed to attract tourists but the province lacked a reputable cross-country road network to draw them in. The following week, Saskatchewan's minister of highways took him to task in the same newspaper. "Mr. Gomery attaches premier importance to the building of a highway for tourist traffic. I do not," wrote the Honourable S.J. Latta. "The Department of Highways … sees a much greater importance to the construction of main market roads designed to provide the best possible means for the producer of grain and other products to convey such to, and necessary supplies from, the market centre."

Fair enough. The minister was thinking of farmers getting their produce to market, and then the grain continuing by train. But in the very same newspaper that Gomery's criticism was published, in fact alongside his column on the same page, was an article reporting that there were now 10 times as many miles of highway in North America as there were miles of railway. For every railway car, there were three motorcars. The future was staring Samuel Latta in the face, and yet he couldn't see it. He was replaced as minister the following year, but conditions hadn't improved in 1924 when C.K. Graham drove through in his Dodge: "In negotiating a wet spot we slid into a washout. Bing! We were ditched. The nearest rancher had a bonanza while the wet spell lasted for it meant at least half a dozen cars a day to be pulled out." And then the next year, Ed Flickenger's film shows the Model T driving through the deep ruts of wet clay roads, with the camera lingering over a rear wheel so caked with mud that its tire chains can barely be seen. Progress was slow, but it was at least steady. By the time Alex Macfarlane drove through, 21 years later, he wrote that the road across the province was dusty gravel, with a few strips of pavement in the towns.

Saskatchewan was proud to be the first province to complete its stretch of the Trans-Canada Highway. "For years, Saskatchewan's pride has been hurt by visitors' harshly derogatory references to its terrible roads, even though they agreed in their own minds with them," wrote the *Globe and Mail* when the highway was opened at Regina in 1957. "They have been irked by the unfavourable comparison of Saskatchewan's trans-provincial highway with the trans-provincial routes in Alberta and Manitoba. Now that Saskatchewan has completed its trans-Canada route before Alberta and Manitoba, the province feels it has turned the tables on its neighbours."

□

The Trans-Canada Highway now bypasses Regina, but just as with Winnipeg, the original highway still runs directly through downtown if you prefer. There are a few small road signs along the way. It's simple: just keep going west on Victoria Avenue beyond the bypass, then turn left on Albert Street for 10 minutes until you reach the ring road. Victoria, then Albert — it seems fitting in a city named Regina. If you take this beautifully treed and leafy route, as Peter and I did, then you'll pass the museum and the art gallery and the impressive stone Legislative Building next to Wascana Lake, and for a while, you'll forget completely that you're in the middle of the prairie. Not that there are any rises or dips to the road.

When I was a summer reporter for the *Leader-Post* in 1988, I covered a story in which city planners considered raising the 20-metre toboggan hill at the Wascana Centre as a use for landfill; they rented a double-decker bus to drive to the summit and get a feel for the extra height. "It was amazing," said a bus rider from the top deck, now 25 metres above the rest of the city. "You could see the entire skyline all around, without any trees masking the horizon."

We drove through to the bypass and continued west on the twinned Trans-Canada, onto the true billiard-table flatness of the fields for the hour across to Moose Jaw. Peter had never seen such expanse and loved it, though the novelty can pass quickly into tedium. I used to make weekend visits to Moose Jaw when I lived in Regina; more often than not, the Moose Jaw correspondent begged to come to Regina instead. The bureau office there was infamous for its fold-out guest couch on which many young visiting reporters had slept off an overindulgent Saturday night and which had apparently never, ever been cleaned.

There are tunnels under the main street, and the marketing-savvy Tunnels of Moose Jaw company offers year-round, hour-long tours. Nobody's quite sure why the tunnels are there. The prevailing theory is they were built as a link between basements for heating the buildings. That hasn't stopped the marketers from selling three different themed tours of the tunnels, hosted by actors in costumes from three different periods: Chinese at the turn of the previous century, when immigrant labourers hid out from racist tax collectors; bootleggers from Prohibition days in the 1920s; and most recently, citizens in the 1950s preparing a nuclear bunker. It seems the only truth behind any of these is that somebody once saw some Chinese people coming out of a basement during a fire, and that a couple of people noticed photos of Al Capone and thought they might have seen him visit Moose Jaw once, when the town was well known for its underground gambling dens and cross-border provisions of illicit booze. The nuclear threat? Why not? In any case, the tunnels are a very popular attraction for the town, almost required after stopping at the Tim Hortons off the highway and checking out the anatomically correct statue of a giant moose.

Another hour farther on, we reached Ernfold, which few people have heard of and even fewer people notice as they pass. It's a strange place of less than a couple of dozen people now, and it's notable because it's the only community in the country that exists actually between the lanes of the Trans-Canada Highway.

The grassy median that separates the twinned lanes is wide enough at many points on the prairie to support the growing of hay, and at the right time of year, you can see the huge rolls lying on the short stubble waiting to be collected and brought to the barn. The people here are practical, and the median is as fertile and well drained as any other field, so it's not left to waste. The farm driveways lead directly onto the Trans-Canada, but they're widely spaced and there's only one direction of traffic for the combine operator to watch for. Approaching Ernfold, however, the median grows wider and wider until the oncoming lanes of the Trans-Canada can no longer be seen. At their widest point, they're four kilometres apart and there are roads between the paired lanes to access the fields and the village.

The original two-lane highway ran along the south side of the Canadian Pacific Railway tracks and squeezed its way through just to the north of Ernfold. When the Trans-Canada was twinned in 1975, there wasn't the space to expand it without moving either the tracks or part of the village, so its planners just swerved its eastbound lanes around to the south of the entire community. There was no urgency to bring the lanes back to closer parallel and, in fact, it avoids a dogleg on the westbound lanes. That means the eastbound road through to the next community of Chaplin — and by extension, the entire Trans-Canada itself, if you discount all its other twists and turns — is two kilometres shorter heading east than heading west.

In its heyday, 165 people lived in Ernfold. Farmers brought their grain to the elevators and shopped for supplies in the village. That was in 1931. When the highway came through, the elevators weren't so important — they didn't need to be spaced every 15 kilometres or so to be accessible to the farmers' wagons, but maybe every 50 kilometres to be reached by their trucks. The last elevator came down in the 1980s when the census showed the population at 91 people, and 20 years later, there were barely half that number of residents left. In 2012, when I first visited, there were 21 people.

Back then, I met Warren Beach, who farmed much of the land between the lanes, and we went for a drive to show me the original graded road that Ed Flickenger would have driven through the gumbo across the province. Alex Macfarlane probably took the same road in his cloud of dust. "It makes it kind of novel," Warren said. "You think of it as like the railway once was: it was the link of Canada, the lifeline of Canada. That's what the Trans-Canada is now. We've always felt here that we're kind of close to civilization, and it's because of that highway. You go 15 miles south of here and you feel you're in the middle of nowhere, but the Trans-Canada makes you feel less isolated." But it wasn't the highway that killed Ernfold, he mused — it was the centralization of everything into the cities.

I called Warren again before I came back to visit with Peter, but he was out of town with relatives. We did get to speak on the phone, and he suggested I call on the village mayor, Christine Bauck, to get her perspective. She was happy to invite Peter and myself up onto her porch to tell us about the community. The population is now 18 people, Chris said, which is three more than just a few years ago, since some new people moved in.

"The cost of living in the city is getting to be too much and too rat-racey, and it's cheap to live here," she said. The town might sell you a plot of

Chris Bauck is the mayor of Ernfold, population 18.

land for a dollar if you promise to build a house, which could cost another $5,000 or $10,000. It's all negotiable. In the town of Morse, next along the highway to the west, a nice home with a garage and a plot of land may well sell for less than $100,000 when it would be 10 times that in Toronto or Vancouver. "Water and sewer here are $340 a year and you can use as much as you want," she said. "In Morse, that'll cost you $120 every three months. It doesn't cost a lot of money to live here."

There are drawbacks, though. All the dilapidated buildings and junked cars, for a start, and the lack of facilities. The restaurant on Main Street was struck by lightning in 1990, burned down, and was never repaired. A tornado came through a few years later, blew out the back wall of the gas station, and threw its furnace into the house behind, which was never repaired. Then a car cut off a semi-truck, forcing it to shunt into the gas station and set everything on fire. Never repaired. The post office closed when it shifted to rural mailboxes. All that limitless water? It's fine for "hygienic use," but you can't actually drink it. And the church on the hill, next to Chris's home? Her husband bought it for a dollar and uses it for storage.

"Last Christmas, or maybe the Christmas before," said Chris, "we were just coming into Ernfold and my husband says, 'You know, in 20 years, this is going to be a memory.' He goes, 'Do you really think our kids, and all this younger generation, give a shit about who lives here?' And he's right. They're like, yeah, so? When our generation goes for its dirt nap, then for sure it'll be a ghost town. But I'm going to continue doing what I do for as long as I can. You might bend me a little bit, but you're not going to break me."

Her short driveway is angled directly off the Trans-Canada Highway, and she has a rock sunk into the lawn next to it. "That rock is there because there are so many semi drivers that fall asleep, and one of these days a semi's going to be in my house," she said, as if this was no big deal. She keeps a dog and her door is always locked, even when she's at home, because she's never sure who might walk in from the highway. Trucks drove by constantly as we talked on her porch, and I asked if the noise was troublesome. "You know what? It don't bother me," Chris said, "but if you guys were to sleep over here, you'd probably think, holy shit!" Her full-time job is superintendent of operations for the Ministry of Transportation, which means she drives the plough in winter and fixes the roads in the summer, and she says she'll never leave. After all, she can look out her living room window and know exactly what kind of day she's about to have.

I asked if Ernfold felt like a special place because of being inside the Trans-Canada Highway — hugged by the arms of its paired lanes, if you will, and connected directly to the world through its asphalt. Chris shrugged. "You know what?" she said. "I've never really thought about it. Never thought about it at all."

◻

We stayed the night in Swift Current, less than an hour down the road. Our motel was the cheapest of the entire drive: $65 for a twin room. "Interesting aroma," said Peter when we walked through its much-repaired door. It was a smoking room, but he preferred to smoke outside where we could sit with a beer on the white plastic chairs, look out onto the parking lot, and listen to the trucks roar past on the highway, not so close and loud as at Chris Bauck's porch. We ate steak at the restaurant across the way but left our valuables locked in the Lexus. My laptop, my camera, and, most valuable of all, the Todd Medal. It stayed securely in its case, hidden under the front seat.

There's a granite monument in town that remembers four hockey players with the Swift Current Broncos, killed in 1986 when their bus skidded out on the Trans-Canada's black ice and flipped down an embankment. They were on their way to play against the Regina Pats, and the four who were killed were in the back, playing cards before they were thrown out and crushed. Twenty-four other passengers survived, but that's an easy statement to make and not so easy to live with. "Trauma impacts everybody differently, and it impacts some significantly more than others," National Hockey League player Sheldon Kennedy told the *Athletic* in 2018. He'd been at the front of the bus and was speaking after the tragic crash of the Humboldt Broncos, which killed 16 players and injured 13 others, far away in the northeast of the province. "Some of our guys [from the 1986 crash] are still dealing with it today. As a community, as a league, as families, it's important for them to know how significant these types of events are on

SASKATCHEWAN

people — and how much damage is done. But they also have to know there's hope. There's lots of hope that people can move on, but never forget — and that's important also."

Less well remembered is the bus crash near here in 1980 that killed 22 men and left only eight survivors; it's still by far the greatest loss of life for any collision on the Trans-Canada Highway. There's a memorial beside the road, half an hour on from Swift Current, and Peter and I paused there to take it in.

It's a lonely place. Some trees on the south horizon suggest there might be farm buildings over that way, but everything else is grassland. The memorial itself is in the crook of a gravel road at the point where it turns to meet the Trans-Canada, and there was a plume of dust from a truck far down that road to the south. And then there was the main highway itself, with widely spaced cars and trucks droning past, not stopping here as they drove west or east. Maybe noticing the maple leaf flag flying from the monument site. Maybe not.

The memorial remembers the wet afternoon on May 28, 1980, when a CPR steel crew that was fixing tracks left work early to return to Gull

The lonely memorial near Webb, which remembers the 22 young men killed in 1980 on the Trans-Canada Highway in a fiery bus crash.

Lake, riding in a pair of yellow school buses. The Trans-Canada was just two lanes then, and somewhere near the town of Webb, an oncoming black Chrysler strayed over the centre lane and sideswiped the second of the crew's buses. The car was driven by two men who had been drinking at the Swift Current Legion. The bus was knocked sideways and skidded over the centre line, directly into the path of a tanker truck loaded with more than 34,000 litres of asphalt oil, heated to 65 degrees Celsius. The tanker exploded with the impact. "It was just a massive horrible, horrible sight," said an eyewitness. "There was a mass of flame and there were bodies all over lying around. Oil was burning and splashing all over. They got their share of it, too, some of the people who were trying to save the others. The whole thing was absolute chaos."

Most of the crew were young men from Manitoba or Newfoundland, living on a train parked at Gull Lake and moving around to wherever the work was needed. At a memorial service two days after the crash, when 500 people filled the First United Church in Swift Current, somebody suggested a collection should raise money for the victims' families. Donation boxes at local churches and banks raised $3,000 that was distributed to the families, about $136 for each person who died. Canadian Pacific Railway returned the bodies to their homes and paid for the funerals, and then a few months after the crash, a bronze plaque was unveiled at the rail tracks in Swift Current that carried the names of the 22 victims. An engineer had started a collection and raised $1,627 from his fellow workers to pay for the plaque, which left $2 to spare. The truck driver survived and the two men in the car were uninjured. They weren't breathalyzed for alcohol at the chaos of the scene. An inquest the following year recommended twinning the Trans-Canada Highway and installing seat belts in buses, and the provincial attorney general said no criminal charges would be laid against the driver of the car. And that was that.

The Trans-Canada was twinned at the site in 1983, though it took until 2008 to twin the entire highway across the province. It also took until 2007 for the memorial we visited to be built near the site of the crash, with help from the local Teamsters. It's a tall cross made from railway track, mounted on a couple of metres of laid track, with a brass plaque remembering the victims. When we were there, some plastic flowers were tied to the cross with string and a small Newfoundland flag. It was sad and sombre, and I wouldn't have noticed it if it wasn't for the maple leaf flag flapping behind in the wind, a flash of red and white against the blue sky.

The township administrator told me the flag was purchased privately by a woman in Medicine Hat, just across the line in Alberta. So Peter and I continued west, out on the wide and smooth Trans-Canada Highway across the lonely prairie, to find her and ask the question: "Why?"

11

Alberta

Medicine Hat is a busy, leafy city just an hour from the provincial border — quite out of keeping with its wide-open prairie surroundings. It just seems to suddenly happen when you drive in on the Trans-Canada Highway, and this is the place to stop for gas or something to eat because there's nowhere else around of any size for hours. Lethbridge is a couple more hours to the west on the single lanes of Highway 3, and Calgary is three hours up the Trans-Canada with really nothing to look at along the way. Like, nothing. Some oil derricks and a few cows, if you're lucky. Medicine Hat, however, has a giant metal teepee frame, and malls and businesses and a thriving tourist industry that loves to quote Rudyard Kipling.

"This part of the country seems to have all hell for a basement, and the only trap door appears to be Medicine Hat," says the mural on the wall of the liquor store downtown, supposedly quoting the famous author from 1907. "And don't you even think of changing the name of your town. It's all your own and the only hat of its kind on earth."

The comment about "all hell for a basement" is a reference to the vast reserves of natural gas beneath the land, and Medicine Hat being its trap door refers to all the wells that tap into that gas. Locals liked to take visitors out to the wells, open the valve of one of them, and toss a lit match onto it. The flame could reach 100 metres in the air.

The liquor store quote is often attributed to Rudyard Kipling, the renowned British author of *The Jungle Book*, among many others, who made a return visit to the frontier city in 1907. "I have always considered Medicine Hat a kind of mascot for me," he said to a newspaper reporter at the time. "I have used it a lot in my stories. I can never get the name out of my head.... Why, how could you be kept down with — I was going to say all hell for a basement — natural gas?" Then three years later, there was a movement to rename the city as "Gasburg," and the local postmaster wrote to Kipling at his home in England: "You know, no doubt, that the name of our city is a translation of the old Cree name of the place," wrote Francis Fatt. "It is rich in Indian traditions, eloquent with war-songs of the Black Feet and the Cree.... In a moment of weakness, our city fathers have decided to submit the question to the vote of the rate payers instead of ordering the proposers to be cast into a den of burning fiery rattlesnakes. Can you help us with a few words of encouragement in combating these heretics?"

Kipling wrote back two weeks later:

> [The original name] hints, I venture to think, at the magic that underlies the city, and as years go on, it will become more and more of an asset. It has no duplicate in the world; it makes men ask questions; and as I knew more than twenty years ago, draws the feet of the young men towards it. It has the qualities of uniqueness, individuality, assertion, and power. Above all, it is the lawful, original, sweat-and-dust-won name of the city and to change it would be to risk the luck of the city, to disgust and dishearten Old-Timers, not in the city alone, but the world over, and to advertise abroad the city's lack of faith in itself....
>
> What then should a city be re-christened that has sold its name? — Judasville.

The local newspaper reprinted both the postmaster's letter and the famous author's reply in full. The proposed name change was voted down 10 to 1.

The unusual name "Medicine Hat" is recognized as a translation from the original Niisitapi word *Saamis*, but in turn it's not so clear where that came from. There's a story about a Cree medicine man being gifted a hat that gave him powers to save his starving people, and another tale about a Cree medicine man losing his hat while his people fled a marauding band of Niisitapi, and any number of variations on the theme. What matters is the local tourism bureau used these stories, and the unusual name, to make the city more interesting for visitors. These days, though, Medicine Hat prefers to plug itself as "Canada's Sunniest City," with 330 days of sunshine a year. Such marketing would have made Rudyard Kipling proud.

□

Peter and I weren't in Medicine Hat for the sunshine, though. We wanted to visit Marina Gilchrist, who is the cousin of Michael Beach, driver of the school bus in Saskatchewan in which 22 people died in 1980. It was a summer job for Michael, who was 24 years old and studying social work in Winnipeg. His dad was a CPR engineer and helped get him the work. By coincidence, Marina is also the cousin of Warren Beach in Ernfold, and she visited the village just a couple of weeks earlier with her husband, Mike, to attend its Cemetery Day. That's when relatives gather from around the country to remember the people buried in the cemetery there.

"We didn't stop at the memorial this time, but we knew it was coming up, and we saw the flag there," said Mike, sitting beside Marina at their kitchen table as we chatted. "We see it every time we go by, and we always acknowledge it. It helps us remember what happened."

The flagpole is relatively recent, and Marina said she paid for it when it was clear the monument committee and the local township wouldn't. It cost just over $500, and since then her two cousins who were sisters of Michael Beach picked up the expense. "When the flag wasn't there, nobody noticed [the memorial]," she said. "Nobody stopped. I don't think they

Marina Gilchrist, at home in Medicine Hat with her husband, Mike, is the cousin of the bus driver killed in 1980's tragic crash.

knew what it was. I wanted people to acknowledge what happened there and remember the people who were killed. For me, it means something. It's a personal thing."

"In our opinion," added Mike, "we thought they were forgotten too fast."

Forgotten by Canada, perhaps, but not by their families far away. "I think about it all the time," Yvonne Edwards told me when I phoned her later. Her older, only brother was Richard "Tommy" Slaney, who was killed that day, age 25. "I think about everything he's missed out on. He loved kids and stuff, but he never met any of his nieces or nephews. His motto was 'live fast, die young, be a good-looking corpse.' He loved the rock and roll."

Tommy had started out as a surveyor with the Alcan mine in St. Lawrence on Newfoundland's Burin Peninsula. When the mine closed, he went out west with his friends to work on the tracks for CP Rail until he could find another surveying job. It was the luck of the draw that he was riding in the bus that was struck. His family at home in St. Lawrence saw the news of the fiery crash on television that night; it was the first they knew of it, and no names of victims were released, but one of the images at the scene showed a workman's hard hat laying on the scorched ground. It was light blue from the Alcan mine. Distinctive. "Mam said, 'That's Tommy's hat,'" remembered Yvonne. "Dad said, 'Don't be foolish, there's thousands of those hats around,' but the next morning, of course, when the RCMP showed up, we knew."

It took three weeks to identify Tommy's body — he was originally misidentified as one of the two Seward brothers, both killed and badly burned, and he was buried by mistake at the Sewards' church in Hodge's Cove three hours away. When the mistake was discovered, his body was exhumed and brought to the church in St. Lawrence, but Yvonne says that, aside from some CPR lawyers who had her parents sign forms to not hold the company liable for Tommy's death, nobody ever spoke to her mother, Theresa, about the tragedy. Not for 30 years. Not until one of the survivors, Gerald Synard, helped arrange a local memorial identical to the Saskatchewan one from three years earlier. It's at the Christ the King Catholic churchyard at nearby Rushoon, a town of a couple hundred people an hour away on the same Burin Peninsula. Eight young men from Rushoon were on the bus — four died and four survived.

"Nobody likes to talk about it," said Yvonne, "but for my mother — she's 92 now — that was the first time, at that memorial service in Rushoon in 2010, that anybody involved with it spoke to her about it. She was really happy for that. Counselling was unheard of back then. It's just the way it was. In Newfoundland, all your families are very close-knit and it's your family and your friends that gathers around you. But nobody ever spoke of it."

Angus Moores doesn't believe that's such a bad thing. He was on the bus that afternoon, and he remembers everything right up to the impact. After lunch, "the rain basically washed the clothes off everyone's backs, it rained that hard," he told me later, speaking on the phone from his home at Rushoon. "Everyone just wanted to get on the bus and have a nice warm-up and have a smoke, and maybe a lot of the guys were already sleeping, because everyone was probably soaking wet." Angus wasn't sleeping, though. "I saw the car coming, yes. I saw the truck. I braced myself around the seat in front of me until the impact happened. I basically waited for the accident to happen. I stayed with the accident until the crash, and then I guess I was knocked out. The hospital had everything set up on the lawn, and I do remember lying on the grass, but I had no idea at the time, with the shock, if I was in an accident or not. I saw all the doctors and nurses there, but I had no idea where I was to."

He had a ruptured spleen and spent a month in intensive care before returning to Newfoundland. He didn't work for a year. "I do not think about it every day," he said. "I am always reminded of it, and yes, it's there, but I never — you've just got to try to not let it bother you. I didn't refuse to think about it, but it's just that I told myself, I got to live with this, right? I don't know why I got saved, nobody can answer that, but I did survive and then I told myself, well, I can't let this bother me as such. I've got to move on and I've got to make the best of it."

Gerald Synard, who pressed for the two memorials to be created, found it more challenging to move on. He died recently from cancer, but he told a reporter at a later memorial service that "there's a lot of survivor's guilt," which only builds each year as the May 28 anniversary grows nearer: "You get pretty on edge. There's all kinds of emotions that start to take over." Another survivor from Rushoon, Mike Lake, told another journalist in 2010 that "even the sight of a school bus gives me the shivers."

When Angus Moores resumed work, he left Newfoundland and went back to CP Rail where he found a job administering the work crews in western Canada. It became a 32-year career, based in Vancouver. He was the person responsible for booking hotels, chasing the crews around British Columbia, Alberta, and Saskatchewan, getting the garbage removed, whatever was needed, that sort of thing. He passed through Webb many times. "Of course, the accident was always on your mind, naturally," he said. "I knew I would be reminded, especially when I first went back and the crews still had the bus. The crews were still being transported by the school buses, right? So my first time on the bus, there was, yes, you know, of course, my mind was different when I stepped on the bus the first time. In 1980, we were just kids. We left Newfoundland, we went to the mainland, and got this great job with CP Rail, and they paid us good money, and hey, we were the happiest kids on the block. It was just a summer job. I lost all my friends, all my buddies. We were like one big family because we worked together so closely."

Angus told me he wouldn't be at the memorial service on the next May 28. "I have to drive past the church every time I pass up the street, and I'm reminded every time that the memorial is there. I know it's there. I stopped going for no particular reason. I had the opening, and I did not want to go year after year and attend the memorial. I haven't gone in a few years. I don't want to be at the centre of 'I survived.'"

But for everyone else, why did it take so long to memorialize the dead? "We were all isolated in different communities and nobody got together," said Yvonne. "They were just too traumatized to talk about it. Especially Gerald. You could see the pain in that man's face. Anytime you spoke to him, you know, it was just something that never, ever, left him. He told me, he woke up and he was in the wheel well of the bus — that's what saved him. A lot of it was survivor's guilt."

She told me her mother will always stop now at the Rushoon memorial when she travels past on her way home to St. Lawrence. Theresa can sit there for hours, and for the other relatives involved in the crash, it gives them some peace. It helps them to share the burden of grief.

And the Saskatchewan memorial? What good does it do there so far from the homes of the victims? Has Yvonne ever been there?

"No, but it's on my bucket list," she said. "I just want to look around at where he spent his last moments. Whenever any of my friends go to the site, I'll give them little mementoes, a little Newfoundland flag, or a beach rock or something from home, just to lay, you know? I think it's important for the people who live there, who helped rescue the survivors, to be able to remember what happened, so they can talk about it too, but once all the people impacted by it are gone, then that will be enough. I don't think future generations are going to remember them like we do. But for now, we need to remember them."

◻

Medicine Hat is where we split away from the earliest pathfinders. Peter and I followed the Trans-Canada Highway up to Calgary, taking the same route as Ed Flickenger and Jimmy Oates, but the original duo of

Thomas Wilby and Jack Haney in 1912 drove their Reo directly west toward Lethbridge on what would become the southern Crowsnest Pass route, carrying Earl Wise and a local guide with them. They were followed by Percy and Bernadette Gomery in 1920, and even by Alex Macfarlane and Ken MacGillivray in 1946.

Macfarlane could have taken the central Trans-Canada route, which was still just a dream in British Columbia over Rogers Pass but quite driveable on the Big Bend road; if he wanted to win the Todd Medal though, he had to abide by its Rule Number 13: "Route taken must be fairly direct and pass through Ottawa, Winnipeg, Fernie, Cranbrook, Rossland, Grand Forks, Greenwood, and Princeton." Clearly, the Canadian Highway Association in 1912 wanted to promote the improvement of the Crowsnest Pass road, and perhaps it was unthinkable then that any other route could be possible. When Macfarlane came through, there was still a roadless gap of about 15 kilometres across Kootenay Lake near Nelson, British Columbia, but there had been a ferry there since 1931. Even if the ferry had to ply its 80-kilometre route along the lake, as it had done in earlier days, Rule Number 5 was clear: "No ferry of more than twenty miles in distance will be permitted, except in British Columbia." The rule about the route could probably have been appealed, but Macfarlane was in too much of a rush for that — he only received the go-ahead a couple of days before setting out from Louisbourg, don't forget. The southern route it would be!

There were no rules to govern Wilby and Haney other than staying inside Canada, and they pressed their way west across the prairie toward Lethbridge, remaining out long past sunset. "I believe there was a road. There were evidences of it every now and then," wrote Wilby. "In the blackness which covered the earth shadowy telegraph poles came and went, the railroad appeared and disappeared, a lonely flag station flashed into sight and out again. We took our bearings by the stars and by the wind which would blow in our faces so long as we kept to the right trail.... We motored by a kind of instinct." They made it late into Lethbridge but drove on the next day, making 40 kilometres an hour now in the wagon ruts across the fields, toward the mountains that rose on the western horizon. They entered the Rockies at Frank, a coal-mining town barely a decade old, which had been decimated in 1903 by a rock slide that killed at least 70 people. More than 100 million tonnes of limestone slid down the side of Turtle Mountain in a swathe a kilometre wide. It's still the deadliest rock slide in Canadian history, and although the town was rebuilt, Wilby found the place depressing as they followed the road cut through the debris.

It was a three-kilometre climb to the top of Crowsnest Pass, on a steep ascent that Wilby estimated at sometimes a 25-degree grade. The passengers jumped in and out of the straining car to lighten the load as it progressed, and "we grabbed it at the sides, the hood, the wheels, the top — by anything, in fact — to save it from slipping backward as the life gave out of the unfortunate creature." But they made it. At the top, they'd reached the Continental Divide and drove into British Columbia.

It was an easier drive across the prairie for the Gomerys. They spotted the whitecapped Rockies from more than 150 kilometres away and were transfixed by them, but as they approached Pincher Creek, "the roads of Alberta, so creditable behind, now fell off shockingly in quality as we neared their end," wrote Percy. "All along we heard the same comment, 'Poor till you get into British Columbia; then splendid.'" Their Maxwell was more powerful than the Reo and had less trouble on the climb to the provincial border at Crowsnest Pass: "The creeping automobile circles on a thread-like road which is nevertheless perfectly safe. Though generally only a few feet wider than the car, there are regular turning out places well marked by two crossed boards on a high pole — and in reality not at all suggestive of cross-bones!"

□

The modern Trans-Canada Highway pushes through close to the centre of Calgary, leaving heavy trucks to take the restricted-access ring road that bypasses to the north and south, but which let Peter and I slow down through the traffic lights and past the storefronts of the six-lane road to the north of the Bow River. It narrows when it passes over the Crowchild Trail, but here it's really just one of many busy streets that get people around the city. Same with the Crowchild, or Highway 1A, which heads to Cochrane half an hour away and is the original Trans-Canada route to Canmore and Banff. It's a more scenic road into the mountains and more relaxing to drive, but the modern Trans-Canada will get you into the Rockies more quickly, twinned all the way.

Ed Flickenger would have driven on the Crowchild in 1925. So would Jimmy Oates three years later. It was smooth dirt in Rocky Mountains Park, Canada's first national park (renamed Banff National Park in 1930), and stayed well graded all the way to the B.C. border on the Continental Divide. Federal money kept the park maintained, which included its roads, as well as the road through Kootenay National Park that continued west into British Columbia.

When Edward McCourt came through on the new highway in 1963, he wrote that its greatest danger was the surplus of scenery with few spots to pull over and take it all in. For him, the better drive was on the older Bow Valley Trail. "One of the finest views in all Canada is that from the turn-out at the top of the great hill above the village of Cochrane twenty miles west of Calgary — a magnificent expanse of river, valley, foothills, mountains, and over-arching sky juxtaposed in a flawlessly balanced harmony, so flawless as to suggest a deliberately contrived artistic improvement on nature. It is a view of which no man can ever tire."

McCourt's son, Mike, who grew up to be a television journalist in Calgary, was so taken with the view that he moved to Cochrane, and I visited him in 2012 to say hello and find out more about his father. Edward McCourt was a professor of English literature at the University of Saskatchewan in Saskatoon and a prolific writer, with a half-dozen novels set on the Prairies to his name. But after he died in 1972, he slipped into near-total obscurity. Part of the reason was, in Mike's words, that his dad had "almost pathological shyness," unwilling to promote his books in person but preferring to let the writing stand for itself. Yet Edward was tenacious and committed: he studied for high school while working full-time on his parents' prairie farm and went on to become a Rhodes Scholar. "His greatest expression was through his writing," Mike told me. "He wrote by longhand, and sometimes he would go into his study at the house in Saskatoon with a page that was blank, and come out several hours later with a page that was

Edward McCourt loved the Prairies and wrote a series of novels, now mostly forgotten, set under the big sky.

still blank. But other times, he'd written a dozen pages and he would be so happy for it."

In 1965, the year *The Road Across Canada* was published, Edward McCourt discovered a canker on his tongue that would grow to kill him seven years later at 66 years old. "His last communication to me was with a note," said Mike. "He couldn't talk to me to tell me that he loved me, but he could write it in a note. It's how he was."

□

The CBC journalists were also impressed by the mountain view in 1960. It had been hot for them on the Prairies, reaching 36 degrees Celsius, and they were happy to reach the cooler foothills of the Rockies. It doesn't sound so different from today. "What I like is when you leave Calgary as we did early this morning, cross the Bow River, and then get your first view of the

Rockies," said Doug Brophy. "It's a bit deceptive — they seem to be quite a distance away, but then almost suddenly you are right at the foothills and, if I may put it this way, it's a delightfully sinister way, the way they take you in, sort of absorb you."

"The next few days should be pretty exciting, Doug, now that we're in the mountains," said Ron Hunka, "and we're getting a chance to see just what this Economy Turbofire V8 on our Chevy can really do, and it is actually just about as exciting as the mountains themselves."

Sadly, we don't know any more, nor how the V8 held out on those mountain roads. This wasn't their last broadcast from the highway, but it's the last that's still known to exist. The remaining week of radio reports is now lost, in which Ron Hunka was given a ride through the unopened Rogers Pass by an engineer in a Jeep, while Doug Brophy and technician Ken Frost laboured around the Big Bend Highway in the Chevy Impala. They reached Victoria on July 28, and all three carried on with successful broadcasting careers. Their month-long journey across Canada was surely one of the highlights. And the CBC phased out all advertising by April 1975.

□

Peter and I took the swift road out of Calgary, past Canada Olympic Park from 1988, and sped into the mountains to stay the night in Canmore. We had dinner with my friends Jeremy and Elle, and they took us on a nighttime walk afterward on a gravel trail up to the dam. "Stay close," said Jeremy. "If we see a bear, there's safety in numbers." A bear? We scoffed at him at first, but the farther we walked in the moonlight, surrounded by trees and hearing the occasional strange noise, the more we realized he wasn't joking. We stayed close and started speaking loudly, so we wouldn't surprise any animal lurking along the way, and we saw little but the dark forest and the darker shade of the mountain peaks.

Canmore is just outside the boundary of Banff National Park, and its animal population isn't protected as thoroughly as those within the park. Even so, just east of town, we'd driven under a bridge being built for wildlife to cross the Trans-Canada, similar to the one south of Sudbury. Until its construction, there had been no fence to keep animals away from the road, and no way for them to cross safely. In 2019, a truck hit a herd of elk on the highway here and killed seven of them; the previous month, another truck killed five elk near the same spot. Pressure from conservation advocates finally convinced the Alberta government to build the wildlife crossing and 12 kilometres of fencing to funnel animals into it at a cost of more than $17 million. At the time, the government estimated animal collisions on Alberta highways cost the province about $750,000 per year in health care and insurance, though some say that's a really low-ball figure. If a motorcyclist should hit an elk, for example, the rider could be killed, which changes the picture considerably. A human life is often valued by government and insurance agencies at about $10 million, which would go a long way to funding safe bridges for wildlife.

Just west of Canmore, Banff National Park is now the international model for how to build wildlife crossings. We drove under six of the graceful, rounded-arch bridges, with grass and trees growing on their tops, but didn't even notice the 38 underpasses beneath us, all fenced beside the highway for more than 80 kilometres. The first underpass was built in 1983, when the road was widened, to try to stop the meat-maker happening up on the asphalt, where more than 100 elk were killed every year by trucks and cars. That was just elk — it didn't account for the deer, bears, wolves, moose, cougars, coyotes, and bighorn sheep trying to follow their natural migration patterns. That Banff underpass copied some small crossings in Europe, where Dutch and French conservationists were trying to protect badgers and other wildlife, and a handful of crossings in the United States, including an underpass in Florida for alligators. In all those cases, the bridges and underpasses were just built and then everyone hoped for less roadkill. At Banff, researchers set up cameras to watch the comings and goings and see what worked and why. They rigged barbed wire and sticky string to collect hair samples. And they stayed at it for 17 years.

"With all those others, they built them but nobody monitored them. Nobody learned from them," researcher Tony Clevenger told me when I called him up later. "A lot of these transportation engineers, they won't build something unless there's proof that it works. Seriously. At Banff, we can see

A dedicated bridge helps wildlife travel safely across the Trans-Canada Highway.

it works, but the cherry on top is having the data to show for it: grizzly bears are using them, elk are using them, moose are using them. There's a nearby underpass that's four metres high, seven metres wide, and a lot of wildlife, we see their tracks in the snow and they walk right past it and they go right to the overpass."

For grizzlies, scientists now know that mother bears and their cubs will almost always use the bridges, while solitary male bears will almost always take the darker underpasses. Critics had believed some carnivores would use the bottleneck of a wildlife crossing to act as a prey trap for hunting, but Tony told me nothing of the sort has shown itself, probably because there are too many crossings as options.

Tony Clevenger is a wildlife biologist who was brought on from Montana State University in 1996 to monitor the crossings at Banff. The report for Parks Canada he co-authored in 2014 with Calgary zoologist Mirjam Barrueto is considered the Holy Grail of highway crossing research because it took the time to study generations of animals using the bridges and underpasses. It counted more than 150,000 animal crossings over 17 years. Highway collisions are now just a fifth of what they were, and that's because the animals' needs are accounted for to move around their traditional hunting and grazing and breeding grounds. The bridges are landscaped with trees and rocks and are now more densely wooded than before, as they've been left to grow in. Whether their users realize they're crossing a highway is up for debate, but over several generations, they've come to accept them as safe paths to the rest of the park.

"If you can't get the breeding females across the highway, you haven't mitigated the highway," said Tony. "That's what genetic connectivity is about — it's not getting the males back and forth to breed females on both sides, it's about getting the breeding females to cross. That was really important to discover — that if you're going to build crossings, you have to build overpasses for the breeding females." If you don't, and the bears are just kept in a huge fenced enclosure even many kilometres in size like a giant zoo, then genetic diversity suffers and the entire species begins to degrade.

I also called up Trevor Kinley, an environmental assessment scientist with Parks Canada's highway engineering services, for his take on the effect of the crossings:

> In the early days, we were looking at the monitoring and scratching our heads and saying, "Gee, there's not a lot of grizzly bears crossing this thing." But you have to think about it, and those underpasses were small and underneath four lanes. Those are long crossings, and if you put a fairly small structure over a long distance, it's like looking through a wrapping paper tube. There wasn't much use at all, so then the idea came up of why don't we build overpasses?
>
> There's been lots of research done, but this is a science that even though it's been around a few decades, it's still kind of in its infancy. I think in 20 or 30 years from now, we'll look back and think, my God, those guys were primitive! But we do know some things. We know bigger is better. You'll get more examples of more species on a larger structure.

But bridges usually cost more money. Then the question becomes: Is it worth it? In 2021, the Nevada Department of Transportation analyzed all the costs involved with a car hitting a deer on the road, including health care for human injuries like whiplash, damage to the vehicle, potential towing, and removal of the carcass. The average cost came out to more than US$8,000, which is almost $11,000 Canadian. Then there's the much higher cost of hitting a rarer bear or wolf: in Yellowstone, a grizzly bear is valued at several million dollars, thanks to its potential as a tourist draw. Clearly, wild animals and highways can be an expensive mix.

"A lot of the U.S. national parks, like Yellowstone, were established as far from — quote unquote — 'civilization' as they possibly could, but parks in Canada were the opposite," said Trevor. "They were intentionally put on transportation corridors — that was the whole point. There was some nice talk about conservation, but frankly, at the beginning, it was about getting tourists and developing less. That's why those parks existed. We've always had this interesting relationship with transportation because we're on these major highways."

But there's also the rail line. There's no fencing around train tracks, nor are there any wildlife bridges or underpasses. The animals don't damage the mighty trains, after all, which just plough through; the only evidence of a collision is the dead animal, and that's assuming it didn't crawl away to be unseen in the woods. At least trains are loud and arrive with plenty of warning, but bears are known to charge them, and that never turns out well. Trevor told me that at least 100 large animals are killed by trains every year in Banff National Park, and there's really nothing anyone can do about it. This science, it seems, is in its infancy.

It is, however, gaining attention. Tony is treated like a rock star at transportation conferences, and researchers hang on his every word. Banff "was a big part in convincing ministers of transportation and public works that these things are effective, and they exist," he told me. "I went down to Argentina and I went out with my friend Diego to see the first overpass built in Latin America for jaguars, because three or four jaguars were killed on this highway. When we walked over it, I asked Diego why this thing was built. And he said, because Banff had one. It's not just the scientific research, it's a mitigation complex you can't find anywhere else. Banff has become the symbol of a gold standard for wildlife crossing mitigation."

ALBERTA

It's a good feeling. Peter and I drove west on the wide Trans-Canada past Lake Louise, close to the border where we would cross from Alberta to British Columbia, and from Banff National Park into Kootenay National Park, and we passed beneath the last of the six wildlife bridges, with their graceful oval arches. Humans aren't allowed on the overpasses, but it was easy to imagine a man up there, standing proud in stage-show buckskins, looking down on the highway and knowing that at least a part of Canada had found its way at last.

LEGEND

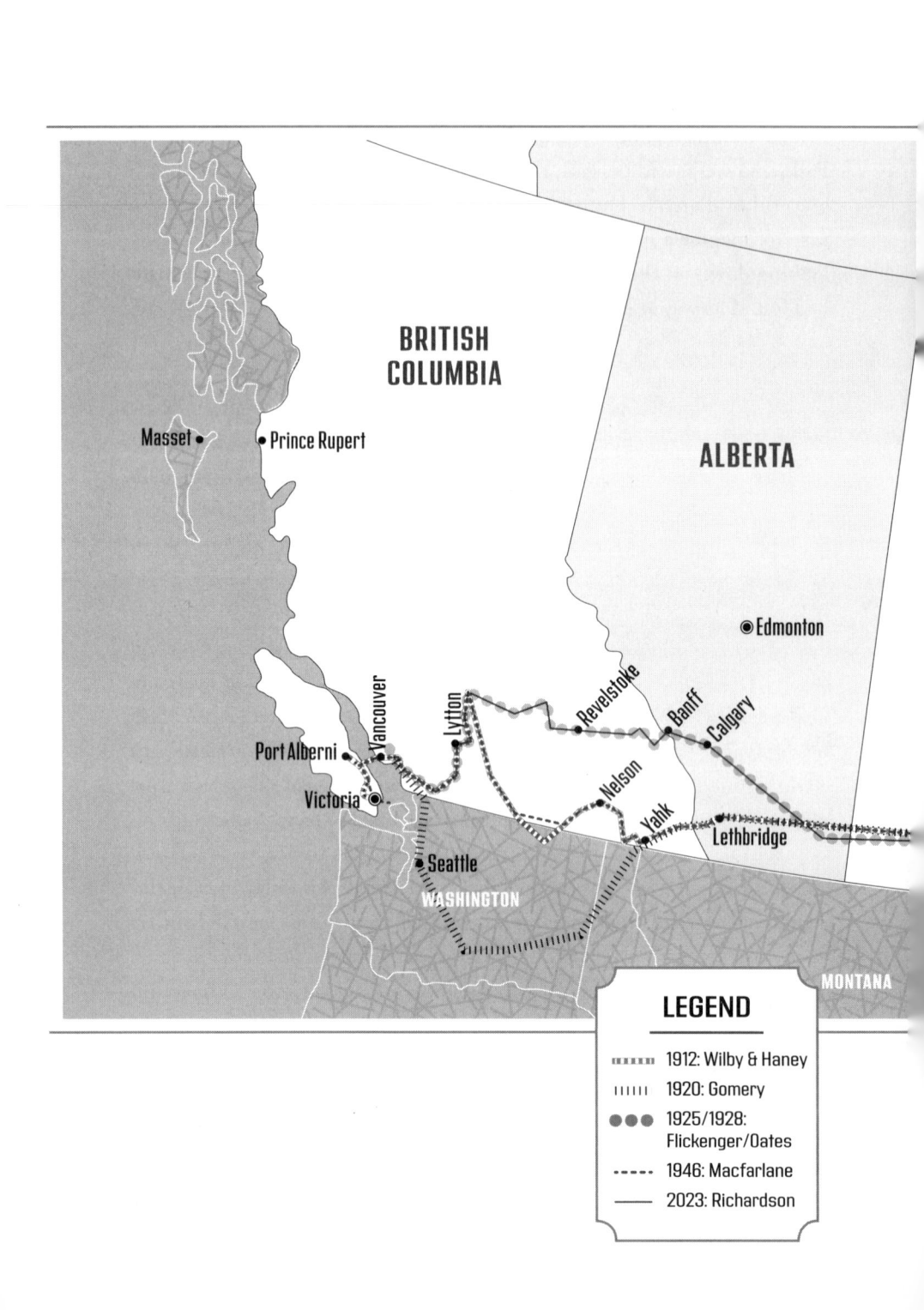

- ▪▪▪▪▪ 1912: Wilby & Haney
- ∣∣∣∣∣∣ 1920: Gomery
- ●●● 1925/1928: Flickenger/Oates
- ----- 1946: Macfarlane
- ——— 2023: Richardson

12

Mainland British Columbia

The original road on the Trans-Canada route to Banff was built from Calgary in 1914, intended as a tourist road to bring visitors to the park. It went into British Columbia nine years later, when it was extended down to Windermere through the newly created Kootenay National Park, and there it met the existing road back up through the Columbia Valley to Golden where the railway comes through. It was a southerly loop of more than 200 kilometres, hewn through the Sinclair Gap with pickaxes, shovels, and dynamite. Ed Flickenger's movie shows the Ford Model T bouncing along through the gap, beneath rock overhangs beside the river and over a rickety wooden bridge barely wide enough for the car before turning back north through the broad valley to Golden.

Jimmy Oates would have taken the new road to Golden over Kicking Horse Pass that opened in 1927. This is the highest point on the entire Trans-Canada Highway — at 1,627 metres, it's almost 300 metres higher than the famed Rogers Pass that's now a couple more hours to the west. Kicking Horse was a much more direct route, halving the distance between Banff and Golden; it used some of the old right of way laid down by the railway before that steep route was replaced by train tunnels through the mountains.

Those spiral tunnels were built in 1909 and became as much of an attraction for tourists as the mountains and the wildlife. Before the road came through, visitors to the park would get off the train and hike 12 kilometres south to watch another train enter the tunnel at Mount Ogden and then emerge 15 metres higher, curling around itself as it progressed through the 891-metre tunnel. This eliminated the steep grade of the original "Big Hill," more than 4 percent, which had needed extra locomotives to push the carriages uphill and brake them downhill, sometimes with a disastrous lack of success. There's a second tunnel a little farther east through Cathedral Mountain that's 100 metres longer, and which again loops over itself to bring the train out 17 metres higher than it entered and then on to the top of Kicking Horse Pass.

These days, there's a pull-off area from the Trans-Canada Highway where you can park and wait to watch for a train to come along and enter the Mount Ogden tunnel. Peter and I did so, and soon enough, a long train chugged through the forest beneath us and entered the tunnel on the far side of a wooded valley. When it came out again a few minutes later, from the other end of the tunnel just above, its tail was still going into the mountain with at least half the train yet to go. Peter loves trains and nerded out completely, and I must admit, it was both hypnotic and satisfying to watch. It was definitely one of Peter's highlights from our long journey.

We drove past Golden, barely noticing when we crossed a bridge high above the Kicking Horse River, and continued on to the pass. Some roadworks slowed us a few times, but we really had no appreciation of just what a challenge this highway was to build. When the Trans-Canada was young in the 1960s, the road was paved and serpentine as it followed the twists and turns of the mountainside, with the river far below, but it's been constantly widened and straightened since then, and now it's in its final stage of improvement to full, modern Trans-Canada standards. It's a $600 million project, with bridges over ridges and built literally on the side of the mountain, but little of this was apparent from the road itself. When I saw photos and videos later of the highway from drone cameras over the valley, I could barely believe it. It's a massive undertaking, now in its final phase, and almost drivers can do is moan about the waits at construction traffic lights.

The B.C. roads were rough going in 1920, and the Gomerys were having a tough time of it. Within a few minutes of leaving Alberta, they met a cowboy whose horse was spooked by their car — so it did happen, sometimes — and which threw its rider and smashed a headlight. The cowboy had ridden up the side of the hill to go around the Gomerys, who paused and then moved ahead slowly, but it was still too much for the animal. A little farther along, after a thunderstorm, Percy almost lost control on the narrow, slippery road; they were high above a river, and when everything began to lurch, they were so close to the edge that Bernadette leaped from her seat to hurl herself clear, but Percy caught it just in time. "I have always thought that the Skipper and I were nearer to death in those moments than at any other time in our lives," he wrote.

They were told the 30 kilometres of road over to Elko had 300 turns, and it was "smooth as braid and, like braid, it is narrow, and laid on the edges of things." Because events happen in threes, it was on that road they met a car coming toward them from around a blind corner driving on the wrong side. The B.C. interior had changed its rules only a few days earlier to switch cars from driving on the left to driving on the right, and the two vehicles hit head-on. (The Lower Mainland and Vancouver Island held out another 17 months before changing to the right, just to totally confuse the issue.) The passengers were mostly uninjured, though Bernadette cut her knee. They were lucky, of course — seat belts and crumple zones were unheard of. The oncoming car was wrecked, but Percy had his Maxwell fixed overnight for $120 (about $1,800 today), and the Gomerys were on their way the next morning.

The road improved for a while to Cranbrook before deteriorating into little more than a rough roller-coaster track, and they were relieved to make it to the American border at Kingsgate. There they crossed into the United States, and although "the Idaho roads ahead were unspeakably poor and rough," they remained south of the line until reaching the Pacific itself. We'll say goodbye to them for now.

Eight years earlier, Wilby, Haney, and Wise had similar adventures on the same route, and they even collected a fourth person, a fruit rancher who came along for the ride to Creston. The roller-coaster road, however, existed only as far south as the settlement of Ryan, halfway to the border, where it petered out into a swamp before reaching the railway community of Yahk. Undeterred, the Reo crew drove into the swamp just as night was falling, followed by a lighter local car that was there for guidance and support; they were anxious to meet with a team of horses ahead, arranged earlier, that would pull them from the mud when needed. The horses weren't there, though, and the two cars slithered along the path. "We were buried to the flanks in the slough," wrote Wilby, "and at times both cars sank to the hubs, listing heavily, grinding and ploughing their way, pounding the tyres to rags, while the engines roared and groaned and the wheels angrily shot the water in inky spindrift over men and trees."

They made it through to Yahk to find there was no road or path forward. The only way out of the settlement was on the railway, which cut west to the

Jack Haney fixes a flat tire somewhere in the woods of southern British Columbia.

road at Creston. It was nine o'clock by now and their guide told them there probably wouldn't be a train for the rest of the night. Probably. That was good enough for Wilby.

Whatever you might think of the guy, Thomas Wilby didn't want to give up on the drive. The four of them stiffened their upper lips and drove out to a crossing and onto the tracks. Haney settled the car with one pair of wheels inside the rails and the other outside, and they bumped along the ties for more than 20 kilometres, chewing up the rear tires on the spikes.

"There was a gasp as one felt the first forward plunge of the car and the white path of acetylene light shot before us into the immense shadows of that forest wilderness," wrote Wilby. "Four pairs of eyes strove to pierce the distance ahead and behind; and every nerve was strained in listening for a possible monster of steel and steam which might dash down upon us at any moment from around a curve or catch us in its swift career from behind! Muscles were tense, ready for the leap to a precarious safety at first sight of an approaching headlight."

Halfway to Creston, they reached a trail where they could leave the tracks and drive high above the railway until they finally arrived in town at three in the morning. "Lucky thing that we came over the tracks in the dark," Wilby writes that the fruit rancher told them afterward. "Those precipices are bad enough to look at from the train, but in daylight in a motor-car — Excuse me!"

Their motoring triumph was short-lived, however. Wilby's book breezes over the next few days, waxing on about the scenery while waning on the details. He doesn't say that they drove north beside the Kootenay River, where Haney found the horseshoe that I carried with me more than a century later in the Lexus. He doesn't describe the long ferry ride over Kootenay Lake to Nelson, where he was forced to put the Reo on a train to be shuttled 40 kilometres through the roadless mountains to Castlegar. And he most definitely doesn't mention that they then drove on the only road out of town, which took them down to the American border, where they had no choice but to cross and detour for 80 kilometres on the roads of Washington State before they could return to Canada and trek their way west to Princeton. You know they all did their damnedest to avoid this, but in 1912, it was unavoidable. The road just didn't exist yet and wouldn't for at least another decade.

◻

Ten years after Wilby and Haney, the City of Victoria offered its own gold medal to the first car to make the drive from Edmonton to Victoria under its own power, using the northern Yellowhead Pass. The most uncertain stretch was through the mountains between Jasper and Kamloops, and on June 17, 1922, an Overland car sponsored by the Edmonton Automobile Club set out to claim the prize. Its drivers, Charley Niemeyer and Frank Silverthorne, followed an abandoned railway track west to Jasper where they met up with P.A. "Baldy" Robb, "a well-known mountain guide," and then bumped their way through to Kamloops on a variety of supply roads and railway lines, both abandoned and active. They cut back the brush and built three dozen bridges along the way.

"They drove their car on the railroads around curves and along precipices where the variation of a hair would have thrown them hundreds of feet to their death," reported the *Ottawa Journal*. "The car wheels straddled the rails, the outer wheel being on the outer edge of the ties. The ties in many instances were projecting out over a yawning space which fell straight to the roaring river hundreds of feet below." At one point, they met an oncoming train: "They were proceeding on the steel toward a tunnel and had not been notified of an extra train. It came belching out just before they reached the entrance. The driver swung off and against a pile of rocks, bending an axle, jarring his friend, but permitting the train free passage."

The following week, another car set out from Edmonton. It was a much lighter Ford, not weighed down by the tools and supplies of the Overland, driven by George Gordon and James Sims. They followed the same route as Niemeyer and Silverthorne, driving over their newly constructed bridges and through their freshly cleared tracks, and both expeditions arrived on the same day in Kamloops. The Overland stayed with the railways and supply roads and pushed on through British Columbia, while the Ford hustled south on rudimentary highways to cross the border into Washington State.

Gordon and Sims would have reached Victoria first, but they missed the final ferry out of Washington, were delayed almost 24 hours, and arrived in Victoria later on the same day. All five of the motorists were exhausted, with the drivers' hands swollen and blistered from manhandling the steering wheels over the ties and ridges. In the end, the city awarded medals to both cars.

Two years later, a pair of young American adventurers drove through to Victoria from Winnipeg, winning the medal Bert Todd had sponsored years before. E.S. Evans was a pilot and wealthy industrialist, while Austin Bement was an advertising man about to start his own agency with the Packard Motor Car Company as his main client. They were both from Detroit and streaked west from Winnipeg at 80 kilometres per hour in a sponsored Packard 226 — it had recently rained and the gumbo roads were freshly graded and now dry, so they were smooth and hard as concrete. The two men were members of the Lincoln Highway Association, promoting the road that crossed between New York City and San Francisco. They wanted to encourage a Trans-Canada Highway as the upper half of a touring loop across the continent and told anyone who would listen that the previous year, more than 150,000 cars had driven on the Lincoln Highway between California and east of the Mississippi River. The two men saw all kinds of prospects for automobile tourism; mostly, they wanted to win the gold medal.

The rules allowed them to drive under their own power on railway tracks — though official permission was now required after the near-miss with the Overland expedition — but they made their way by road over the mountains through Princeton and up to the Fraser Valley before resorting to the rails. "Out of the 264 miles that we motored through the Fraser canyon from Boothroyd, BC, to Hope, BC, I walked at least 125," Evans told the *Victoria Daily Times*. Put aside the math that the actual distance between the towns at the time was 63 miles, or about 100 kilometres, and instead sympathize that the men fitted flanged train wheels to drive on the rails but the gauge didn't fit properly and the car derailed at every curve. After less than two kilometres, they put the rubber tires back on and bumped their way slowly along the ties through 17 tunnels and over 150 trestles. I'm sure it seemed considerably farther than it was. "With four passengers, two railroad men having been picked up as aides, and 600 pounds of baggage, the car carried more than a normal good roads load during two days of the most severe treatment to which an automobile could be subjected," reported the *Manitoba Free Press*. At one point, they made it through a tunnel just four minutes before the train arrived.

The two men were awarded the medal by Bert Todd himself at a luncheon in Victoria and took it home to Detroit to present to Packard executives. They relished their success and the attention it garnered: Austin Bement opened his own Packard dealership in New Rochelle, New York, and E.S. Evans went on to set the record in 1926 for the fastest circumnavigation of the world, circling the globe by air, road, and rail in 28 days, a full week quicker than the previous holder.

In fact, the first person to drive across British Columbia from Alberta, staying entirely within Canada and not using railway tracks (though taking an 80-kilometre lake ferry), was Perry Doolittle in September 1926. He was the founder of the Canadian Automobile Association and "Mr. Trans-Canada Highway" himself, who had driven Ed Flickenger's Ford Model T on the rails of the Quebec City bridge the previous year. The road was now built from Yahk and from Nelson, all the way through to Princeton and up to Lillooet. The only portion not driven on the road was the long ferry ride to and from Nelson along the length of Kootenay Lake; the final road that links Nelson to Creston to avoid the ferry wouldn't be finished for many years, not until 1963 after the opening of the Trans-Canada Highway itself. Doolittle was successful because his hard-earned reputation preceded him: he was allowed to drive on the road beside the Fraser Canyon before it was officially opened the following year. That was the last stretch of highway that needed completion to avoid any transport by rail.

To make his point about how viable the new road was, Doolittle drove alone from Banff to Vancouver in five days, then drove back to Calgary and up to Edmonton for the annual meeting of the Canadian Good Roads Association. He admitted it was a strenuous journey: he dodged fallen rocks on the mountain roads, drove for hours over washboard ruts, and at one point pressed through 25 centimetres of fresh snow that needed tire chains. But he made it regardless. As a route between Calgary and Vancouver, however, it wouldn't catch on until 1949 when the much more direct highway was opened between Princeton and Hope. This cut more than 300 kilometres from the driving distance that no longer needed to loop all the way up to Lillooet. Before then, it still made much more sense for most motorists to cross over into Idaho or Washington for the faster American roads.

"The coming Trans-Canada road doesn't mean a direct highway in a straight line," said Doolittle. "It will be made up of many routes, all interconnected." It was always expected to travel through the central mountains, and in 1928, work crews began chipping away at the missing link between Golden and Revelstoke. The simplest road followed the looping Columbia River as it flowed north from Golden for about 150 kilometres, turned on a hairpin, and then flowed back south for the same distance to Revelstoke. The provincial government paid for construction in the west valley, while the federal government funded construction in the east valley, and when everything was hastened by the coming Second World War, the two crews met at the top in October 1939. The Big Bend Highway was 300 lonely kilometres of three-season dirt blasted through dense forest and solid rock, and after it opened to motorists the following summer, it was pronounced a marvel of engineering. Motorists, however, thought differently. That August, a reader of the *Albertan* wrote:

> The "marvel of engineering" … must apply to the marvel of how so many potholes and so many rocks protruding from the worn road bed could possibly have asserted themselves in so new a road in so short a time.
>
> The vibration of continuous pounding and bumping for a hundred and ninety odd miles from Golden, going west, and the narrow winding road, with sharp bends and hardly sufficient straight-a-way at any point to enable one to pass a slow car in safety (and believe me there were hundreds of them crawling gingerly along with anxious and nerve-wracked faces of drivers and passengers) is what

so many are complaining of and the reason why so many dread the return journey from the coast.

It was clear to everyone that the Big Bend was merely a stopgap. The true Trans-Canada would have to be a much more direct, all-weather paved road. There were still those who wanted it to take the northerly Yellowhead route across the Prairies, past Saskatoon and Edmonton, before dropping down through the mountains to Vancouver, but the route we know today won out in 1956. The decision was made to send the highway through the Selkirk Range and over Rogers Pass, following the route of the national railway.

That wouldn't be easy. The 1,323-metre pass was deadly, with 10 metres of snowfall every year that could tumble down its slopes at any time. Sixty-two men were killed in 1910 when they were buried by an avalanche as they tried to clear the way for a train that was itself blocked by snow; it's still remembered as Canada's worst railway loss of life. "The snow got a hold of me and what it didn't do to me. Why, it done everything," recalled survivor Bill LaChance, a fireman on the snowplough train. "It pulled me out twice my length the way it felt, and then it just doubled me all up and rolled me." This

The Big Bend Highway quickly gained a reputation as a bone-jarring nightmare for motorists.

came only three days after a pair of trains in the Washington State Cascades were swept into a canyon by an avalanche and another 96 people were killed. The tragedies were the last straw for the CPR, which gave up on the line it built over the pass and spent the money to drill an eight-kilometre tunnel straight through the mountain instead. When the Connaught opened in 1916, it was the longest tunnel in North America.

Highway engineers, however, weren't so deterred. Most of the road was in Glacier National Park, which meant its construction was well funded with federal dollars, and some of it could follow that original railway. Much of the challenge was in learning how to control the deadly slides of snow. Earth mounds were placed strategically on the slopes above the highway where the snowpack can routinely be more than three metres deep — if the snow slips, the mounds will break it up and dissipate it. Dikes were dug to direct avalanches into safe areas. Scientists skied to multiple sites daily to analyze the snow for its density, temperature, and water content, developing an expertise in forecasting when an avalanche might be close. When that happened, the Canadian Army fired a howitzer cannon at the snowpack, triggering small, easily controlled slides. As the highway began to take shape, snowsheds were constructed in selected areas that acted like tunnels to protect the highway, so any avalanche would slide over the top of the road and safely down into the valley below. The highway over Rogers Pass took five years to build and cost $40 million, which would be more than $400 million today, but it was the final direct link, and when it was finished, the highway was ready to open.

☐

The federal government announced in early July 1962 that the Trans-Canada Highway would be declared open with a ceremony at Rogers Pass in September. It wouldn't be complete — there were still plenty of roads to bring up to standard and even construct, notably in Quebec and Newfoundland — but the route would be navigable by the average motorist between Victoria and St. John's. It took a half century of work, but for John Diefenbaker's Progressive Conservatives it was a triumph, and when British

Columbia's premier, W.A.C. Bennett, learned of the ceremony, he wanted a piece of the glory. So he announced his own ceremony for the end of July when B.C. Highway 1 would be opened nearby at Revelstoke.

Federal engineers stated the highway's snowsheds wouldn't be ready for motorists on the planned opening day of July 30, and they warned the road would be immediately closed again, but the provincial government called their bluff and went ahead anyway. Buses would bring spectators to the site on the highway 13 kilometres east of Revelstoke, and on the day itself, which was declared a public holiday in town, some 250 invited dignitaries attended a lunch and then travelled out to the site. Only a half-dozen low-level federal officials accepted their invitations. Traffic, however, was nuts. Cars were lined up almost to Revelstoke waiting to cross, and at the other end of the pass, in Golden, police opened the road four hours earlier to allow cars to come through from the east. The Feds waited until that day to confirm the highway would remain open after all and motorists streamed in to experience it. Some 5,000 cars were estimated to be lined up at the big blue ribbon on both sides facing both directions, their passengers waiting in the 35-degree heat for it to be cut by Bennett and Gordon Taylor, Alberta's highways minister. The event was hosted by Phil Gaglardi, British Columbia's highways minister, a man who could never resist an audience. Speeches were made. "It's your highway," Gaglardi told the crowd. "You paid for it. Now enjoy it!" Eight people fainted from the heat. The ribbon was snipped at three o'clock and the cars drove through and were still crossing bumper to bumper hours later. Three cars collided near the top of the pass and two of them had to be towed away.

A week or so later, 7,000 kilometres to the east, a dozen cars dipped their wheels in the Atlantic Ocean at St. John's and began driving across the country on the not-quite-opened Trans-Canada Highway. There was a car to represent each of the provinces, one for Canada, and the final car carried the press. The road across Newfoundland, of course, was far from complete: one of the participants called it "a dusty, unfinished endurance contest pitting car springs against nature," but the convoy made it through to Vancouver in four leisurely weeks, in time to turn back east and join the prime minister's ceremony at Rogers Pass on September 3.

Everybody turned up on time for the one o'clock event, including the Regimental Band of the Princess Patricia's Canadian Light Infantry, which was to play a medley of Canadian folk tunes appropriate to each province as their coats of arms were unveiled on the $25,000 monument beside the highway. As many as 3,000 people were present in chairs and on bleachers and just standing to watch the proceedings. They had no trouble reaching the site on the warm, sunny day; at least 100,000 cars were estimated to have already crossed Rogers Pass in the month since the B.C. premier opened the road. Just as at the opening of the Canso Causeway to Cape Breton seven years before, everyone was in a good mood, and the snowcapped majesty of Cheops Mountain and Mount Macdonald made for a stunning backdrop. Not everyone was there, however: only five provinces accepted their invitations to send their highways ministers. Quebec and Manitoba sent their deputy ministers, Prince Edward Island sent a member of its legislature, and both Newfoundland and New Brunswick sent nobody. Newfoundland's minister of provincial affairs said the province didn't want any motoring tourists because its highway just wasn't ready, and New Brunswick "found it difficult to spare a person at this time."

The ceremony went on without them. And went on. And went on. It didn't help that the truck carrying the band's instruments got lost and turned up late, so the Princess Pats stood mute while a lone bagpiper piped in Prime Minister John Diefenbaker. It also didn't help that 14 different dignitaries seized the moment to make speeches, some of them rambling and at times nonsensical. The Saskatchewan minister told the crowd how much he'd enjoyed "travelling on the highway here in Quebec," and British Columbia's effusive Gaglardi told them, "I want to thank God personally today for the beautiful weather he has given us."

The prime minister finally stepped up half an hour late to unveil the provincial plaques and then took the microphone to address the assembled crowd. "This ceremony marks another step in the completion of the dreams of the fathers of confederation," he said. "The dreams of a united and growing Canada that will move forward in faith that Canada's destiny will be even greater and that it will remain an independent nation." Stirring words indeed, which nobody at the ceremony heard because Diefenbaker had grabbed a microphone for a radio station instead of for the public address system. Then he placed the last shovel load of asphalt into a freshly cut hole in the smoothly paved road, tamped it down, and declared the Trans-Canada Highway open.

"In the event," wrote District Supervisor Jim Webb in his memoir *Tales of a Highwayman*, "the band did get their instruments in time for a tune or two as the last of the succulent roast beef was being polished off by the hungry guests. But the conducting and playing were uninspired; I could see their hearts weren't in it."

In 1962, the federal government estimated the highway cost $700 million in new construction, of which Ottawa paid $450 million, and the total cost was closer to $1 billion when improvements to existing roads were

Prime Minister John Diefenbaker declared the Trans-Canada Highway open at the Rogers Pass in 1962, though hundreds of thousands of motorists had already driven on it over the mountains.

included. But that wasn't the end of it. "Today's official opening does not mean that the Trans-Canada Highway is completed," wrote the *Globe and Mail*. "It's actual completion date is scheduled for Dec. 31, 1963." Wishful thinking, indeed.

☐

The monument is still at the original picnic area on top of the pass, and Peter and I pulled over to look at it. It's two parabolic wooden arches of Douglas fir within a low circular stone wall that holds plaques for each province; one arch symbolizes the joining of Canada through Confederation, while the other represents the union through road and rail. A wooden box hangs from the arch and displays plaques on each of its four sides, telling the story of the highway and the railway and listing the dignitaries invited to the ceremony — half of whom weren't actually there. A family walked their dog nearby, and several others wandered over to read the plaques in the 20 minutes we hung around. When I'd come this way in 2012 with my son, Tristan, we stayed much longer. It was on my birthday, 50 years to the day since Premier W.A.C. Bennett opened the road three hours after I was born. The CBC had arranged for me to chat with numerous radio hosts across the country for their afternoon shows, and I sat in the car and answered the same half-dozen questions, trying with dubious success to explain the difference between the official openings on July 30 and September 3. Cell reception was poor at the top of the pass and some of the calls dropped off, including my live chat with the station in Prince Edward Island. There was a hotel there at the top, and I got us a room with a phone for the rest of the interviews, but the building was gone in 2023. Literally gone. It was closed a few years ago and demolished so you would never know it existed. I stood at the site with Peter and wondered how long it would take the mountains to reclaim the highway here if mankind suddenly disappeared. Not too long, I figured.

☐

THE DRIVE ACROSS CANADA

The monument for the Trans-Canada Highway, at the site of its opening on the Rogers Pass, is made from a pair of wooden arches that symbolize the joining of Canada.

Copious snow still falls over the Selkirks every winter, and the Trans-Canada here is kept open by the world's largest mobile artillery avalanche control program. Technicians dig deep pits at high elevations to analyze the snow, usually skiing over to numerous sites, and their information helps forecasters to predict the likelihood of avalanches. If necessary, the Canadian Army fires off guns to trigger small, controlled snowslides on any of more than 100 sculpted paths. Parks Canada employs a senior avalanche officer to direct soldiers with the Royal Canadian Horse Artillery, who move 105 mm C3 howitzer cannons to any of 17 different positions along the Trans-Canada, where they fire shells at defined trigger zones to set off the slides, shooting at snow up to five kilometres away. On average, they do this 20 times in a season, and the Trans-Canada is closed for up to a couple of hours each occasion. The Parks Canada website estimates it costs the Canadian economy more than $68,000 for every hour the highway must be closed. This avalanche control is known as Operation Palaci, and the same Parks Canada website says it's the longest-running Canadian Forces operation, domestic or expeditionary, in Canadian history.

Peter and I saw nothing of this, of course — snow can fall at any time of the year at such altitudes, but the day was warm for us in the Lexus. It was the same for Edward McCourt in 1963, who wrote, "No doubt the Rogers Pass Highway was fantastically difficult to build, but it is child's play for even the timidest tourist to drive."

☐

At Revelstoke, you can still travel north on the road that used to be the Big Bend Highway. It's paved and smooth now and takes you to the Mica Dam, two hours away, but it ends there and it's known as "the road to nowhere." There was no need to maintain the Big Bend after Rogers Pass was opened, and most of the eastern leg of the road was flooded by Kinbasket Lake when the dam was built in 1973. Peter and I were headed west, though, where the highway narrows and becomes squeezed in the Eagle River Valley. There's a plan to widen and even twin the Trans-Canada all the way through to Kamloops, but "I've heard that plan for the last 40 years," said Gary Sulz, the mayor of Revelstoke, when I met him in his office. It was just a few weeks before he planned to retire as the local funeral director. He said he was acutely aware of the dangers of an inadequate highway that's busy with truck traffic.

"I'm the guy who gets to go out to the accidents to bring in the deceased," he said. "There's nothing worse than getting called out at Christmastime for a motor vehicle accident, and pulling a family of children out of a car who have died because the road wasn't cleaned, or they didn't have the right tires, or there were transport trucks on the road that just slid into each other."

Gary blamed much of the road's carnage on heavy truck traffic, and on the poorly trained or unlicensed drivers who stay out too long on the highway to meet deadlines and targets. It's more than 200 kilometres to Kamloops and much of that Trans-Canada Highway is two-lane road. Cyclists avoid it. There's nowhere for those trucks to go when they slide out on a corner, or when a car underestimates the distance needed to safely pass.

"Back in the day," he told me, "we thought this highway was quite an engineering feat, but now, we look at it and it's just a two-lane road."

What's the solution? Often, the road here is narrow because there's a tall mountain on one side and a river or lake on the other. Where to put the extra lanes? I called the B.C. Department of Highways to ask why they don't just blast tunnels through everything, as the Europeans do. The department's chief engineer told me it all comes down to money, and a tunnel can easily cost two or three times as much as an exposed road. These days, with modern safety standards, any tunnel that's more than 250 metres must have sophisticated ventilation, access to electricity, water for fire suppression, and escape routes. It must also be within reach of a fire department, and all those things combine to make it expensive.

"In Europe, they have a lot of people living in a small geographic area, so their tax base is much higher than ours," said Ian Pilkington, talking over the phone from his office in Kamloops. "We're a relatively small population in a very vast province. The only European country that's kind of comparable to us would be Norway, but their oil revenues are starting to dry up and they're thinking they can't just build tunnels everywhere anymore. They've actually been coming and starting to ask us about how we do this work in this mountainous terrain without tunnels."

Not only are tunnels costly, but British Columbia's shifting tectonic plates tend to fracture the rock, which means it might need to be reinforced with expensive liners if the tunnel is to be stable. It can be done — it's just a question of how much the government is prepared to spend, and normally it's cheaper to blast away a rock wall or skirt over the top of a lake.

These days, said Ian, any new highway also has to take future climate change into account to cope with floods and fires. It also needs to be sensitive to the cultural nature of the land. "We're engaging the First Nations communities well in advance in anything we do, and they're becoming a partner in our designs," he told me. "This is something new to us. As designers we always just think of the technical side of what the issue is, but now we're thinking about the cultural side and trying to understand how this impacts our First Nations communities. This is a new world that we've never dealt with before. Way back when, we kind of ploughed our way through the province without asking where these things are, or if they're logical where they are, so that's a huge part of our decision-making process now that we've really embraced."

The original Trans-Canada route certainly never considered any part of Canada's Indigenous heritage, aside from bringing tourists to gawk at the "natives." An even worse cultural transgressor, of course, was the railway, which linked Canada as a nation but was oblivious to the First Nations ownership of the land it tracked across.

The site of the Last Spike at Craigellachie is just a half-hour west of Revelstoke, right beside the Trans-Canada Highway, and Peter and I stopped to see it. Nowadays, it's a gift shop and a large stone cairn, right beside the working railway line. Peter bought train souvenirs, and I studied the famous photo on display of Sir Donald Smith in 1885, driving home the Last Spike of the Canadian Pacific Railway to declare the track open across the nation. He's surrounded by men in hats, but I won't retell the well-recounted story here. It offends me, because of the abuse of the 17,000 Chinese workers who were essential to build the railway, none of whom are in the photograph.

□

The road twists and turns gently past Shuswap Lake to Kamloops and then most traffic heads south on the wide Coquihalla Highway. From here on, if you take the Coq, the route is twinned all the way to the Pacific. It's an easy four hours to Vancouver in good weather, though in bad weather, it might be 15 minutes of fame on *Highway Thru Hell*. The Trans-Canada doesn't take this route, however. It stays west to travel between the rolling grassy hills of desert country, following the wide Thompson River Valley to Cache Creek, before turning south toward the Fraser River. It lets the heavy trucks take the fast, twinned route down the Coq and instead becomes a less-frenetic tourist road, popular with RVs and touring motorcycles, as well as pickup trucks for the residents.

Wilby, Haney, and Wise came through this area in the Reo, slogging up from Princeton some 200 kilometres to the south, in order to loop back down through the Fraser Canyon. Ed Flickenger left the railway tracks before Revelstoke, then drove this way. There's movie footage of the Model T meeting a pair of cowboys in "the last vestige of the penny novel west," according to the title card, and the horses don't seem bothered in the least by the car. The engine was likely shut down while Flickenger worked the camera from over by the fence. The road seems to grow more narrow and higher above the river, becoming a single-lane track, before the Ford stopped at Spences Bridge to put on its steel railway wheels for the last time. The road through the canyon wouldn't be driven until the following year, when Perry Doolittle took it while still under construction.

In 1928, Jimmy Oates probably came this way, too, though his final route is uncertain. His original journal is lost, and all we know is from newspaper reports and the selected journal pages of his biographer's book, *Aurora to Ariel: The Motorcycling Exploits of J. Graham Oates.* We do know that he rode between the railway tracks through the Connaught Tunnel to Revelstoke, so he surely then followed the Fraser Canyon south, as Doolittle did, since it was still the only available road to the coast. Perhaps he went back onto the railway, but probably not. Almost any road was preferable to constant rhythmic pounding on the track ties.

Even Alex Macfarlane and Ken MacGillivray sped north from Grand Forks, near the American border, on the long loop up to Spences Bridge before heading south again to Vancouver. "We had intended to go from Princeton to Hope but our road map was more hopeful than exact, for the road it showed was not built," Macfarlane wrote in his journal.

The GPS was accurate for Peter and me, though when it brought us down the valley to Lytton, it didn't show that the village was completely and utterly destroyed.

□

We arrived at Lytton the day before the two-year anniversary of the community's destruction. A fire swept through in the afternoon of June 30, 2021, and burned most of the 100 or so homes to the ground. Two people were killed and everyone was affected in some way, including the 2,000 First Nations residents who lived on nearby Indigenous land. Its main street leaves the Trans-Canada to head through the village before crossing the river to the First Nations reservation and then on up to Lillooet, but everything was fenced off. Almost nothing existed of the buildings I remembered from pausing here with Tristan: the restaurant, the bank, the museum. All now was just flat gravel behind tall wire fencing. Construction trailers were dotted around, but nobody seemed to be working anywhere. The place was empty. It was hot — and eerie.

It was much hotter in the days leading up to the fire. For three days, Lytton recorded the highest temperatures ever seen in Canada, peaking at an official 49.6 degrees Celsius. That's in the shade. "There was a boil water advisory happening," resident Melanie Delva told me when I spoke to her later. "I remember trying to stay cool and still boil water. My goal was to keep the temperature below 30 degrees. I'd found what felt like the last inflatable kiddy pool in all of Canada, and I'm 41 years old, but I blew that thing up and I set it out on the front lawn and I sat in there, then went in and boiled water. It was the cycle."

On the afternoon of June 30, Melanie and her wife, Erin, were inside their rented house, lying on the hardwood floor, trying to stay cool. Blackout curtains kept out the sun, and blankets hung over the porch for extra shade. It was noisy in the dark room. A friend lent them a portable air conditioner the day before that didn't quite fit in the window, and it rattled and raged without respite, while helicopters dropped constantly down to the river a few hundred metres away to scoop water to drop on the fires burning in the forest. They were scrolling Facebook on their phones when a train passed on the tracks close behind their house, and its horn honked more than usual. Melanie saw a just-posted Facebook video of a train nearby on fire. Erin got up, opened the blinds, and saw flames everywhere — their house was already on fire. At the same time, Melanie, still checking her phone, spotted a live video of their house burning with flames on all sides. The two women opened the front door and saw fire at their propane tank, between them and their truck. They escaped out the back, grabbing only their small dog, Dexter, and a box of paperwork.

"I remember the sound," said Melanie. "It was just this unbelievable roar mixed with screaming. I don't know that a day will come when I don't hear that sound. When we went into the bedroom, there was fire at all the windows and I could hear the flames crackling in the walls and the ceiling, and there was smoke coming from all the outlets. We ran out to the truck, checked our neighbours, and got out of there. I remember, we turned down an alley and there was just smoke and we couldn't see a thing. That was the only time I was scared. I thought we might get stuck. We had to throw it in reverse, but couldn't see a thing."

They drove the hour up to Lillooet, where nobody yet knew Lytton had burned, before following backroads to Merritt, where they found other evacuees and a hotel room. "We went to Walmart and bought pajamas and dog food and shampoo," said Melanie. "We had ashes on our faces and were covered in soot. I still had debris in my hair. Parts of the house were in my hair."

I also spoke on the phone with Denise O'Connor, Lytton's mayor. Like I said, it seemed as if nobody was at home that day we drove through. In any case, there were few homes to be at. "The reality is, they didn't even start removing the debris until June of last year," she said. "I don't know why. I keep saying that someday, there's going to be an investigation or an audit or something, and the story will come out about why everything's taking so long."

Not everything was burned, though. In the centre of town, the Church of St. Barnabas still stood next to its village hall. It was surrounded by flattened gravel, but there was the Anglican church, its low shingled roof intact. Green trees and bushes grew in its garden. The day after we came through, the hall hosted a lunch after a blessing ceremony for the rebuild, the first gathering since the fire. The parish minister, Reverend Angus Muir, told me later the church's survival was helped by the asphalt street at its front, which acted as a firebreak, though other buildings on its side of the street were gone. "Even though there was some fire between the rectory and the church that burned the grass and whatnot, and burned a post off, it didn't burn the church because it's cement and stucco. But it's amazing they survived, for sure."

St. Barnabas may have survived, but the area's other churches burned to the ground. It seemed to me, standing in the hot sun looking at the grey, flattened area that was once a green and vibrant town, that the whole place was cursed. This wasn't the first fire Lytton's experienced, and just up the road, Cache Creek was still digging out from a spring flood that swept away half its downtown. Twenty minutes down the road, the village of Boston Bar was almost decimated a few months after the fire when an atmospheric river took out the Trans-Canada — and much of the lower mainland east of Vancouver — and its residents were isolated for weeks. No highway. No train. Medical services were supplied by helicopter, which was the only way to reach the place. So why on earth live there?

I asked the question of Melanie, who left the hotel in Merritt, after just two weeks, to return to the area. She and Erin set up a borrowed camper on the river just south of the village and lived there for three months before moving onto the nearby reservation. Melanie was born in Manitoba, but Erin is Nlaka'pamux and born there. Even so, they could live anywhere in Canada. Clearly, I wasn't the only person to ask this question:

> So many people said to us, why did you go back? The fire wasn't even out. What the fuck were you thinking? The one thing that Indigenous folks have taught me is that when God gives you to a place — not when God gives a place to you — that place is family. And just because your relative gets raped, or just because your relative goes through trauma and gets hurt and damaged, you don't leave that relative. You don't abandon that relative. We've been given to this place. My wife's people have been given to this place. I'm not speaking for the other non-Indigenous folks. I'm speaking as a person who's married into the Nlaka'pamux nation and who's learned what it means to be a relative to this place, and who's still learning to be a relative to this place.
>
> So climate change and climate disaster and human ignorance and human stupidity have raped and damaged our relatives. We don't abandon our relatives because they're abused by others. And this is our place. We know this place. This place has rivers that feed us. It has fields of wild food. I give offerings, sometimes parts of my hair, or tobacco, before I take from it. This place loves us and

feeds us. The fire? That's not the land. That's not the place. That's humanity's ignorance. So we don't blame the place for that. We love this place.

☐

If there's anywhere that will make an atheist believe in God, it's British Columbia. The mountains reaching to the sky; the sheer force of the elements. At Hells Gate, the narrowest point of the Fraser Canyon, twice as much water pours through the narrow gorge at its spring peak as over the wide Niagara Falls. The Fraser River isn't something to be trifled with. Simon Fraser knew that when he made his way through in 1808: he had to sometimes walk beside the sheer cliff wall on short planks suspended above the torrent, placed there by the Indigenous people who knew to respect the land.

In 1863, pioneers built a wagon trail along the cliffs above the water, blasting away at the canyon walls before the land flattened out to the north, creating a supply route to the goldfields in British Columbia's central Cariboo region. The trail was narrow and dangerous, sometimes suspended over the river, but it was the only way through, and when the railway was built after the gold rush, it took over much of the route of the Cariboo Road. The way wasn't driveable until Perry Doolittle's new road went through in 1926, higher up the cliffs.

"Picture yourself driving an automobile around the edge of a building 155 stories in height, with no railing to guard you," Doolittle told the *Toronto Star* upon his return. "Well, that's the impression you would get … away up there on a road where no cars would pass you, with no hint of a guard rail or wall along the edge that seemed to drop clear to the bottom of things, and with a straight up wall on the other side from which crumbling stones bounced from time to time, sometimes threatening to come through the roof of the car or puncture the gas tank."

Twenty years later, the drive was no less spectacular. "I've driven about a million miles, and that is the toughest mental hazard I've yet met," wrote Alex Macfarlane. "The road is a one-way strip and narrow.... Down there somewhere about 4,000 feet below, the Fraser River was foaming along, but as I was driving I left Ken MacGillivray to watch the scenery and concentrated entirely on the job at hand. In an occasional glance at him, I saw that with that careful flyer's eye, he was picking out the likely spots where the distant river seemed a bit smoother. They are good roads all right, but when you've been driving along a shelf of rock half a mile or more above nowhere, you find yourself beginning to wonder if it wouldn't be a good idea to forget the cost and make them just a bit wider."

That stretch of road, actually about 800 feet above the river, didn't exist in 1912, and Wilby was forced to send the Reo on a train to the south end of the canyon. He knew it was too far to risk driving on the rails again. Until reaching Lytton, though, he, Haney, and Wise had given it a damn good try to make it through. They travelled on the wider Cariboo Road, pulling over for wagon trains hauled by teams of 10 or 12 horses, until the road grew narrower and darkness fell. And then the gas tank for their headlights ran dry:

> We had still ten more miles to shelter, but our big acetylene lamps went out, leaving us in total darkness on a dangerous curve. We pulled up, lit the lamps again and crept onward. Once more the lights went out; the gas in the cylinder was exhausted. To advance without lights meant certain death, and our small oil lamps were next to useless, being hung too high above the roadway to give us a view of the dangerous ledge.
>
> The situation was desperate. We could not camp there, nor could we apparently progress until daylight, since to walk ahead with our feeble light only served to increase the danger of a fall over the precipice.
>
> It was the extra driver from Saskatchewan who finally came to the rescue. Taking one of the oil lamps, he stretched himself at full length along the mudguard next to the outer edge of the road, reached out his arm so as to bring the lamp close to the ground, and boldly gave the signal: "Go ahead!"

Ten miles on one's stomach, holding a light over a sheer drop of hundreds of feet is a devilishly unpleasant *rôle*! Inch by inch we crept on. Moment by moment the poor fellow grew stiffer. A sudden jolt and it seemed as if we must throw him down the bank. A flicker of the light, and it seemed as if we all, car and passengers, were already over the brink. We were incessantly rounding a series of bluffs, twisting and turning in short, sharp curves that shut out the road ahead. Conversation languished. The unfortunate man progressing on his stomach gave vent to his emotions only in occasional grunts.

They reached Lytton, had dinner with some rowdy Swedes, and went to bed. "Got stuck with an empty gas tank and had to drive 15 miles in to Lytton without lights, over dangerous roads," wrote Haney in his diary before turning in. I really don't blame them shipping the car south on the train.

☐

It's an easy drive now, of course. The two-lane road passes through trees at Jackass Mountain, and there's little sensation of being high above the river. There are only occasional glimpses of Hells Gate Canyon 240 metres below. At Hope, at the far end of the canyon where the Coquihalla Highway and even the southern road from Princeton join the Trans-Canada and the faster traffic resumes, the last couple of hours of highway to Vancouver seem anticlimactic to the cross-country driver. It's wide; it's flat; once it reaches Abbotsford, it's suburban. The recently conquered mountains are in your rearview mirror, and fresh ones lie to the north, capped with snow for much of the year. The Fraser River isn't filled with logs. Starbucks and White Spot seem to be at every junction.

Peter and I drove through, barely slowing on the graceful Port Mann Bridge, its soaring suspension cables reaching high above us as everything else had done since entering the province. The Port Mann is a new bridge, opened in 2012 to replace the one built for the Trans-Canada in 1964, which was one of the longest arch bridges in the world but became overwhelmed by Vancouver's traffic. The new Port Mann carried tolls to help pay its billion-dollar price tag, though the B.C. government removed these in 2017 and moved the annual cost over to general taxes — it learned its lesson from New Brunswick in how to stay popular with voters.

It must have been a triumphant arrival at the Pacific for all of the pathfinders. Well, most of them. Percy and Bernadette Gomery drove up from Portland and Seattle, where they missed the welcoming party from the local automobile club sent out to greet them, and just went home instead. Percy said later his outstanding impression of the journey was how few people live in Canada.

Jimmy Oates, true to form, got a rock caught in his drive chain on the last leg into Vancouver and was almost pitched from the seized bike into the river, but he somehow kept control and slewed to a halt and freed it. On the edge of the city, he met the mayor travelling with a pair of motorcycle cops who'd come to escort him to an official lunch. The mayor must have been brave, stupid, or just ignorant of Oates's many mishaps over the 21 days of the journey, because he asked for a ride in the sidecar and the two of them carried on to the city hall together. After lunch, they travelled to English Bay to dip Toby's wheels into the Pacific. "C.C. Wakefield's 'Castrol' — that's the whole story," Oates told newspaper reporters. "That standard motor oil brought me through." His was the first machine to be driven entirely across Canada on its regular rubber tires, from ocean to ocean, and he took a few days for a rest and to replace its frame before riding down to the U.S. border. He returned to Toronto on American roads, crossing back to Canada at Detroit. It took a while — he stopped many times along the way to completely rebuild the engine and the wheels.

The rest of us, however, have a little farther still to go. The scenic tourist route travels into the city and then through beautiful Stanley Park and over the Lions Gate Bridge to North Vancouver, and Peter and I took the time to explore the city and the park. Then we headed back to where the Trans-Canada skirts the east of the city, rejoined the highway, and drove over Burrard Inlet on the Ironworkers Memorial Second Narrows Crossing.

This bridge collapsed during construction in 1958, and 79 workers fell into the water; 18 died, some drowned by the weight of their tool belts. A diver also died during the rescue mission. Stompin' Tom Connors wrote a song about it, but most people these days just think of it by its original name, the Second Narrows Bridge, and curse its stalled traffic during Vancouver's extended rush hours.

There was no traffic for us, though. It was late in the evening, and we had tickets booked for the last ferry out of Horseshoe Bay. Just like the ship to Newfoundland and the ship to Prince Edward Island, the MV *Queen of Cowichan* is a part of the Trans-Canada Highway. When we finally made it to the metal ramp and onto the deck for the sailing to Vancouver Island, we knew we were on the last leg of our drive across Canada.

13

Vancouver Island

It was late when we arrived in Nanaimo. I was lucky when I booked the crossing two weeks earlier — this was the Canada Day weekend and most every ferry was full. There are several routes to the island from Vancouver, and I considered them all, but only the Horseshoe Bay–Nanaimo crossing is considered part of the Trans-Canada Highway. Fortunately, there were still a few spaces available on the last sailing of the day.

There's long been talk about building a bridge or a tunnel across the Strait of Georgia. It looks simple on paper: the shortest ferry travels about 50 kilometres, and that's the length of the Chunnel between England and France, so it can surely be done. You could cut it to almost half that length by going between the mainland and Galiano Island and then linking from there, and there's a single bridge in Louisiana that's longer than that. There's even a 55-kilometre combination of bridges and artificial islands and a tunnel that links Hong Kong across the sea with Macau. And after all, British Columbia's chief engineer told me that if you have the funding, you can pretty much engineer a solution to anything. So, if they could build a bridge to Prince Edward Island, why not Vancouver Island?

It turns out, there are a few reasons. For a start, the Strait of Georgia is 10 times deeper than the Northumberland Strait. There's no bridge anywhere in the world that has its pillars sunk into water so deep — deeper than the height of the Eiffel Tower. The record is held by a Portuguese bridge in Lisbon that's in water 79 metres deep, or about a quarter the depth of the Strait of Georgia's 365 metres. As for a tunnel, the deepest in the world is in Norway at 300 metres, but it's not very long; the best comparison is with the rail tunnel in Japan that links the island of Hokkaido to the main island. It's more than 50 kilometres long and 240 metres deep. The B.C. tunnel would need to be significantly deeper because there's a layer of soft silt on the sea bed up to another 450 metres thick that any bored tunnel would need to pass beneath. There are a couple of other options: a submerged floating tunnel that's held in place by chains to the sea floor, which sounds feasible in theory but has never actually been built anywhere to prove it can work, and a floating bridge that's never been constructed at anything like such length or depth. In practice, just forget them until somewhere else takes the risk first. Add to this the occasional seven-metre waves and six-metre tides, and the earthquakes, and the 45,000 ships that pass through the strait every year, and the ferry seems the only reasonable option.

It could be done, of course, but somebody has to pay for it. Studies are made periodically as engineering methods improve, but the latest estimate is the cheapest fixed-link crossing would cost $15 billion to construct, plus servicing and maintenance. If that was paid for by tolls, spread over 100 years, the one-way cost could be as much as $800. So the ferries will be plying the waters here for a while.

It took a couple of gentle hours to reach Nanaimo. From there, it's an hour and a half down to Victoria on the Trans-Canada Highway, but Peter and I had a detour to make first.

☐

The original white "Canadian Highway" signpost is long gone, but there's a copy in the Alberni Valley Museum, safe in a glass case with some other curiosities from the time. It was made in 1967 and planted close to where the original post had been placed, guarded by the doctor's dog. This was a part of "Amalgamation Day" when the towns of Alberni and Port Alberni finally joined to form the City of Port Alberni, and it stayed in place until a snowplough hit it the following winter. Perhaps that's what happened to the original too.

The first post was still there when Thomas Wilby and Jack Haney drove into town in 1912, though I hope the dog was long since released. It was just the two of them again — Earl Wise left at Vancouver to return to Saskatchewan. They arrived 52 days after leaving Halifax and five months after it was installed, when those hundreds of motorists gathered to call for a Trans-Canada Highway. It was a fairly straightforward trip across the island for the Reo: what had been a two-day haul just a few years before was now a drive on "ideal gravel roads through forests of giant pine and fir — that was Vancouver Island, a paradise of the motorists," wrote Wilby. "For miles we travelled through a veritable forest tunnel of timber, the car dwarfed to insignificance by trees which shot up to the sky and barred the sunlight from spreading banks of fern and flower."

Little has changed. Many of the trees are still there, though when Peter and I came through, the road was only reopened that week. A forest fire, one of hundreds that summer that sprang up all across the country, had burned close to the road and closed it to traffic. The ancient stand of Douglas firs at Cathedral Grove was threatened, but in the end, the fire left them alone and so did we — the footpaths were closed off and visitors weren't permitted to wander among the ferns and squint up at the high canopy. We pressed on, inconvenienced by the clearing of debris from the road but delayed only an extra half-hour. The week before, traffic to Port Alberni had to be escorted along an old logging road and took all day, so we didn't complain.

In Port Alberni, we met David Hooper, a volunteer at the local transportation museum. He took us to the city's other museum to see the signpost and also down to the park at the end of Johnston Road where it meets the river that flows into the Alberni Inlet. This is about 40 kilometres from the Pacific itself, but it's close to the quay where the ships docked. The CPR had its terminus nearby, and in 1912, this area was the most westerly point in Canada that was navigable by road. The signpost was planted here, and a

THE DRIVE ACROSS CANADA

sign in the little park explained its story. When we looked around, the buildings from the old photos were gone and long since replaced, but we realized we were standing exactly where the cars had been. It was a strange sensation, even after travelling to so many of the same places as the pathfinders, to know we were there.

"A few years more and the transcontinental motorist will find a post yet further west than Alberni, on the actual western shore, looking out across the blue Pacific to an unobstructed view of the horizon beyond which lies the Orient," wrote Wilby optimistically. He was being a little hasty: the road wasn't extended through to Ucluelet and Tofino until 1961, but those towns have benefitted tremendously from the tourism that such convenient access provides. Tofino even declares itself to be the end of the road and has its own sign at the wharf, stating PACIFIC TERMINUS — TRANS-CANADA HIGHWAY — TOFINO BC. It's made of steel and planted in concrete, the modern equivalent of the doctor's dog, to stop it from being stolen like its wooden predecessors, as happened several times with souvenir hunters. Old-time Tofino residents

David Hooper, seen at the Alberni Valley Museum with its copy of the original "Canadian Highway" road sign.

244

claim they were promised the status back before the Trans-Canada was actually built, before Highway 4 to Tofino was even constructed, and say they were double-crossed by the politicians, but it makes no difference. It was never going to happen. Even Port Alberni isn't connected to the Trans-Canada. "I've heard the double-cross story," Mayor Perry Schmunk told Victoria's *Times-Colonist* in 2012, "but most Tofitians believe that we are, without question, the official — maybe only in our minds — terminus of the Trans-Canada Highway."

For the record, even if the Trans-Canada did go to Tofino, it wouldn't be the point farthest west. The alternative Trans-Canada along the Yellowhead, which travels to Prince Rupert on the coast, continues by ferry to Haida Gwaii, and the highway travels there to its true terminus at Masset, which is more than six degrees of longitude west of Tofino. And the Alaska Highway, which runs through northern British Columbia and the Yukon, reaches the Alaska border at the 141st meridian, which is almost nine degrees west of Masset. That's officially the farthest west that any Canadian highway touches, just in case the question ever comes up in a pub quiz.

We had lunch with David, and I asked what he would say to those motorists who drove to Alberni in 1912 for the highway promotion gathering. "I'd congratulate them for doing what they did," he said. "You think about it — how optimistic they were. This was the new age of the automobile and they really were optimistic. Look at how intrepid they were, setting off on those lousy roads, on a great enterprise. I don't think people are quite so optimistic these days." And when our server came to check on us, I asked if she knew about the signpost, and the gathering, and the fight for the cross-Canada highway. She was probably in her twenties and told us she'd lived in Port Alberni for the past couple of years. "Really?" she said. "I never heard that story. How about that. Would you like dessert?"

□

There's a grainy silent video on YouTube shot in 1912 from a car driving on the Malahat Highway, which is on the road that heads down from Nanaimo to Victoria. It's believed to be from the official visit of the Duchess of Connaught that October, filmed by an inept government cameraman, who was fired from his official position the following year because his films were of such poor quality. The Canadian Automotive Museum believes it's the oldest existing footage shot from a moving car in Canada, and it places Wilby's glowing depictions of motoring paradise into context. The road is muddy and narrow, little more than a slippery black track with steep drops into the rotted stumps and fallen trees of the forest. It's relatively smooth, at least, and a night-and-day difference from just four years before.

The Malahat Highway would never have been completed in 1911 — or its construction even begun — if it wasn't for the bloody-minded perseverance of Major James Francis Lenox MacFarlane, who moved to the area in 1903. MacFarlane — no relation to Brigadier (Retired) Alex Macfarlane — was an Irishman who served with the British Army in India and retired to Canada to become a farmer. He didn't have much choice, his great-grandson told me, because he'd had an affair with a chorus girl and his wealthy wife wrote him out of her will. When she died, his grown children paid him £2,000 to leave Ireland for one of the colonies and never return. That's about $360,000 today, enough for a fresh start even though he was already more than 50 years old, and he chose Canada because he'd heard the hunting and fishing were exemplary. Except he moved to Alberta and installed the chorus girl and their handful of new children in a sod-hut farm just south of Edmonton where he was a terrible farmer and rapidly ran short of money. Just a few years later, he moved again, to a 40-hectare farm he bought sight unseen at Cobble Hill, north of Victoria on the other side of the Malahat Ridge.

There was a wagon trail leading around the ridge that could reach his property, but it was barely passable except on horseback. The railway was inconvenient. It took MacFarlane and a friend three days to push and pull the wagon through to the farm, about 80 kilometres of strenuous hauling on the steep, circuitous track. Victoria was reachable by boat and rail, but by wagon? Forget it. Except MacFarlane refused to forget it. He set out to get a proper road built.

"He was a proponent of the highway for personal reasons, not because he believed in public transportation," said John MacFarlane, the great-grandson of the Old Major, as he was known, when I called him later. "He wanted to get from his farm to Victoria to drink, but that was a two-day journey and that was too long for him. He'd bought a sailboat and tried to commute using that, but it was too slow."

There was no road either north or south from Cobble Hill, so he went to Victoria to lobby for one. He was told there was no suitable route that was reasonably direct and a road wouldn't be possible. Such a shrug must have grated on the Old Major. "He was an irascible character," said John, "and politically, he was a pain in the ass." For the next three years, he plotted out a potential 30-kilometre route, sighting it from his sloop in the sound and from a borrowed handcart on the railway, and pounding pegs into the trail he trekked through the forest. His artillery experience had taught him how to survey, but when he presented the results to the minister of lands in Victoria, the work was dismissed: he was unqualified and his research was considered irrelevant. Locals started calling the proposed road "MacFarlane's Folly."

The Old Major wasn't a man easily dismissed. He called for a meeting of the Cobble Hill Farmers Institute, and though only three other farmers turned up, they passed a resolution calling for a new road; MacFarlane understood the media and made sure the papers ran the story. The resolution and its coverage got the attention of the Victoria Board of Trade, the Tourist Association, and the Automobile Association. The government was still on the fence about the road, so MacFarlane gathered signatures from every resident he could find along the route. When he pasted the sheets together, they measured three metres long. Finally, this was enough to prompt the minister of lands to have MacFarlane's proposed route checked by a civil engineer, who declared it was the only possible way through and quite feasible.

Around the same time, the Victoria Automobile Club made a trial run to Nanaimo. Bert Todd was one of the participants, as reported in the *Vancouver World* after the drive:

> One portion alone mars the way, and that is the passage of the Sooke hills. The need of a change in the route of the road is badly needed, and motorists are taking a very deep

interest in the move to have a road opened around Saanich Arm which would overcome the steep climb over the Sooke hills. The new road would be of inestimable value to the general public as well as those who love the auto. The autoists have long cherished the hope that the road will be built and looked for a grant towards it in the estimates this year. The government has promised to have it surveyed, and it is yet hoped something will be done at once to take away this one objection to the run from Victoria to Duncan, Nanaimo and Alberni.

The dual offensive on the reluctant government was too much to resist, and the B.C. Legislature approved $25,000 to start construction. It took three years to build, and when it was ready, the Old Major crashed the opening. "He was not invited to the ribbon-cutting. He went the night before and did what they called 'hanselling,'" said John — an inauguration of the road with considerable, if inappropriate, imbibing. "He drank a bottle of whiskey with the crew who were just finishing off the highway. Then in the morning, as they were about to cut the ribbon, he drove his horse and buggy through the ribbon and drove over the Malahat."

The road was open, but it was still a dicey proposition to drive. The ascent and descent of its 356-metre summit was steep, and early motorists had to carry extra water for their overheating radiators. Spare tires were also a good idea, as well as nerves of steel for meeting oncoming vehicles on the narrow track, built on the side of the ridge with no guardrails. "The mist used to get so bad, we'd have to pull over and wait for it to clear. The [carbide] lights wouldn't cut through it," one early driver told journalist T.W. Paterson. "Once you got rolling, you didn't change your mind. There were stretches of that road which seemed to go on forever without a place to turn around."

It was good enough for the Victoria Automobile Club to drive to Alberni the following April and lobby for a Trans-Canadian Highway, and it was improved slowly but surely over the years until it was paved in 1956, ready to become the Trans-Canada itself. Even now, however, it's two or three lanes of highway with a low concrete wall for its median, and when there's an accident or event that closes it, traffic grinds to a halt and the road is cursed by its drivers.

Never by Major Lenox MacFarlane, however, who could finally take his buggy easily to Victoria to find a drink. He lived at Cobble Hill until 1935 when he accidentally burned down the farm. Its long driveway was lined with empty bottles he'd consumed of Burke's Old Irish Whiskey, one for every day of his life he claimed, buried upside down for their bottoms to reflect the light, and their glass exploded in the heat of the flames. He moved to Victoria where he became such a fixture that the newspaper ran a news story each year to announce his birthday. He died in 1940, six years before his namesake drove over his highway to complete the first coast-to-coast Canadian road trip and claim the Todd Medal.

□

Brigadier (Retired) Alex Macfarlane and Squadron Leader (Retired) Ken MacGillivray were met near Cobble Hill by members of the Victoria Automobile Club and escorted over the Malahat Highway to a lunch in the city, and then on to Oak Bay to dip the Chevy's wheels into the Pacific Ocean. He was formally presented with the Todd Medal at a banquet that night at the Empress Hotel, paid for with the $500 (plus interest) Bert Todd had set aside all those years before. "Brig. Macfarlane, in accepting the medal, said it had been his desire since before 1914 to make a trip by automobile across the continent," reported the *Victoria Daily Times* the next day, on May 22, 1946. "He had not found the roads too bad in crossing but spoke of receiving a number of thrills in travelling the Fraser road when the edge seemed extremely close. At times, coming through the mountains and the snow, the car had had to slow to Intermediate and Low to come through, but once over the peaks the driving had been better, he said."

For its part, General Motors was proud of its Chevrolet's achievement and bought large advertisements in newspapers across the country that summer to proclaim the news. "Another 'first' for Chevrolet" announced the ad, describing the Todd Medal and showing photographs of the car and Macfarlane. In one of the photos, the car is seen with its front wheels in the

Alex Macfarlane's medal-winning drive was advertised proudly by Chevrolet, though his partner, Ken MacGillivray, was barely mentioned.

water at Oak Bay. "After 4,743 miles of rapid, trouble-free driving, Brigadier Macfarlane and his co-driver dip the front wheels of their Chevrolet in the Pacific Ocean — to win the A.E. Todd Gold Medal." Macfarlane is named nine times in the ad; MacGillivray is never identified.

Twenty-one years earlier, Ed Flickenger was given a warm welcome when he brought the Ford Model T over to Victoria on October 20, 1925, though it was more of a ceremonial visit than anything else — the car came direct on the ferry from Vancouver where the movie had ended with dipping the wheels into the ocean. Nonetheless, it was an impressive achievement of 7,715 kilometres, of which 1,373 were driven on railway tracks. "Where the mighty Pacific laps the marge of Vancouver's shore," reads the film's final title card, "the pioneer reaches its final goal making new history to be added to the annals of Mackenzie, Fraser and Lord Strathcona who crossed

Canada by caravan and rail." Right. A bit purple perhaps, but not untrue. The *Victoria Daily Times* reported:

> Whenever it was possible to go by road the Ford made the trip and the wheels were changed no less than eleven times during the journey. At one point, they changed to go over a stretch of road four miles long. Every time the wheels were changed, it meant the losing of two hours' time.... On the whole, the roads across the Dominion were good according to the officials, the worst part of the journey being their trip through the Prairies where they ran into several snowstorms.

The mayor of Victoria poured a bottle of Atlantic water that Flickenger carried from Halifax into the Pacific at the city's harbour, then signed the scroll alongside the signatures of all the other mayors. After that, Flickenger drove the car over the Malahat to a civic banquet in Duncan, and the rest of the story is unknown. Nobody knows what happened to the car, and the scroll was lost. The hour-long movie was shown in theatres the following year, but it was then also lost; it took almost 50 years before a copy was discovered in a cabinet at Ford's advertising agency. But that's okay — Perry Doolittle and the Good Roads advocates had made their point.

And then there was Thomas Wilby and Jack Haney, back at the beginning in 1912. They came from Alberni, as we did, and were escorted over the Malahat by a group that included A.E. Todd himself. Wilby delivered the multitude of letters to the mayor of Victoria, and then after a stop at the Parliament buildings, he and Haney drove with their entourage to Oak Bay to dip the wheels for the last time. "Mr. Wilby went through the ceremony of mingling the waters of the Pacific and the Atlantic in a flask which he had brought over from Halifax," reported the *Victoria Daily Times* on October 19. "He poured Atlantic water into the Pacific and then filled up his flask from the sea. 'An A.P. cocktail,' he said with a smile, as he raised the flask to his lips." The account doesn't say if he actually drank it, but it does, at least, mention "his skillful chauffeur, H.V. Henry." Poor Jack just couldn't catch a break.

Thomas Wilby pours his Atlantic water into the Pacific while Jack Haney sits at the wheel of the Reo and various dignitaries crowd the car to watch.

◻

Peter and I drove over the Malahat on Canada Day and followed the Trans-Canada Highway all the way into town, right to its farthest point where it ends with a stop sign at Dallas Road, up against the shoreline of the Pacific Ocean. This is beside Beacon Hill Park, and unlike at its eastern end, there's a large sign that proclaims itself to be Mile Zero. Alongside it is an impressive statue that commemorates Terry Fox, because Terry had hoped to run to this point. Steve Fonyo Beach, dedicated to the one-legged Canadian runner who did make it this far from St. John's with his own Journey for Lives in 1984, is just down at the water. We parked and took photographs. It was a warm day and sunny, and the flowers were in full bloom. We chatted with some guys who rented an apartment at Mile Zero House on the corner, and they said it was no big deal to be able to walk out their front door and drive all the way to Quidi Vidi Gut, if they should want to, which they didn't, but they would like one of Peter's cigarettes. I also chatted with their superintendent, the husband of a woman I'd spoken with in 2012, and he told me he believed his house to be at the end of the highway, not the beginning. Kind of like Oz at the end of the yellow brick road.

The area was so beautiful and the weather so perfect that we had a true feeling of accomplishment. We drove to Oak Bay, as Wilby, Haney, Macfarlane, and MacGillivray had done, the horseshoe, badge, and medal safe in the glovebox, then inched the Lexus down a boat ramp into the slowly rising tide. I poured out my plastic bottle of St. John's salt water, and the cool Pacific Ocean lapped at the front wheels just as the cold Atlantic had lapped at the rear wheels, and our long journey was finally complete.

Mark, at the wheel, and Peter dip the Lexus into the Pacific at Oak Bay to complete their drive across Canada.

Epilogue

Just to throw a wrench into everything mentioned so far, the very first person to drive a car across the B.C. mountains, from the Prairies to the Pacific coast entirely within Canada, was actually an American, Charles Jasper Glidden of Boston, who did it in 1904. You read that right — eight years before Thomas Wilby and Jack Haney made their attempt. Stay with me here. Glidden was a wealthy man who'd sold his telephone business to Alexander Graham Bell and loved to drive, usually with his wife, Lucy, and he would promote road-building along the way. He'd already driven north of the Arctic Circle in Europe, and at 47 years old, he saw the B.C. Rockies as just one more challenge for his money to conquer.

Charley Glidden was too impatient, and far too rich, to wait for roads to be built. He used his many connections with railway barons to get permission to drive on train tracks when convenient, and made the most of their availability. That was how he'd crossed the Swedish Arctic Circle, which had worked out well enough. This time, he wanted to carry on to travel right around the world, so he and Lucy shipped their car to Chicago and drove from there up to Minneapolis. Then they changed the regular wheels on their Napier Limited — so open it didn't even have a windshield — for steel flanged wheels, and left them on for the rest of the drive to Vancouver. There was no bothersome swapping around. The Gliddens employed a chauffeur, of course, who is rarely identified, of course, but he didn't do any driving because Charley much preferred to be at the wheel. The "chauffeur," Charles Thomas, was there to look after the car's maintenance and mostly just along for the ride.

It was a leisurely journey that took 28 days from Minneapolis, but much of that time was spent out of the car, appreciating local sights and enjoying the luxuries of Canadian railway hotels. The actual driving took just 60 hours over a dozen days, and the 24-horsepower Napier could hit 100 kilometres per hour when the wind was right. The Gliddens and their chauffeur wore long waterproof automobile coats, with caps and goggles, to stay comfortable while maintaining the brisk pace. "As we could stop much quicker than a heavy train, we generally preferred for that reason to follow rather than lead a fast train," Glidden told a reporter from Vancouver's *Daily Province*. "In some cases we came up close behind some of the fast trains — so close that we could talk to the passengers on the rear car. But we only held that position for a while as a rule, for the dust and cinders generally proved uncomfortable, unless there was a side wind." It must have been like a roller-coaster ride, but without the loops and twists. "It is really delightful travelling along the rails in a motor car," he said. "There is an absence of all side rocking and jarring, such as is experienced in a train travelling at high speed."

The Gliddens reached Vancouver on September 18 and stored the car while they returned home to Boston for a few months. Then they returned and shipped it to Hawaii, and then Fiji, and then Australia, and then carried on around the world. They travelled for two years and had such a good time they did it all over again in 1908.

The point of this story is to illustrate that if you throw enough money at a project, it can be done, just as the Americans built their enormous interstate system so rapidly by just spending more than US$100 billion and watching it take shape. Also, in those first years of the 20th century, automobile technology was progressing far more quickly than road-building technology. It wasn't just that cars were popular and their sales

EPILOGUE

were growing exponentially every year; it was that cars were becoming more capable and their need for expensive roads couldn't keep up. One might argue that our highways still haven't caught up. Highway 401 north of Toronto has as many as 18 lanes, one of the widest roads in the world, but it still clogs to a standstill at rush hour.

Done right, however, a nation's highway system can be an effective part of our need for swift and simple transportation. You want proof? In 2016, four guys in a rented Volkswagen drove the 5,800 kilometres from Vancouver to Halifax in less than 65 hours, staying inside Canada and not driving at excessive speed, swapping around drivers as they grew tired but spending less than five hours stopped. More impressive, in September 1973, Toronto racer Roy Eastwood left Sydney, Nova Scotia, on his bored-out BMW R75/5 motorcycle and rode alone on the traditional route of the Trans-Canada Highway through Sault Ste. Marie to Vancouver in 83 hours, 48 minutes. He was 30 years old at the time and tried to maintain 145 kilometres per hour all the way. Even so, "I never really took this run too serious," he told *Cycle Canada* magazine. "If I had, I could have knocked the time down considerably."

His record solo ride — faster than two others that set their own records in the previous year — was certified by the Canadian Motorcycle Association, which was clearly horrified and promptly announced it would no longer sanction any more coast-to-coast record runs. So now the American-based Iron Butt Association only certifies motorcycle rides that take place within a certain number of hours that it deems safe and legal: you'll get a certificate for completing the Trans-Canada Quest run between Halifax and Vancouver without leaving Canada if you do it in less than 90 hours, and the Trans-Canada Gold run must be made in less than 75 hours, with time-stamped receipts to prove everything. Short, mandated rest stops aren't included in those times. More than 30 motorcyclists have so far earned their Trans-Canada Gold certificates, and considerably more have earned certificates for the slower Trans-Canada Quest.

Only one rider, however — Thane "Inthane" Silliker, of London, Ontario — has earned a Trans-Canada Gold Insanity certificate for riding from Halifax to Vancouver and then back to Halifax in less than 150 hours, not including a mandated 12-hour rest period halfway through. On a separate ride three years before from downtown Halifax, he reached downtown Vancouver in 59 hours, 51 minutes. He made that run in 2001 on his Honda ST1100 motorcycle and saved distance by taking the alternative Trans-Canada Highway through Northern Quebec and Northern Ontario, and the Coquihalla Highway. Taking the ride far more seriously than Roy Eastwood, he connected an extra gas tank and even rigged up a catheter tube so he wouldn't have to waste time in a washroom. The tube went down the inside of his riding pants and drained beside his boot, so when he stopped for gas, he just stood over a drain at the same time to relieve himself, while also eating a banana for his meal. "It wasn't until I outfitted my bike and private parts with additional plumbing that my dream of being the fastest became realized," he told me. "It was a hell of a long ride, but it was never boring."

Just think about that for a moment. Less than 100 years after Charley and Lucy Glidden took a record-breaking 60 hours to travel 2,900 kilometres, Thane Silliker took the same time to ride exactly double the distance, all within Canada, because now the road was built. It may not have been legal, or even responsible, but it was quite possible — even, perhaps, taken for granted.

◻

It's a shame that few of our pathfinders lived to see the completion of the Trans-Canada Highway, or even any kind of a highway that linked the country from coast to coast. Thomas Wilby's book *A Motor Tour Through Canada* was published in 1913 while Sir Robert Borden was prime minister. Reviews were mixed. The *Times Literary Supplement* said: "There is rather an excess of commonplace philosophy and a vast amount of useful information for those who think of following in his wheel tracks — a wild adventure which shall be postponed, so far as we are concerned, until Mr. Borden's road-making policy is being carried out." The book never named Jack Haney and never identified the car they drove. A professional photographer who accompanied the party on Vancouver Island, Richard Broadbridge, took

EPILOGUE

a photo at Cathedral Grove that shows Wilby and Haney and three other men posing with their cars beside a tree. A large sign on the grille of the Reo reads REO, but the reproduced photo in Wilby's book has neither the sign nor Haney — they're airbrushed out. None of the book's other photos show Haney, or at least not clearly enough to be identifiable. I expect Wilby felt he'd covered his sponsorship contract with the promotional pamphlet he'd written for Reo, but maybe he was upset by something else, or just still disliked the driver. They left Vancouver separately and never met again; Wilby never did return the two suitcases he'd borrowed at the start of the journey.

"Wilby was a louse," wrote Haney's future wife, Glen, in a 1968 letter to a friend. "We have no pictures of the eastern part of that trip. Jack took Wilby's pictures and Wilby took Jack's and spoiled them all. When Jack got to Toronto, he had them developed and found out what he was doing." Whether it was intentional or Wilby was just an awful photographer, none of the photos he took are clear — they're all blurred or out of focus.

Thomas Wilby found work as an editor with the *Christian Science Monitor* in Boston, then travelled with his wife for a year in Europe and the United Kingdom before falling ill. He died on November 17, 1923, in Bath, England, age 56, with no children to continue his name.

Jack Haney returned to a hero's welcome at the Reo factory in St. Catharines, where he was the guest of honour at a company dinner and was presented with a gold watch and a $50 bonus (about $1,300 today). He went to some car shows with the scratched-up car, but Reo closed its Canadian production line the following year and moved all assembly back to Michigan. The car was apparently converted to a delivery truck and eventually scrapped. Haney stayed in Canada and started a taxi garage in St. Catharines, where he married his girlfriend, Annie Glendinning Swan, known as "Glen," in 1914. They had a daughter and a son, and eventually he helped establish an independent repair garage that was open 24 hours a day, seven days a week. He helped fix machinery used for the building of the Welland shipping canal between Lakes Erie and Ontario, and even assisted in the opening of the local airport in Niagara Falls.

Haney had always been a healthy man, but his heart began to fail him. In 1928, he felt a sharp pain in his chest while hauling a deer out of the bush, and then a month later, walking home for lunch, he had a mild heart attack. He recovered, but his coronary thrombosis grew worse, and over the next seven years, weakened him so that he often couldn't get out of bed and rarely worked. The garage suffered for it and eventually closed, causing the family to lose their home and move in with friends. Jack Haney died on March 26, 1935, just a couple of weeks after his 46th birthday.

"My dad never spoke much about the trip," his daughter, Ferne, told biographer John Nicol in 1997. "When he did, he called Wilby 'Sir Thomas,' but he never said a bad word about him."

It was Earl Wise who fared the best among the three — the gangly young man who travelled from Regina with his legs hanging out of the Reo, sometimes even riding on the hood, once stretching out beyond the headlight above the Fraser Canyon. "He got out on the fender to steer me," wrote Haney in his account for the company magazine. "A little oil remained in one of our oil lamps, and with its aid he was able to pick the trail. We came very near going over the precipice into the Fraser River at one sharp turn.

Jack Haney's lucky horseshoe, a 1925 Canadian Automobile Association grille badge, and the Todd Medal itself, all carried by Mark in both the 2012 Camaro and 2024 Lexus across Canada.

EPILOGUE

We just stopped in time. When Mr. Wise noticed where we were, he gave the danger signal — 'whoa!' I understood what he wanted as soon as I heard it. Anybody within a mile of us would." Wise returned to Michigan and put himself through university, where he earned an engineering degree and eventually helped design California's iconic Highway 1 along the Pacific coast, which included plenty of guardrails on the corners high above the ocean. He died in April 1954, a month after retirement at age 65.

Such highways were the dream of Perry Doolittle, "Mr. Trans-Canada." He continued to advocate for a cross-country road and firmly believed it was just a matter of time and political will, but his health began to fail at 70 years old and he was forced to retire from medical practice. He stayed on, though, as president of the Canadian Automobile Association and was re-elected in 1933 despite being too unwell to attend the annual general meeting. Perry Doolittle died at home three months later on New Year's Eve, age 73. Toronto's *Globe* remembered him as an indefatigable promoter of road safety and practical use: "Once, when the Ontario Legislature sought to restrict the speed of motors to eight miles an hour," it reported, "he took the entire Parliament for a ride and convinced them ten miles an hour was not 'scorching.' They changed the bill." That February, the Ontario Motor League agreed to establish a monument to Doolittle that would be placed "wherever the final link of the Trans-Canada Highway is completed," and the cairn was finally dedicated in 1964 at the midway point beside the Montreal River south of Wawa.

Ed Flickenger, the Ford photographer and filmmaker who stayed with the Model T all the way across the country, died in 1944 at a comparatively young 59 years of age. What he'd done was "impossible," remembered the *Windsor Daily Star*: "He fought his way through Maritimes roads so narrow that trees and bush had to be chopped in places to squeeze the car through.... Despite the tough going, the Model T averaged 120 miles a day for the entire trip. The record established on the first transcontinental automobile trip set the pattern for other pioneers to keep pushing road-building horizons."

Before Flickenger's railway run, Percy and Bernadette Gomery had pressed through as best they could from Montreal, returning to Vancouver just as we do today — no heroes' welcome or congratulatory banquet for them, but instead pulling up outside their front door and getting a nonchalant greeting from their daughter, who wanted to know what gift they'd brought her. Percy went back to work at the Canadian Bank of Commerce where he stayed as manager of the Kitsilano branch until retirement in 1939. In that time, though, he wrote another travel book, *Curve: Go Slow — A Romance of Pacific Coast Highways*; a novel, *End of the Circle*; and then, after the Second World War, a final travel book, *Hot and Cold Laid On*, set in England and co-authored with Bernadette. Percy died in Vancouver in 1960, age 79, and Bernadette died there in 1969, both of them remembered fondly by their two daughters and their grandchildren.

Perhaps the most adventurous later life was lived by Jimmy Oates, who returned to the Isle of Man and hatched another plan with Ariel to promote British goods in Canada. In 1934, he brought a new Ariel 500 cc single-cylinder motorcycle with a sidecar to Halifax and rode it to Sault Ste. Marie. It sounds as if he was well in form. "Picked up some bad petrol which made the motor run so hot it melted the grease on the rockers," he wrote in his journal on September 12. "Ran into a swarm of grasshoppers and was forced to wear over-trousers to stop them going up my legs."

This time, however, when Oates reached Winnipeg after riding through the United States from Duluth, he set off north on the railway for Churchill, way up on Hudson Bay. And for this trip, he rigged an extended axle and metal guides for the motorcycle wheels so he could ride on the smooth rail itself, as Flickenger had done with the Ford Model T. It sounds great in principle, but in practice, the bike kept hopping off the rail; other times, frost and ice made the metal surface so slippery there was almost no purchase. "This riding on a narrow ribbon of steel is very hard on the nervous system," he wrote on September 27, as winter was setting in, "and I prefer to ride 500 miles on the road to 100 on the rail." Even so, he reached Churchill in frigid temperatures, returned as a stowaway in a grain wagon on the train that was shipping his motorcycle, and continued to Vancouver, avoiding the B.C. mountains by taking the same American route as the Gomerys. When he finally made it back to Montreal, he found Ariel had changed ownership,

EPILOGUE

his sponsorship had disappeared, and he had to work his way home on a creaking cargo liner.

Jimmy Oates went on to promote competitive trials riding on the Isle of Man, open a motorcycle and car dealership in Liverpool, and during the Second World War, taught dispatch riding to the British Army. When the war ended, he was appointed head of the Roads and Road Transport Section of the Control Commission Germany, where he helped rebuild the German road transport system in the country's British Zone. He always kept an interest in Manx motorcycle racing and eventually died in 1972, age 75 — "a slight man in stature," remembers his biographer, Bill Snelling, "but undoubtedly a person with incredible strength of purpose and character."

And then there was the Todd Medal winner himself, Brigadier (Retired) Alex Macfarlane, the first person to drive across Canada on all-Canadian roads. His passenger, Ken MacGillivray, went back to a career in public relations and became the PR director for Chrysler of Canada, but died at just 55 years old in 1963, after fighting illness for more than a year. The brigadier, however, purchased the Canada Hair Cloth firm from his wife's family in 1947, which he ran as president in St. Catharines even after divorcing his wife, before retiring in 1974 to Winnipeg where he died six years later, age 90. "He drove right up until the end," his grandson, Jim, told me. "I'm sure it was a Cadillac. He was confident. Outgoing. A man's man. He was bigger than life."

□

In 1925, Dr. Perry Doolittle told some 500 delegates at a convention in Manitoba that he envisioned the future Trans-Canada Highway as a leafy avenue stretching between Halifax and Vancouver. "Trees will be planted where the scenery demands this particular form of beautification," reported the *Winnipeg Free Press*, "and he had received assurance from Ottawa that all the trees wanted would be provided, and expert advice furnished as to the kind that should be planted in certain sections. With beautification of this kind, Dr. Doolittle declared, the Canadian transcontinental highway would be the most attractive on the continent, and would eclipse even the Lincoln highway in the United States."

It's a nice idea, but this image demonstrates the difference between vision and reality. There are plenty of attractive, landscaped parkways in the country for motorists to enjoy on leisurely drives, but, ultimately, roads are there because we need to get somewhere and to do so quickly with a minimum of effort and fuss. It's one thing to drive through Regina's leafy boulevard on the way to lunch but quite another to want the same thing driving five hours from Regina to Winnipeg, or 65 hours from coast to coast. New Yorkers discovered this in the 1930s with the parkways that spread out from the city and prohibited commercial vehicles, built to help lure them into their cars and out to the cooler countryside — ultimately, drivers just wanted to get to where they were going on the fastest roads possible. These days, people don't even care about looking at the scenery, which they've already seen on TV. They'd much rather be stimulated by their phones, whether they're in the passenger seat or behind the wheel. For younger people especially, who often have little other reference, the actual driving is just a chore.

"The new highways are too impersonal," says Teresa Willett. "The Trans-Canada is like the Route 66 of my country," says Phil Duprey.

EPILOGUE

And yet it doesn't have to be onerous. In Kamloops, Peter and I met a couple staying at our motel who had come from Vancouver Island and were on their way home to Crystal Beach, near Fort Erie, Ontario. Phil Duprey and Teresa Willett had long dreamed of driving across the country and had already been Down East; this was the Out West leg, and it was on their bucket list. This time, they'd driven the Trans-Canada to return the ashes of Teresa's grandmother to the sea at Nanoose Bay.

"When we came back today along the Fraser Canyon, I was like, this is the Trans-Canada I remember," Teresa said. All four of us were enjoying a beer at the end of the day on the balcony outside our rooms, sitting on plastic deck chairs with our feet up on the railing. "I think the new highways are too impersonal. You're losing touch with the people who helped build it. To me, we're losing a part of our history by bypassing that to make it faster."

It had been a hot drive for them. The temperature was in the high thirties, but the air-conditioning was broken in their Honda and they'd had the windows wide open all the way, music cranked to hear it over the wind noise. She shrugged. "We're doing this old-school," she said.

"I'm a proud Canadian," said Phil. "The Trans-Canada is like the Route 66 of my country. Maybe it was bigger in the 1960s and 1970s when people were travelling and that's all there was, but I just want that nostalgia for the old Trans-Canada. You know, when you're flying, it's about the destination, but when you're driving like this, it's about the journey."

I reminded Peter of this when I took him to the seaplane terminal in Victoria for the first of his flights home. It was the day after Canada Day. The wheels were dipped and the fireworks fired. We leaned on the railing and looked out at the harbour, at the same place where the mayor poured Ed Flickenger's flask of Atlantic water in 1925.

"You know, I was just winding you up," said Peter. "I never really was scared by your driving. It's been a good trip. Canadians are incredible people. Canada's a wonderful country, and this was a wonderful way to see it."

I nodded. I knew. We'd say goodbye and then I'd deliver the Lexus to Vancouver and fly home myself. I'd be back through my front door in Cobourg after five hours of flying and complaining about the cramped seats and rubbery food. I mentioned this to Peter.

"It doesn't have to be that way," he said, and turned to look at me. In all our driving together, we rarely got to look each other in the eye. "We've still got the key. Why don't we just drive back? Maybe take a different route, over the Crowsnest or the Yellowhead, through those trees on that Northern Ontario road? There's a few choices. Why don't we do that instead of just rushing back to the rest of our lives? What's the hurry? What's stopping us from making the drive?"

Nothing was stopping us. Nothing at all.

Acknowledgements

Many people helped with the research and preparation needed for *The Drive Across Canada*. Special thanks must go to Romaric Lartilleux and Danielle Petruccelli of Toyota Canada, who provided me with the Lexus RX 500h, a prototype SUV built in Cambridge, Ontario, that Peter and I drove for 14,500 kilometres, and which never put a wheel wrong. Also, my editor at the *Globe and Mail*, Jordan Chittley, who encouraged me to write a series of columns about the drive, as well as a column about the Trans-Canada Highway itself that appeared on the printed newspaper's front page on Canada Day. Even after years of working as a journalist, it was still an old-fashioned thrill to pick up the newspaper in Port Alberni and see my name above the fold.

Ian Jack and Kristine D'Arbelles at the Canadian Automobile Association also assisted with preparation, and it was a comfort to know the CAA would rescue us if the car ever broke down. Which it didn't.

Nancy Macfarlane of St. Catharines generously (and with great trust) lent me the Todd Medal to carry on the journey, as did her late husband, Jim Macfarlane, in 2012.

Lorne Findlay and his son, Peter, of Vancouver drove across Canada in 1997 in a 1912 Reo identical to the car driven by Jack Haney and Thomas Wilby, and their comparatively trouble-free experience was an inspiration for my own drives. They took me on a tour of Vancouver in the Reo in 2012, and the car broke down then, but it was soon back on the road. Lorne died in 2019, and now Peter owns the Reo and it's still running today, alongside an immaculately restored 1910 Russell-Knight.

Many writers and researchers laid the groundwork for telling the story of the Trans-Canada, and for this, special thanks are due to authors David Monaghan, Daniel Francis, John Nicol, Rudy Croken, and Bill Snelling. Many archivists assisted directly, including Anne Cox at the Canadian Broadcasting Corporation (CBC), Hannah Grant with the Ford Motor Company, Betty Brill with the Nipigon Museum, Katie Braithwaite with Heritage Park in Calgary, Tammy Bradford with the Creston Museum, Dumaresq de Pencier at the Canadian Automotive Museum in Oshawa, and Helen Booth at the St. Catharines Museum, who lent me Jack Haney's lucky horseshoe for the journey.

Much of the historical research for *The Drive Across Canada* came from newspaper reports that I found through my subscription to Newspapers.com, while many other reports, both current and historic, came from the archives and websites of the CBC. The CBC's growing collection of stories is a rich and irreplaceable national resource that must never be allowed to diminish.

Across the country, we enjoyed the kindness of friends, including Peter and Mardi Gullage, John and Debbie Poirier, Zac and Raquel Kurylyk, Julia Sinclair-Smith, Paul Williamson, Dale Johnson, Jeremy Kroeker and Elle West, Janelle Somerville, and Keith Morgan. Many others gave me their time to tell their stories, and these included Michelle Higgins, Mandy Francis, René Roy, Elias and Margaret Osmond, Joe Roberts, Ron Barrington, Terry Best, Lloyd and Audrey Adams, Jackie Gaulton, Yvonne Edwards, Angus Moores, Carol and Bob Hyslop, Bill Casey, Ken O'Brien, Kevin MacDonald, Darcie Lanthier, Jill Marvin, Gerald and Velma Stone, Howard Gibbs, Neil Graham, Kari Gunson, Said Abassi, Ed Nyman, Marlene Turner, Doris Mengelberg, Frances Fry, Bryan Cowie and Kelly

ACKNOWLEDGEMENTS

Durst, Laurie MacNevin, Warren Beach, Christine Bauck, Marina and Mike Gilchrist, Tony Clevenger, Trevor Kinley, Tony Einfeldt, Gary Sulz, Ian Pilkington, Melanie Delva, Denise O'Connor, Angus Muir, David Hooper, John MacFarlane, T.W. Paterson, Leonard and Louise Rousseau, Thane Silliker, Prunella Reynolds, and Phil Duprey and Teresa Willett.

Online, I was assisted by the media departments of every provincial government, but special thanks must go to the thoughtful and informative email responses of Hicham Ayoun of Transport Canada. Thank you, too, to transport ministers Kim Masland of Nova Scotia, Jeff Carr of New Brunswick, and Ernie Hudson of Prince Edward Island for taking the time for personal interviews.

At Dundurn, I benefitted from the enthusiasm of Kathryn Lane, Meghan Macdonald, and Erin Pinksen, while editor Michael Carroll's diligence both improved my writing and saved me from many small slips of the keyboard.

Eric Sweet, a keen and experienced traveller in his own right, was committed to creating helpful and meaningful maps from my long lists of Canadian towns.

Randy Paisley's enthusiasm for my previous book, *Canada's Road*, gave me the inspiration to finally complete the research for *The Drive Across Canada*, and I must also thank George Saratlic at General Motors, who lent me the convertible Camaro I drove across Canada in 2012. I wish I owned that car.

My wife, Wendy, gave me all the time and encouragement I needed to prepare this book, and of course, I must thank Peter Faulkner, who is as good a friend now after six weeks on the road together as he's been in the four decades we've known each other. Here's to the next one, Pete.

Appendix: Rules for the Todd Medal

1. Tour to be between Halifax, Nova Scotia, and Victoria, British Columbia, over a continuous route and, excepting for ferries, the tour must be made entirely under the car's own power.
2. Tour to be run east or west, at entrant's option.
3. Any car and any person shall be eligible to compete.
4. The Medal to be awarded to either driver or owner of car, according to whichever of the two registers with the Canadian Highway Association, Victoria, B.C., for that purpose at the start of tour.
5. No ferry of more than twenty miles in distance will be permitted, except in British Columbia.
6. Travelling on railway tracks is not permitted.
7. Competitors to start whenever they please and to take their own time.
8. Tour to be in no sense either a speed or reliability trial.

9. A careful log of the route travelled is to be kept. A copy of this log to be turned over to the Canadian Highway Association, Victoria, B.C., at the end of the tour.
10. Route shall not go outside Canada.
11. Entrant's log book must be endorsed at least once in every hundred miles by city or town official, postmaster, police constable, any prominent merchant, Chamber of Commerce, or automobile club official.
12. In conspicuous positions on the car, in large letters, must be displayed one or more signs worded "Canadian Highway," and one or more signs worded "Halifax, Nova Scotia, to Victoria, British Columbia," or vice-versa.
13. Route taken must be fairly direct and pass through Ottawa, Winnipeg, Fernie, Cranbrook, Rossland, Grand Forks, Greenwood and Princeton.
14. At termination of tour, competitor or driver and one of the passengers will be required to make statutory declaration that the rules of this contest have been observed throughout.
15. Tour is under the auspices of the Canadian Highway Association of Victoria, British Columbia, and any additional conditions or alterations in conditions, or determination concerning interpretation of rules is to be under the direction of and at the discretion of the Board of Directors of the Canadian Highway Association, whose decision shall in all cases be final.

Selected Bibliography

Aubert de Gaspé, Philippe. *Canadians of Old: A Romance*. Montreal: Véhicule, 1996.

Clevenger, A.P., and M. Barrueto, eds. *Trans-Canada Highway Wildlife and Monitoring Research, Final Report. Part B: Research*. Radium Hot Springs, BC: Parks Canada Agency, 2014.

Croken, Rudy. *Ban the Automobile: Instrument of Death: The History of the Early Automobile on Prince Edward Island 1900–1919*. Rudy Croken, 2017.

Durnford, Hugh, and Glenn Baechler. *Cars of Canada: A Craven Foundation History*. Toronto: McClelland & Stewart, 1973.

Emerson, Diana, et al. *In-Service Road Safety Review — PTH 1 and PTH 5 Intersection*. Winnipeg: Manitoba Transportation and Infrastructure, 2023.

Francis, Daniel. *A Road for Canada: The Illustrated Story of the Trans-Canada Highway*. North Vancouver, BC: Stanton Atkins & Dosil, 2006.

Gomery, Percy. *A Motor Scamper 'Cross Canada: A Human-Interest Narrative of a Pathfinding Journey from Montreal to Vancouver*. Toronto: Ryerson Press, 1922.

Grey Owl. *The Collected Works of Grey Owl: Three Complete and Unabridged Canadian Classics*. Toronto: Prospero Books, 2004.

Gunson, Kari, et al. *Best Management Practices for Mitigating the Effects of Roads on Amphibians and Reptile Species at Risk in Ontario*. Toronto: Ontario Ministry of Natural Resources and Forestry, 2016.

MacIntyre, Linden. *Causeway: A Passage from Innocence*. Toronto: HarperCollins Canada, 2006.

McCourt, Edward. *The Road Across Canada*. Toronto: Macmillan Company of Canada, 1965.

Monaghan, David W. *Canada's "New Main Street": The Trans-Canada Highway as Idea and Reality, 1912–1956*. Ottawa: National Museum of Science and Technology, 1996. publications.gc.ca/site/eng/107054/publication.html.

Nicholson, Karen. "A.C. Emmett and the Development of Good Roads in Manitoba." *Manitoba History* 27 (Spring 1994).

Nicol, John. *The All-Red Route: From Halifax to Victoria in a 1912 Reo*. Toronto: McArthur & Company, 1999.

———. *Jack Haney*. Toronto: Fitzhenry & Whiteside, 1989.

Richardson, Mark. *Canada's Road: A Journey on the Trans-Canada Highway from St. John's to Victoria*. Toronto: Dundurn, 2013.

Snelling, Bill. *Aurora to Ariel: The Motorcycling Exploits of J. Graham Oates*. Isle of Man: Amulree Publications, 1993.

Stewart, Walter. *My Cross-Country Checkup: Across Canada by Minivan, Through Space and Time*. Toronto: Stoddart, 2000.

Sullivan, Kristian. "The French Counts of St. Hubert: Local History as Social Commentary." Saskatoon: University of Saskatchewan, 2009. web.archive.org/web/20100620233600/http://sha.org/about/conferences/documents/Sullivan_Kristian_TheFrenchCountsofSt.Hubert.PDF.

Warner, Charles Dudley. *Baddeck, and That Sort of Thing: The Book That Brought Alexander Graham Bell to Baddeck, Nova Scotia*. Baddeck, NS: Deja Vu Press, 2015. First published 1874.

Webb, J.R. *Tales of a Highwayman*. Banff, AB: J.R. Webb, 2009.

Wilby, Thomas W. *A Motor Tour Through Canada*. Toronto: Bell & Cockburn, 1914.

Image Credits

3 Port Alberni Museum Archives
4 Library and Archives Canada/Canadian Intellectual Property Office fonds/a029919
6 Ford Motor Company
7 Bill Snelling
16 Mark Richardson
22 Mark Richardson
24 Unknown
30 Mark Richardson
36 Jim Macfarlane
43 Library and Archives Canada/Department of Employment and Immigration fonds/e011000018
48 Lorne Findlay
52 Mark Richardson
60 Mark Richardson
68 Mark Richardson
75 Mark Richardson
84 Mark Richardson

- 92 Mark Richardson
- 96 Library and Archives Canada/e010752830-v6
- 109 Mark Richardson
- 116 Mark Richardson
- 122 Mark Richardson
- 126 Lorne Findlay
- 133 City of Vancouver Archives
- 145 Bill Snelling
- 147 Town of Wawa Heritage Committee
- 150 Nipigon Historical Museum Archives
- 172 Ford Motor Company
- 174 Mark Richardson
- 184 Ford Motor Company
- 188 Mark Richardson
- 191 Mark Richardson
- 198 Mark Richardson
- 205 Mike McCourt
- 208 Mark Richardson
- 216 Lorne Findlay
- 222 Internet Archive
- 226 Library and Archives Canada/National Film Board of Canada fonds /e006580621
- 228 Mark Richardson
- 244 Mark Richardson
- 250 General Motors
- 252 Library and Archives Canada/Canadian Intellectual Property Office fonds /a029912
- 253 Mark Richardson
- 260 Mark Richardson
- 264 Mark Richardson

Index

Abegweit, MV, 66
Adams, Lloyd, 17, 20, 149
All Red Route, 182
Anne of Green Gables, 62–63
Aubert de Gaspé, Philippe, 99–100

Barrington, Ron, 25
Bauck, Christine, 188–90
Belaney, A.S., 93–97
Belcourt, Father Georges-Antoine, 56–57
Bement, Austin, 219–20
Bennett, W.A.C., 9, 224
Best, Terry, 25–26
Binns, Pat, 78
Borden, Sir Robert, 258
bridges
    Confederation, 51, 58, 67–69, 119
    Louis-Hippolyte, 104–6, 119
    Port Mann, 238–39
    Quebec City, 101–2
    Seal Island, 41
    Second Narrows, 239–40
    wildlife, 129–30, 206–11

Brophy, Doug, 73, 76, 111–12, 148, 206

Canada Highways Act of 1919, 108, 110
Canso Causeway, 43–46, 117
car brands
    Austin, 183
    Cadillac, 2, 164–65, 263
    Chevrolet, 7, 10, 38, 73–74, 76, 87–88, 109, 112, 148, 171, 206, 249–50
    Ford, 6, 37, 49–50, 57, 88, 101, 143, 171–72, 218, 250–51
    Lexus, 10, 16, 72, 74–75, 82, 253
    Maxwell, 132–34, 138, 139, 168, 203, 215
    Napier, 255–56
    Overland, 218–19
    Packard, 219–20
    Reo, 4–5, 47–48, 88, 126–28, 182, 252, 259
    White Steamer, 2
    Winton, 1
Carberry crash, 87, 173–77
Clevenger, Tony, 207–9

Clubb, William "Billy," 165–66
Cowie, Bryan, 160–61
CPR steel crew crash, 191–93, 197–201
Crocker, Sewall, 1, 11

Delva, Melanie, 233–36
Diefenbaker, John, 9, 19, 223–25
Doolittle, Perry (doctor), 5–6, 49, 101, 160, 171–72, 220–21, 232, 236, 261, 263
Duplessis, Maurice, 104, 114, 117
Duprey, Phil, 264–65
Durst, Kelly, 160–61

Eastwood, Roy, 257
Edwards, Yvonne, 198–99, 201
Eisenhower, Dwight E., 8, 118
Emmett, Arthur Coates "Ace", 170–71
Evans, E.S., 219–20

ferries
    Newfoundland, 12, 17, 32
    Prince Edward Island, 8, 53, 58–59, 66–67
    Vancouver Island, 240, 241–42
Flickenger, Edward, 5–6, 10, 49–50, 88, 101, 132, 143, 159–60, 171–72, 184, 185, 204, 213, 220, 231–32, 250–51, 261
Fox, Terry, 16, 158, 252
Francis, Mandy, 28
French counts, 180–81
Frost, Leslie, 115

Gaglardi, Phil, 224, 225
Gap at Wawa, 143, 146–49
Ghiz, Joe, 67
Gibbs, Howard, 121–24, 131
Gilchrist, Marina, 197–98
Glidden, Charles Jasper, 255–56
Gomery, Percy, 132–38, 139–41, 168–69, 183–84, 202, 203, 215, 239, 261–62

Gooch, Donald, 183
Gordon, George, 218–19
Graham, C.K., 167–68, 185
Grey Owl. *See* Belaney, A.S.
gumbo soil, 167–68, 171–72, 183–85
Gunson, Kari, 129–30

Haney, Fonce Val "Jack," 5, 10, 47–49, 79–80, 82, 88–89, 98, 102–3, 125–28, 139, 159, 166–67, 170, 182, 202–3, 215–18, 237–38, 243, 251–52, 258–60
Higgins, Michelle, 21–23
highways
    Alaska, 245
    Big Bend, 114, 206, 221–22, 229
    Cabot Trail, 42–43
    Cariboo Road, 236–38
    Crowchild Trail, 203–4
    Crowsnest, 202–3
    Lincoln, 219, 264
    Malahat, 245–49
    U.S. Interstates, 8, 72, 118, 175, 256
    Yellowhead, 11, 218, 222, 245
Hooper, David, 243–45
Hudson, Ernie, 61, 67
Hunka, Ron, 73–74, 76, 87–88, 112, 148, 206
Hurricane Fiona, 29–33, 40, 61
Hyslop, Carol, 52–53

Inco Superstack, 139

Jackson, Horatio Nelson, 1, 11

Kinew, Wab, 176
King, William Lyon Mackenzie, 8, 110, 114
Kinley, Trevor, 209–10
Kipling, Rudyard, 195–97

Lanthier, Darcie, 64–65
Last Spike (railway), 231

INDEX

Latta, Samuel J., 184–85
left-hand drive, 89, 215
Lesage, Jean, 9, 104, 118
Lord, Bernard, 78
Louisbourg, Fortress of, 38–39
Lyons, Harry, 148
Lyons, James, 165–66
Lytton fire, 232–36

Macdonald, Angus L., 44, 45
Macdonald, Father Stanley, 45
Macfarlane, Alex (brigadier), 7, 10, 35–38, 87, 98, 101, 112, 138, 155–56, 171, 185, 202, 232, 236–37, 249–50, 263
MacFarlane, James Francis Lenox (major), 246–49
MacGillivray, Kenneth, 7, 35–38, 87, 98, 112, 155, 171, 202, 232, 237, 249–50, 263
Magnetic Hill, 74–76
McCourt, Edward, 18, 23, 27, 41, 60, 87, 98, 117, 131, 132, 139, 159, 179–80, 204–5, 229
McCourt, Mike, 204–5
McDougall, Lauchie, 27
McManus, Gus, 150, 153
Mengelberg, Paul, 157–58
Monaghan, David, 8, 108, 109, 110, 112–13, 115–17, 119
Moores, Angus, 199–201
Moose Jaw, tunnels of, 186

Needham, Healy, 149–55
Niemeyer, Charley, 218–19
Nyman, Ed, 149

Oates, J. "Jimmy" Graham, 6–7, 50–51, 80–81, 88, 98, 101, 143–46, 160, 171, 204, 213, 232, 239, 262–63
Operation Michipicoten, 146–48
Operation Palaci, 228

Pearson, Lester B., 19, 24, 66
Pearson's Peak, 24–26
Pilkington, Ian, 230
Plan B protest, 63–65
prisoner-of-war camps, 157–58

Roblin, Sir Rodmond, 167
Rogers Pass, 9, 19, 206, 222–29
Roy, René, 29–33

Scrymgeour, J.L., 49, 171–72
Silliker, Thane, 257–58
Silverthorne, Frank, 218–19
Sims, James, 218–19
Smallwood, Joseph R., 18–19, 23–24
specifications, Trans-Canada Highway, 77, 117
St. Laurent, Louis, 114–15
Stewart, Walter, 62–63
Stone, Gerald, 85–87
Sulz, Gary, 229
Synard, Gerald, 200

Tobin, Brian, 78
Todd, Albert "Bert" E., 2–3, 5, 7, 36, 220, 247, 251
Todd Medal, 2–3, 5, 7, 10, 35–38, 47, 165, 171, 190, 202, 219–20, 249–50, 260, 271–72
tolls, 51–53, 59, 68, 77–79, 125, 175, 239, 242
Trans-Canada Highway Act, 104, 115
tunnels
    highway, 104–5, 230, 241–42
    spiral, 213–14
    wildlife, 129–30, 206–11
Turcott, Al, 146–49

Vessey, Robert, 63

Ware, Elijah, 55–56
Wawa goose (statue), 148–49
White, H.W., 164–65

Wilby, Thomas, 4–5, 12, 47–49, 79–80,
    82, 84–85, 88–89, 98, 102–3, 107,
    125–28, 139, 140, 159, 167, 170,
    181–83, 202–3, 215–18, 237–38,
    243–44, 251–52, 258–59, 260
Willett, Teresa, 264–65
Winters, Robert, 114, 117–18, 131
Wise, Earl, 182–83, 202, 215–18, 231,
    237–38, 243, 260–61
Wyman, George, 2

About the Author

Mark Richardson is a veteran journalist and a graduate of Ryerson Polytechnical University, now Toronto Metropolitan University. He worked as a reporter at the *Regina Leader-Post* and the *Ottawa Citizen*, as well as working for CARE Canada in central Africa, and in London, England, as a television news producer. He returned to Canada to work as an editor for the *Toronto Star* and has been a regular contributor to the *Globe and Mail*'s Globe Drive section since 2016.

Mark is the author of two novels, and two published non-fiction books: *Canada's Road: A Journey on the Trans-Canada Highway from St. John's to Victoria*, published in 2013 by Dundurn (Toronto); and *Zen and Now: On the Trail of Robert Pirsig and the Art of Motorcycle Maintenance*, published in 2008 by Knopf (New York and Toronto).

For more information about Mark, and to see more photographs and links from *The Drive Across Canada*, see his website at markrichardson.ca.